T0336436

IN THE DARK OF WAR

A CIA OFFICER'S INSIDE ACCOUNT
OF THE U.S. EVACUATION FROM LIBYA

SARAH M. CARLSON

FIDELIS
BOOKS

A FIDELIS BOOKS BOOK
An Imprint of Post Hill Press
ISBN: 978-1-64293-471-7
ISBN (eBook): 978-1-64293-472-4

In the Dark of War:
A CIA Officer's Inside Account of the U.S. Evacuation from Libya
© 2020 by Sarah M. Carlson
All Rights Reserved

Cover Design by Cody Corcoran

Post Hill Press
New York • Nashville
posthillpress.com

Published in the United States of America

To those who continue to serve in dangerous places over-
seas, you are not alone.

TABLE OF CONTENTS

PREFACE

ON JULY 26, 2014, the US Mission evacuated Tripoli, Libya, as civil war broke out in the country. While surrounded by militia forces, the entire US Mission conducted the emergency destruction of our facilities and evacuated more than 150 US personnel overland, in armored vehicles, through hostile territory, amidst active fighting, and in a heightened terrorist threat environment.

The civil war started in Tripoli on July 13, 2014. Thirteen days later, we initiated the evacuation at approximately 0500 in Tripoli and arrived in Tunis, Tunisia, the following morning at 0700, twenty-six hours later.

The following story is based on real events and my first-hand observations while I served as a CIA officer as part of the US Mission in Tripoli, Libya. I worked closely with the officers described herein. It is told from my perspective and that of my colleagues and friends who led the evacuation. This accounting covers the span of a year, with the primary concentration on the evacuation.

My main objective with regard to individual officers described herein was to protect their true identities. The officers are based on real people, but no true names are used and all call signs have been changed. In addition, most of the officers are a blend of more than one individual to incorporate personnel changes, turnover, conceal the number of officers, and account for personal breaks occurring throughout the year. I slightly altered the timing of arrivals and departures of incoming and outgoing personnel as a result.

The US Ambassador, as the President's designated representative and the most senior State Department official in a country, represents former President Barack Obama's Administration in this narrative and is not solely reflective of a single individual.

The dialogue is not verbatim. I instead attempted to capture the general atmosphere, my memory of conversations, and anecdotes conveyed to me. All the events described herein occurred and are detailed to the best of my ability. I attempted to honestly and accurately capture the events and actions of all the US government personnel in Libya.

I served as a counterterrorism analyst with the US Government for more than a decade, including in the Central Intelligence Agency (CIA). As a former CIA officer, I am required to submit all written or oral material intended for public consumption to the CIA's Publication Review Board (PRB) with the objective of excising any classified information or sensitive operational details. This is a requirement placed on all former employees in order to protect the secrecy of CIA sources and methods. I complied with that requirement.

I chose not to use redacted text in this account. I wanted no distracting, blacked out phrases or missing pages of information. I instead worked with the PRB to choose alternate language I felt conveyed the same meaning and intent, while also protecting our national security, which was my highest priority.

"The bravest are surely those who have the clearest vision of what is before them, glory and danger alike, and yet notwithstanding, go out to meet it."

—*Thucydides*— The Peloponnesian War, *2.40*

CHAPTER ONE

EVACUATION: THE ANNOUNCEMENT

(JULY 24, 2014)

"Net call, net call, net call. There will be an all-hands in five minutes in the office," came the radio call from Harbor, our acting chief. All officers located on the compound the afternoon of July 24, 2014, paused to listen to his announcement, including me.

I scowled in concern at my radio before turning to Nomad, a security officer and former Navy SEAL, who sat beside me inside the relative safety of our villa. Nomad and I met the previous October and we helped and relied on each other. He protected the other officers and me, while I warned him about the things in Libya from which we needed protection. We would need much protection in the coming days.

"Is this it?" Nomad asked me. "Decision time on whether we remain in Libya or evacuate?"

"I think so. The SVTC with Washington D.C. just concluded," I said. Government leaders in Washington held the SVTC, or secure video teleconference, to determine whether or not the entire US Mission would evacuate Tripoli, Libya, including myself, Nomad, and the other officers under Harbor's command.

I knew the chances were high the entire US Mission would evacuate soon and, if it happened, I knew my colleagues and I would help lead it. I heard from the ambassador, she planned to recommend a full-scale evacuation to the president and his administration.

Until a few days prior, the ambassador claimed she was staunchly against leaving and repeatedly emphasized to all personnel the US administration would not lose Libya. It could not fail.

Now they'd waited too long, despite the warnings. Now we had few options for escape.

I glanced back at my radio listening for responses. None came. I then prepared to walk to the office. I donned my body armor, holstered my Glock 19 pistol, slipped my knife into my boot, and grabbed my radio.

"What do you think they decided?" Nomad asked me as he re-holstered his Glock and picked up his rifle.

We'd been listening to music, trying to drown out the sounds of heavy artillery exploding around us. It hadn't stopped for weeks and each concussion sent a jolt of fear through my heart.

An intense firefight also raged nearby throughout the morning and we both needed a short break. I definitely needed the break while the SVTC occurred. I knew it would decide our collective fate.

"Up until a few days ago, I'd have guessed we were staying. Now I'm fairly certain we're about to drive to Tunis," I replied.

"Driving through active fighting in a war could be even more dangerous than staying at this point. At least here we have bunkers, food, water, and weapons."

"I agree. It's extremely risky."

"What about the southern airfield? We finished the reconnaissance about an hour ago and it seems like a good option," said Nomad.

"I think it's the best option too, but I heard the ambassador may have already decided on another route," I said. *And not a safe one*, I thought.

"The coastal road then?"

"No, I think the southern road. Even though part is through hostile territory, we know for sure they're looking for Americans all along the coastal road," I said. We were being hunted by extremists and trapped in militia crossfire—there were no safe options. I prayed we'd make it out alive, unharmed. And when doubts overwhelmed me, I clung to my faith instead.

We needed to make it out alive and I'd do everything in my power to ensure we did.

Nomad and I left our villa together to walk to the main villa, which housed the office on the compound. It was still early afternoon and hot. It was late July 2014 in Libya and sweat dripped off us within seconds of being outside wearing our heavy body armor. The sand stuck to the sweat, creating a gritty paste on any exposed skin. We walked as quickly as possible to the main villa as rockets and artillery continued to explode around us. Others walked ahead of us but no one said a word.

The sky looked dim even though it was early afternoon. Black smoke filled the air and the smell of spent artillery and burning fuel surrounded us. I glanced toward the sound of the closest heavy weapons fire and hurried forward when I heard the distinctive whine of incoming.

I dreaded that sound.

We quietly filed into the office where Harbor, our acting chief, waited motionless and grim in the corner. Once all hands were accounted for, Harbor stepped forward and broke the tense silence.

"Well, who wants to take a road trip?" he asked.

"You tell us boss," quipped Moe, a security officer, who sat closest to Harbor.

"We do. The evacuation is a go. The plan is to use the route officers conducted reconnaissance on last fall, through southern Libya, and into Tunisia. That leg will take about four or five hours. Once we cross the border, we'll drop off the Marines at an airfield and continue to Tunis. The drive to the airfield will take approximately one hour, and the drive to Tunis another four. We will leave Saturday morning. Between now and then we'll focus entirely on conducting a thorough emergency destruction of this compound. Any questions?"

"What about our personal belongings, weapons, and gear? What do we take with us?" asked Belle.

"Weapons and medical kit for sure and anything you would normally have in your go-bag. Otherwise only what you can carry on your lap. The rest you leave behind. Anything else?" asked Harbor. A go-bag contained the bare essentials we would need to survive in hostile territory and we carried them with us at all times in Libya.

"What's the security situation like on the route?" asked Moe.

"Captain will cover that separately with the security officers. There's a section that goes through particularly hostile territory. However, U.S. Africa Command (AFRICOM) will be providing air support. They announced plans to have an Intelligence Surveillance Reconnaissance (ISR) or drone aircraft, F-16s, and several Osprey near our convoy in the event security deteriorates and we need immediate military assistance or medevac," he replied.

"What's the contingency plan if there's heavy fighting Saturday morning?" I asked. "Based on our latest data, since fighting began nearly two weeks ago, the early morning hours have seen the greatest concentration of heavy weapons fire and it's only been increasing."

"There is no contingency," Harbor replied gravely. "We leave Saturday. Now, let's get started with destruction. We have a lot to do in a very short amount of time. Gambler, please take it from here."

Gambler, the information security officer, stepped forward next to Harbor.

"Everyone grab a screwdriver or a hammer. We start with the computers—pull the hard drives first. Everything must be completely destroyed, then burned. It's going to be a long night."

Pandemonium erupted as every officer stepped forward to pick up a tool or ask questions. The room buzzed with chatter.

I'd heard of other facilities that underwent some phase of destruction or evacuation, such as "no paper holdings" or "ordered departure," which we already experienced in Tripoli.

I was not aware of any other recent examples of US facilities that underwent an emergency evacuation overland through hostile territory. The closest I could think of in comparison was the evacuation from Benghazi, Libya, and that happened less than two years prior, and in the same country.

US personnel in Libya operated in the shadow of the September 2012 Benghazi attacks and they were never far from our thoughts. Pictures of our lost colleagues hung on the wall in the main villa below stars engraved into a special plaque. We worried a similar attack could happen in Tripoli, especially since extremists associated with Ansar al-Sharia, the group that conducted the Benghazi attacks, threatened more American diplomats in Libya, and entered Tripoli to participate in the fighting around our location.

Nomad walked over to me and stood by my side for a moment. Not touching, but close enough to feel the warmth of his arm.

"This is unreal," Nomad whispered to me.

"I can't believe we're giving up when there are other options available," I said. "I thought our mission here was important. I want to believe, need to believe, our sacrifices mattered. Otherwise, what was the purpose? Did the ambassador and our colleagues die in vain? Did our work here mean nothing?"

"I thought it was important too," said Nomad, "Worth risking our own lives. You warned repeatedly this war was coming."

"But the administration did nothing. We were forced to sit back and watch the country collapse around us. And for what?"

"I don't know anymore. How'd we get here?" asked Nomad. He walked over to the center table, picked up two hammers, and handed one to me.

He meant the question rhetorically, but I let out a deep, thoughtful sigh. I was already reflecting on the past year and how things went so terribly wrong. I thought I could make a difference in Libya, for the better.

I looked forward to serving my country in Libya. I debated about it for weeks beforehand and talked about it at length with my mother. My mother agreed that if I felt led in that direction, I should go. She supported me and said I shouldn't second-guess my path and couldn't know how God might use me. So, I made the choice to go.

That night I felt even more worried. I worried about the threats we'd face on the drive out. As an analyst, I knew every one of those threats. And I worried, because it was my job to warn the others about those threats. What if I missed one? What if I wrongly assessed one? What if I couldn't convince the ambassador a threat was real? What if someone died, because of some failure on my part?

As I started helping the others with the destruction phase, I let my mind wander back. I thought about my choices. That long series of choices that make up each individual's life—the successes and failures, the good ones and the bad ones. I felt personally responsible for each one of mine. I based my choices on my values and faith and I thought about the choices that led me to Libya and the ones I made since my arrival.

After a year-long, thoroughly predictable, descent into war, we were now at the precipice. Our final days. And I didn't believe we'd all make it out alive.

CHAPTER TWO

FLASHBACK:
WELCOME TO TRIPOLI

(SUMMER 2013)

I landed at Tripoli International Airport in July 2013, months after the Benghazi attacks. I could feel all eyes on me as I walked off the plane and through the airport toward Customs and Immigration. A tall, blonde, clearly American woman was totally out of place.

It can sometimes sound really cool to people when I tell them I served my government overseas and it felt cool the first trip. Not so much by the time I landed in Libya. By then I knew how dangerous it was and how one error could mean the difference between living and dying.

The attacks in Benghazi the prior year amplified the danger in the entire region. Those attacks were the culmination of a series of security incidents from the previous summer, targeting Western diplomats in Benghazi. Just that spring, an attack occurred in Tripoli against a Western embassy. I wondered if it would lead to a similar series of attacks.

The stares in the airport ranged from simply curious to leering to openly hostile. I also spoke Arabic and therefore could understand some of what the Libyans said, although the dialect would take some adjustment. I had no hope of blending in, although I wore long dark pants, long dark shirt, boots, and hung a scarf around my neck that concealed most of my hair, which fell in a low ponytail down my back.

I didn't like the attention, but I held my head high and tried to walk with confidence toward the arrivals area and the local facilitator, Ali.

I felt most on edge my first time arriving in a new country, or at a new airport, when I traveled in an official capacity. I felt particularly vulnerable in Libya since I was fully aware of the threat environment, how much I stood out there, and I carried no additional weapons to defend myself upon arrival other than my self-defense skills.

My mind raced through alternate options of something going wrong. I considered what I'd do if I couldn't identify Ali, what I'd do if he wasn't there, how I would find a phone, how I could find another way to contact the US Embassy, whether I should remain inside the arrivals area, and so on. I prayed I'd find him quickly.

As I thought through the options and scanned the arrivals hall, Ali spotted me, waved, and walked in my direction. I felt relieved to see him and said a short thanks. I strove to maintain awareness of my surroundings as he ushered me quickly through Customs and Immigration.

Unfortunately, my luggage was delayed and still in Germany, but he promised it would arrive soon. I nodded as Ali explained, all the while watching the Libyans customs officials out of the corner of my eye.

I saw the customs officials were actually Zintan militia members. I researched the tribes before departing Washington, but as luck would have it, I sat next to a knowledgeable Libyan on my flight into the country. His name was Muhammad. I discussed the tribes with him at length on the plane and he added additional context to my prior research.

The Zintan fought in the Libyan Revolution against former leader Muamar al-Ghadafi. They were a tribe, but within that tribe there was a military council and a large militia. The tribe organized the militia into different segments, and there were multiple names for the militias that fell under the Zintan tribal umbrella.

Muhammad told me one of those Zintan militia segments formed the security force at Tripoli International Airport. The force was paid by, and nominally fell under, the authority of the Libyan Ministry of

Interior (MoI), but I believed their loyalties ultimately remained with their tribe.

The other major militia in the greater Tripoli area was the Misratan militia. They were from the coastal town of Misrata, east of Tripoli proper, and like the Zintan, also fought in the Revolution.

The Misratans maintained a large militia, larger by some accounts than the Zintan, but they fell under the pay and authority of the Libya Shield that ultimately fell under the Ministry of Defense (MoD). I believed they too remained loyal to their own city and tribe.

The Zintan and the Misratans formed an alliance of convenience in the fight against Ghadafi, as tribal elements in Libya often did for a common cause, but later went their separate ways.

Muhammad told me that in the spring the Misratans entered Tripoli, staged an armed sit-in, and forcibly demanded the implementation of the Libyan Political Isolation Law. That law barred all former regime members from the current government. While most of the Misratans left the city after their demands were met, some remained. Muhammad believed the Misratans viewed the Zintan's control of Tripoli International Airport, and influence in the Libyan government, with mounting discontent.

As I considered the militia dynamics, I hoped the Zintan would be able to get my luggage soon, since everything I needed for the next year was in those bags. I only had enough in my backpack to get by for a few days.

I followed Ali out of the airport and into the Libyan sun.

It was hot. Hot and humid. I guessed it was over 100 degrees. Tripoli also has a distinct smell. It smells dirty and sandy, not as pungent as Cairo and not as clean as Amman. It was somewhere in the middle with an extra dose of humid from the Mediterranean Sea.

I continued to follow Ali to an armored vehicle in the VIP section with red diplomatic plates. Two security officers waited there for me and introduced themselves as Moe and Triage. When they noticed I didn't have any bags, Ali explained the situation.

"I hope you have enough clothes in that tiny backpack," said Triage, "By the time you get your luggage there will only be socks left."

"I hope they're nice socks," said Moe.

"This happens a lot, huh?" I responded. They were the complete opposite of me—a shy, former preacher's kid, turned CIA analyst—in nearly every way. And even though I had an angelic look, my old CIA group chief didn't call me quietly ferocious for nothing. I could hold my own.

So, I smiled at their teasing—they didn't look the type to be joking with me about socks at Tripoli International Airport in Libya. It was a little bit surreal—hold the little. They looked like action figures who had grown to life-size and busted out of their plastic and cardboard packaging somehow. They wore loose shirts over their considerable bulk, which I thought probably concealed armor and weapons. I knew they did so to avoid unwanted attention. They looked formidable anyway.

I'd heard a great deal about the security officers before arriving in Libya. Due to several prominent international events, they became well known at CIA Headquarters and beyond. They were exactly who I wanted by my side and guarding my back in-country.

Most of the security officers had extensive US Special Operations Forces backgrounds and fought non-stop in America's wars since the war on terrorism began in Afghanistan in late 2001. They were assigned to protect us during dangerous operations in designated war zones.

In Tripoli, the security officers supported every movement outside the compound, including picking up and dropping off all personnel from the airport, which they considered a dangerous operation given the high criminal and terrorist threat in Libya.

As we drove, Moe and Triage told me about life on the compound, pointed out various sites along the short route—such as the MoD training school—and mentioned some generalities about the security situation.

The airport was located south of the city and the embassy was located halfway between the airport and the city sitting near the edge of Zintan territory. The main road led into the downtown area of Tripoli, where a variety of smaller neighborhood militias operated. I was assigned to the embassy's residence compound, a short drive from the embassy facility, and Tripoli International Airport.

The Libyan government tried to assert its authority in various ways since the Revolution, but in reality it remained a fledgling government, and very little law and order existed. The roads and buildings remained damaged since the bombings during the Revolution. The police were few and far between, so as a result, traffic was a nightmare and crime ever on the rise. Wrecked and burned out cars lined the road and everything I could see while driving looked dirty and in disrepair.

I kept reminding myself not to stare too wide-eyed or look too much like I was completely out of my element, but I felt like it. I wanted to fit in, but I knew it would take a while before I felt any level of comfort or familiarity with my new "home." And I was a long, long way from home.

I was born in Pennsylvania while my father attended seminary, although my parents were both from the state of Washington, and later returned there. They planned to become missionaries overseas, but the Bible Presbyterian Church asked my father to serve as a minister at a small, rural church in Ohio farm country instead. They chose to go.

After my parents divorced, we returned to the Pacific Northwest. My mother changed denominations, but we continued to attend church regularly. I attended services every Sunday morning, Sunday evening, and Wednesday evening until I graduated from high school. I also went to summer Bible camp every summer from sixth grade until I graduated.

And I loved it. I really did. I had a wonderful childhood in the church, out exploring nature, and with my brothers. It wasn't always easy, but it was wonderful.

My mother, then an underpaid secretary and single mother of four, went out of her way to protect us and make our simple, ordinary lives extraordinary. She turned the struggles into adventures. She taught us the importance of intangible values and impermanence of things.

She also raised me, a girl, with the same values she taught my brothers, which was uncommon among her peers. She raised me to be strong, honorable, and know my worth. I remember hearing her tell us about my grandfather and great-uncles from the time I was a little girl.

"Did you know your grandfather had three brothers and one sister?" my mother asked my brothers and me at the dinner table.

I paused with a heaping spoonful of mashed potatoes near my mouth, my ten-year-old eyes sparkling with wonder.

"She had four brothers?" I asked. If three brothers were already an epic adventure of mud, bugs, and tree-forts, four must be even more spectacular. I was intrigued.

"Yes, and your grandfather's brothers all served in the US Military during World War Two," she explained.

"Like grandpa?" asked my wise older brother. He was eleven and proud that our grandfather flew in the Air Force as a flight engineer.

"Well, grandpa was too young to enlist then, but his older brothers all fought to protect our country. All the way on the other side of the world."

"Why?" my younger brother who was eight, asked through a mouth full of food.

"Because some bad men from far away attacked our country in a place called Pearl Harbor. Those men hurt a lot of innocent people. Your great uncles wanted to protect our country from those bad men and others like them, so they couldn't hurt any more innocent women and children. They wanted to make sure nothing similar ever happened to our country again."

"Did they die?" I asked, already worried even though I didn't know my great uncles.

"Not in the war. They all came home. They were heroes. I remember my grandmother telling me about it. She thought something bad might happen to one of her sons, because that can happen in war. After it ended and victory was declared, they all came home for dinner one night. She fixed a delicious meal, set a beautiful table, and then looked around at her sons, all alive, healthy, and back from the war and she started to cry."

"Like a baby?" My youngest brother was only seven.

"Yes, like a baby, but they were happy tears. Her sons came home and she was so thankful."

"Would you cry like a baby if we all came home after the war?"

"Of course."

It was Memorial Day and my mother was remembering her uncle. He died not long after that dinner at his mother's house. It was one of his last meals with his family. He flew airplanes and on a training mission in the Northeast region of the United States an engine gave out. He could bail or divert the plane from crashing into a populated area. There was not time for both. He chose to give his life to save others.

That was a story my mother relayed often. Her uncle was a hero, in the war and in saving those people after the war, and she was proud.

We also talked about the service of my grandfather, his other brothers, and my mother's siblings, who also served in the armed forces.

I grew up hearing my grandfather's stories about how he flew out of Tehran shortly before the Revolution, served in the Korean and Vietnam wars, and flew in the Berlin Airlift.

One uncle was a rocket scientist—an actual rocket scientist—for the Air Force.

My stepfather served in the Vietnam War and was stationed in Thailand with the Air Force. He told us many fascinating stories about the intense heat, large bugs, and strange food. And of course, the war.

Ours was, and still is, a proud military family.

My mother raised my brothers and me to be that way. She wanted us to be heroes too, even if we chose not to serve in the armed forces. She wanted us to focus our attention outside of ourselves, help others, and serve God in all we did. She instilled in us a strong sense of duty, honor, faith, and the high cost of our freedom.

Once we reached the compound, Moe and Triage reminded me to put together my go-bag, and I thanked them for the ride and information. Then I went looking for my point of contact, NorthFace. I was an incoming analyst replacing NorthFace, who was in Tripoli for the last year, including during the Benghazi attacks.

The analysts back at CIA Headquarters loved NorthFace, and I only had a few days of overlap with him before he left. I wanted to spend as much time as possible talking to him about the current situation in Libya and the prior year.

I saw NorthFace waiting just inside the entrance to the main villa.

"You have a call sign yet?" He handed me a radio and we started walking to the office.

"Not yet."

"Pick one, before they choose for you. That'll be the name you use here." He slowed his walking as we got closer. "Everyone has a call sign for security reasons. Just mark it on your radio, phone, and add it to the board in the office and team room."

NorthFace brought me around the office, introduced me to everyone, including my outgoing boss, who was also in Libya the prior year during the Benghazi attacks and would soon be departing.

"Chief, do you have any specific expectations for me as analyst?" I asked.

"Yes, I expect you to know everything about Libya. Inside and out." His face was sardonic yet unflinching. "We need you to be the fountain of all knowledge."

No pressure, I thought, *just know everything about everything in Libya.*

"I understand. I'll be prepared to drop that knowledge whenever required," I said with a smile, trying to joke and relieve the immense pressure I felt. *How on earth could I know everything?* I'd only just arrived, but I was confident I'd learn quickly.

"Knowledge bombs!" he replied enthusiastically. "Exactly what I want. NorthFace will explain the job and you let me know if you have any further questions."

Then NorthFace and I started discussing Libya and the job. He began by giving me the general briefing given to all newcomers who arrive in the country. He described how it was formerly a state sponsor of terrorism, later provided some of the largest numbers of foreign fighters during the height of the Iraq war, and, post-Revolution, teetered on the precipice.

He explained that once a week the chief required the analyst to provide an information briefing to the ambassador and senior embassy staff, also referred to as the country team. He thought I'd get along quite well with the embassy staff on the country team and I looked forward to meeting them.

In addition, there was a Read Book. The analyst put "The Book" together, which included all intelligence reporting that mentioned Libya in any way, with a specific focus on any reporting obtained by the CIA, and all analytic finished production from the week. I paid close attention as he explained how he provided the briefings. I decided I'd follow his example and gradually shift to my own briefing style later.

The following morning the embassy country team arrived in the afternoon for the briefing and to review The Book. I met the ambassador for the first time. She was a short lady swathed in designer things, from her makeup to her shoes and her handbags. Even the ambassador's leather planner appeared high end and expensive, and greatly contrasted with our standard-issued government pens and notebooks. The ambassador also brought her dog, which surprised me.

During the formal briefing, NorthFace highlighted various new developments with a focus that week on the Federalist movement.

I knew the Federalist movement centered itself in eastern Libya, near Sirte, and was eventually led by a man named Ibrahim Jidran. The Federalists wanted to divide Libya into the three autonomous states that existed under former rulers—Tripolitania in western Libya, Cyrenaica (or Barqa) in eastern Libya, and Fazzan in southern Libya.

To achieve their goal, the Federalists that month shut down oil production at all the major ports and fields in eastern Libya, which accounted for the majority of oil revenue. Since over 95 percent of Libya's economy depended on oil revenue, they would be in for a world of hurt if the ports were not reopened soon. The Federalists held the oil hostage in exchange for recognition of their movement and implementation of their demands for autonomy.

I researched the Federalist movement before arriving in Tripoli, but I did not have much depth on the subject matter. I was not an economic analyst. My expertise was counterterrorism.

For many years I focused on al-Qa'ida central leadership's attack plans external to South Asia. However, in the fall of 2011, a few months after the raid that killed Usama Bin Ladin, I shifted my focus to Libya.

I obtained the position in Tripoli in early 2012, before the Benghazi attacks further destabilized the country. My primary motivation was always to prevent further terrorist attacks against the US homeland and the West, which was my specific area of expertise even within the counterterrorism realm. I knew certain places in Libya were quickly becoming a terrorist safe haven. Given its proximity to Europe, directly across the Mediterranean Sea, it was a natural launching pad for external attacks.

Documents found in the raid that killed Bin Ladin detailed al-Qa'ida's interest in coordinating with the former Libyan Islamic Fighting Group (LIFG) members to send fighters to Libya, possibly with the intent to launch attacks.

I aimed to prevent that from happening.

I was equally determined to prevent an attack from happening against Americans inside Libya, including against my colleagues.

During the next several weeks, I threw myself into my work with vigor. I wanted to get up to speed on all the issues and specific requirements so I could start adding value to our work as soon as possible.

I soon established a general daily pattern. I woke early and was usually one of the first into the office. I checked my email for immediate requirements. I ate breakfast outside on the porch and scanned the Internet and social media, in English and Arabic, for the latest developments.

I quickly discovered social media was the best source for immediate, force protection-type information. Locals frequently posted about road closures, shootings, and protests. The information was usually posted first in Arabic, then later in English.

I immediately notified the security officers' Quick Reaction Force (QRF) in the team room if I heard rumor of any incidents that could impact their moves for the day. Security officers referred to operational movements around the city, simply, as moves. No matter which security officers were in the room, they always stopped what they were doing and listened to me when I passed information. Although I remained partial to Moe and Triage, I quickly gained great respect for all of them.

Moe frequently joked that the security officers' primary mission was to go rescue others, because of the many problems the embassy staff encountered thus far. And they always called QRF. The problems ranged from a flat tire, to unknown individuals trailing an embassy vehicle, to a locally employed staff stealing a diplomatic armored vehicle, to a militia firing on the ambassador's convoy. Moe and Triage also said they would rather deal with an incompetent militia member than a terrorist, but I was not as certain. Both could cause serious damage and were equally as problematic.

I spent the majority of each day in the windowless office. I read every news article and piece of intelligence related to the country, wrote reports, and coordinated with the analysts back in Washington, but rarely left the compound.

At some point during the day, I'd take a break and run laps around the compound. The run around the compound was more like an obstacle course. I had to trudge through sand, cross uneven pavers, hurdle low walls, climb stairs, and dodge concertina wire, and the occasional poisonous snake. We had a small gym there, but I hated running on a treadmill and I always preferred being outside. The security officers often referred to it as the prison yard. I eventually came to view it that way as well.

I didn't log off my computer and leave the office until late at night. I mostly kept to myself. I didn't feel I fit in at all among the warriors and other officers. I was the brain, the geek-in-residence. I was also shy, and usually exhausted by the end of the day, and there were so few women. I enjoyed men's company, but it wasn't the same as having another woman around.

I read my Bible and emailed my mother almost every evening before bed to reassure her all was well. My mother functioned as my tether to the world and I felt so thankful for her love and support, even from so very far away. She prayed for me every day, probably every hour of every day, and regularly sent me quotes and happy anecdotes to encourage me. Whenever I called her, she prayed for me before I hung up. For my safety, wisdom, and a hedge of protection around our compounds and personnel.

I didn't sleep well at night. Even then, occasional booms from gunfire or fireworks resounded in the night, the sound woke me every time.

And although it was dangerous, I wanted to be there because I believed in the mission, wanted to serve my country, and I hoped I could make a difference with my life.

CHAPTER THREE

EVACUATION: PREPARING FOR THE WORST

(JULY 24, 2014)

The afternoon of the evacuation announcement on July 24, 2014, the Zintan continued to oppose the Misratan-aligned-forces who operated under the command of an entity calling itself Operation Dawn. The two opposing forces engaged in heavy weapons fire and fighting in the territories surrounding the embassy. The focus of the heaviest fighting remained at the Zintan-controlled Tripoli International Airport, located south of our location.

Operation Dawn also targeted other Zintan strongholds in our vicinity and thus the compound lay in the direct path of heavy rocket and artillery fire that Operation Dawn aimed at the Zintan.

As a result, Gambler required all officers to wear body armor as we participated in the destruction. Officers took turns assisting with the initial destruction phase and then organizing go-bags and emergency gear. While the evacuation was planned for Saturday morning, a day and a half away, a lot could happen before then and we all needed to be prepared to leave at a moment's notice.

Nomad and I fell in the first group assisting with destruction.

I wore tan low-profile armor, which was slightly smaller and lighter than the standard-issue green armor, but its weight still felt uncomfortable in the heat. I pulled my long hair back in a ponytail, my neck stayed damp with sweat. I guessed it was in the low hundreds and extremely humid. I wiped my brow, adjusted my Glock in the holster and two extra magazines in the pouch on my hips before I stepped toward the destruction fire with my arms full of computer parts.

It was the biggest contained fire I'd ever seen, which I thought was quite noteworthy considering it was made up entirely of non-flammable equipment. Moe and Flash started it with some incendiary grenades from the extensive weapons supply in the security officers' storage container.

We decided to use the huge ditch dug between the perimeter walls—it was originally going to be used for an extra bunker on the compound in the event of an emergency, such as during rocket or other heavy weapons attacks. However, construction for that bunker hadn't started, which made it an ideal location for the destruction fire.

"Don't breathe in that smoke," Nomad cautioned me as I stood near the edge and threw the parts down into the fire.

"I'll be careful." The smoke looked gnarly. I tried to avoid breathing anywhere near it.

"You think our medical insurance covers this?" Moe looked around at the rising smoke.

"Yeah right. I don't even want to think about what I'm breathing in right now," Nomad scanned the area. "Between this fire, the artillery and rocket smoke, and the burning fuel over at the depot, Triage thinks we'll all be lucky not to get sick."

I tried not to imagine the cancer forming in my lungs and walked in a wide circle back to the truck to stay away from the huge plume of thick, black smoke exuding from the fire, which only added to the haze in the air. The sky already looked heavy from weeks of gunfire. The truck was nearly empty when Nomad and Moe joined me. We all threw one last armful onto the fire.

Weapons fire and explosions rang out around us. I resisted the urge to duck my head.

"Well," said Moe, "I need to take a break to pack up my bag. You two done that yet?"

"Not yet, I'll go back to the villas with you." I looked at Nomad with the same question in my eyes. He nodded in agreement.

Moe opened the door to the truck. "Let's roll then."

We jumped inside and sped back toward the inner wall. We passed Triage driving the next truck out to the fire with Tunes and Belle. We waved at each other as our vehicles passed. Computers and electronics loaded down Triage's truck. We'd first removed the hard drives, driven nails through them, and physically destroyed every device before taking it to the fire.

"You think we'll finish up with the office today?" Nomad asked me.

"I don't think so, Gambler said it would take at least twenty-four hours and he wants it to be extremely thorough."

"How thorough?"

"Like, nothing left in the entire room. Computers. Wires. Desks. Pictures. Maps. Pens. Everything. All in the fire."

"Boo," said Nomad.

Moe drove past Captain and Robin next, talking with a linguist by the main villa.

"They look worried," *and exhausted*, I thought, the linguists in particular looked ready to drop. Our linguists were phenomenal and I knew they'd been worked even harder than usual during the last several weeks.

Since Harbor made the announcement, Captain focused entirely on preparations related to the evacuation route with his contacts. As head of the effort, he held responsibility for planning the route. Officers conducted a reconnaissance trip there the previous fall. Now, with the assistance of a linguist, Captain and Robin called militia contacts all along the route to ensure we would have safe passage for the evacuation, or determine what the militias would require in order to obtain safe passage.

"We're here," said Moe, and I opened the door to exit.

Nomad turned in the other direction. "You go on ahead. I need to finish up a few other things and I'll join you in a bit."

I nodded and closed the door behind me. As I did, a GRAD rocket exploded nearby and I flinched at the loud explosion. I could feel the concussion deep in my chest. I hated flinching at the sound. I thought I'd be used to it by then and felt frustrated at myself. I figured it kept me on my toes though, and we needed to be alert.

I marched into the villa and up the stairs to my room. Nomad stayed in the same villa, he was Triage's roommate. I thought Triage and Belle were probably the only ones on the compound who knew for sure about my relationship with Nomad.

I entered my room and took off my body armor. I started setting things out on the bed I claimed. I tried to stay away from the window as much as possible. The last rocket seemed to have set off a spate of fighting and I continued to hear explosions and gunfire to the northeast. I figured it was actually closer to the embassy, but hard to tell. Either way, it was loud and close enough to worry me.

I drew a deep breath and decided to repack my go-bag first. It was a small messenger bag, with a paracord bracelet strapped to the outside. The security officers liked to tease me about the paracord because it was hot pink, but it was a gift from my good friend, so I always kept it there anyway. I'd be upset if I needed rope and didn't have it available. Also hooked on the outside was a small squeeze flashlight.

Inside my go-bag, I packed a notebook and pen, the same one I used for briefings with the ambassador. I had a few Bible verses written in the back, including my favorite, Psalm 139: 7–12. Next was my wallet, which had my passports, currencies, and various cards. I squeezed my medical kit in beside that. Triage put together a special medical kit for me that included some extra combat gauze, an epipen, and two tourniquets, or blow out kits as the security officers called them. I had a bottle of water, granola bars, and headlamp jammed in beside that.

In front of all that was where I normally put my Glock and extra ammo. I wore it on my hip since the fighting started, but I knew I'd be issued an extra Glock and ammunition later in the evening that I would need to add to my bag.

I had an extra knife in the front pocket of my go-bag, in addition to the one I kept tucked in my boot. Finally, I tied my headscarf to the outside strap.

With that done, I picked up my small backpack. I, along with everyone else, would have to leave behind almost everything we owned. I stared for a long minute at my closet, trying to decide what I needed to take versus what I wanted to take.

A sustained volley of heavy weapons fire nearby prompted me to move more quickly. I grabbed an extra pair of jeans, three t-shirts, underclothes, and my flip-flops so I'd at least have something to wear other than boots at the end. I also took one extra headscarf and some jewelry.

I usually wore my compass necklace in Tripoli, especially after the fighting started. It was practical because it was a working compass.

In addition, I packed the only gift I obtained for my mother in Libya. It was a tiny, silly looking elephant. My mother collected elephants, and everywhere I traveled in the world I tried to buy one for her. After telling him the tradition, Nomad saw the elephant when he was out one day on a move and picked it up for her. I wrapped it in my t-shirts and shoved it in my bag.

Nomad walked in as I threw basic toiletry items into my bag, including toothbrush and toothpaste, deodorant, and brush.

"Hello beautiful," I ran over to give him a hug. He leaned down to hug me, because even though I was tall, he was much taller.

As I stepped back, he stared searchingly into my eyes for a long minute. "Doing okay?"

"I'll be okay," I said, staring back, "You?"

"I'm tired."

I was too. We all were. No one could sleep much with the constant explosions, rockets, and weapons fire.

"Maybe they'll stop fighting for a while tonight," I was trying to be optimistic.

He didn't reply, but he didn't have to say anything. We both knew the reality—chances were, we'd be awake most of the night again.

"Stay with me while I pack?"

"Yes," I said with a fake drawl. I liked to tease him about his accent, which he tried to hide most of the time. It always became more pronounced when I distracted him though.

But then our radios squawked.

"A-lyst. A-lyst. Harbor."

Nomad pulled his radio from his belt and handed it to me. Mine still sat on the table by the bed.

"Go for A-lyst," I said into the radio.

"I need to see you in the office," It was Harbor.

"Yes, sir. On my way."

Whenever my bosses, Harbor or Reebok, called for me I responded quickly, especially in our current circumstances. It was usually important. I hustled to get back in my body armor, strap the radio on my belt, and place my Glock in the holster as I walked to the door. Nomad waited there for me. He clasped my arm reassuringly for a moment, and then pulled the door open for me, I hustled out toward the office and the main villa.

Once in the office, I strode to Harbor's desk. I passed the huge shredder on my way, where other officers painstakingly shredded every scrap of paper. I mean every piece, regardless what it contained, even if it was blank. It looked just like in the movies and the grinding drone and haze of pulverized documents only added to the incessant thrum of destruction around me.

There were only a handful of functioning computers left in the office. By then it was almost dinnertime. Harbor looked up when he heard me walking over.

"I need to send an update on the fighting back to Washington. Would you log on and send me one of your usual assessments?" Harbor was scanning the room. "Just like the ones you normally send in the morning. They want to check on our status, see if we'll be okay until Saturday."

"Of course, sir. As I'm sure you can hear, heavy fighting is still ongoing—I've been checking for updates via open source periodically throughout the day. The locations of fighting seem consistent with what we've seen the last forty-eight hours. I'll quickly research any new information and type it all up for you right away."

"Thank you. I'm going upstairs to pack. Please call me when it's ready."

"Yes, sir."

Harbor left to pack while I stayed behind, alone in the wrecked office, to write a short update while the others ate dinner. While I waited for my classified account to boot up, I walked over to the Marine command room right outside the office, to get an update from the Marine Staff Sergeant. He was the most senior Marine on the compound and in command of all Marines there. On the radio, they referred to him as 1-Actual, but I always called him by my nickname for him.

"Hi, Hunter. How close were they today? I could hear the whine of some of those incoming."

"Yeah, most of the outgoing were within one klick, or kilometer, of our location. Seems as though the return fire is getting closer to hitting the mark. You probably heard the whine on that incoming fire, also about a klick or half a klick out," said Hunter.

"You have a list today?"

"No, ma'am. There were so many fired today we couldn't keep count. We stopped around 200 rockets and anti-aircraft weapons fired, but some of those launches had simultaneous fire, so we just can't put an accurate figure on it."

"I understand. Still fired out from the southwest toward the southeast?"

"Yes, ma'am."

"I thought I heard gunfire toward the northeast too, was that up by the embassy?"

"Yes, same locations we discussed before. I think you're right—they're still fighting over the military barracks and militia camp."

"Okay, thanks for the update. You getting any sleep? How're the guys holding up?"

"Not much sleep, but we're still trying to do shifts. The red alerts don't really allow for much rest though." Hunter looked exhausted, but alert. He was by far the most capable Marine I'd worked with and his leadership of the Marines under his command constantly impressed me.

"Please tell them I said thank you, and thank you, too."

"You're welcome, but there's really not much we can do besides watch. We're on a completely defensive mission here, not offensive. We monitor. We prepare to guard. That's it. There's nothing we can do to stop it."

His frustration was evident and I could understand. All the personnel felt that way from one perspective or another.

"Well, it matters to me. So, thanks," and then I returned to the office to type the update.

"Evening Update to Militia Fighting in Tripoli, Libya" was shorter than my usual updates, but I'd been more focused on destruction and preparation than usual. I essentially wrote the same update I gave Harbor moments before and incorporated new intelligence and the details on rocket and anti-aircraft fire the Marines observed. I also added my assessment that the tide was turning, based on the intensity and proximity of fire and social media commentary, it appeared as though Operation Dawn gained even more ground.

IN THE DARK OF WAR

I focused on writing my update until I heard Captain walk into the office.

"Good evening," he said. He always acted formal and proper, even though we'd known each other for months.

"Good evening, Captain," I said, "Were you able to make contact with the militia commander?"

"Yes, he came for a meeting in the front villa. We were able to negotiate an escort on Saturday morning."

"That's good news."

"Well, sure, if they actually show up," Captain replied.

"Don't worry, for you and the money you promised, I'm certain they will," I said.

"They posted the Chalk vehicle and seat lists upstairs, did you see?"

"No, I haven't been upstairs in a while. I just finished this update for Harbor. I'll call him now and go look. Am I in a good vehicle?" I meant the people, not the actual vehicle, but that didn't translate.

"Yes, a Toyota Hilux, with the extra fuel supply."

He said that like it was a positive, but I didn't agree. I worried about riding in a vehicle with all the fuel and knew it could easily be ignited. If hit, the fuel would cause a massive explosion and I'd have no chance of surviving.

"At least I'd go out with a bang," I was trying to make light of my own fear, but he looked stricken and didn't laugh, "Captain, I'm joking. You okay?"

"I need to get this work done."

"Okay," I replied and picked up my radio. "Harbor, Harbor."

"Come back for Harbor."

"The update's ready for you now, sir." I logged off and walked upstairs to see the whiteboard with the Chalk list. A Chalk was a small section of the larger convoy, made up of a few vehicles traveling together in a group with varied departure times.

I saw a big crowd gathered around it and already heard complaints about who was with whom in which car and why. It was like middle school all over again, seeing the seating chart for the first time. I never liked middle school.

I also didn't like crowds and decided to grab dinner first. I walked over to the dining area and looked at the food. Our cook went all out. I figured he was cleaning out all our food supplies, the spread looked delicious. I chose some salmon, chicken, beef, and salad. I hadn't been eating much and knew I needed the sustenance for the days ahead. At that point, no one knew when we'd have our next meal, if at all.

I loaded up a plate and went to sit at the warrior table. I preferred to eat outside, even when it was hot, but with the constant heavy weapons fire it was not allowed. Even then, impacts from the explosions rattled the windows.

I sat alone at the table and the other officers shuffled all around the room focused on different tasks in preparation for the evacuation. I pulled out my iPad and loaded up the Libyan social media pages to find out what the locals said about the fighting.

On social media, there was more of the same rhetoric. The fighting had escalated into some kind of existential threat to the future, with the secular-aligned militias on one side and the Islamists on the other. Both also expressed willingness to fight long and hard for their beliefs.

I read, ate, and waited until the whiteboard cleared, then walked over to see who would be in my ride. Then something else caught my eye first.

Nomad would lead the evacuation.

I stopped reading. My heart thumped double time. I knew he had combat skills, obviously, and was an exceptionally capable officer. He was a great driver. But still, it placed me even more on edge. He'd drive the lead vehicle with Captain, who was also a former Navy SEAL. At least he was with Captain and Dolby, which he'd like, but I worried.

I tried desperately to contain my feelings as Dolby walked up.

"Dude, I'm leadin' the charge!" He sounded happy.

"I saw that."

"Oh yeah. Gettin' the hell outta here."

I ignored him and looked through the rest of the Chalks. I was in the third Chalk. Obi and Flash were in the lead vehicle of my Chalk with Harbor. There were several vehicles full of Marines from the embassy, then my vehicle. I was with Stitch, Tunes, and Whirlwind. As a senior officer, Whirlwind should be in the front right seat, as tactical commander and the shooter, but I was listed there.

"Dolby, why am I listed as right seat?" I paused, then added, "Serious answer, please."

"Dude, okay—wait—yes. You are in the right seat position of your vehicle because you were deemed most capable of carrying out that duty."

"Deemed by who?"

"Does it matter? It's awesome. You'll totally rock it."

"Oh my God," was all I could manage. I most definitely was not a warrior.

"Seriously though, Whirlwind isn't doing well, do you really want him as shooter? You think he can protect you if things go south?"

"He's not a bad guy. He has very good intentions."

"Sure, and the road to hell's paved with them. Is that where you want to go?"

"Of course not."

"And that's why. We know you can. Plus, there's your archery, the knife in your boot, and the Glock on your hip, which most people still aren't carrying if you hadn't noticed. These are all indicators."

"Indicators of what?"

"Your capability." His tone was serious for once.

"But I'm just an analyst, not a warrior." I was worried but I held it together, trying with every fiber of my being not to let it show.

"Dude, you're more than 'just an analyst'," Dolby smiled around the wad of chew in his mouth.

Then he walked away with his usual bouncy step.

Not buying it, I thought, *our options must be pretty limited if Dolby, of all people, tried to encourage me and make me feel better about my role.* It was nice of him to try, but I wasn't that naive and knew a security officer with a Special Operations background would never pick me over a fellow warrior, not if he had any other option. Not a chance. I thought I, as an analyst, would be a last resort for that role.

"Oh my God, please help me," I whispered my prayer.

CHAPTER FOUR

FLASHBACK: FAUX COUP

(LATE SUMMER 2013)

Later in the summer of 2013, a few weeks after I arrived, I began to feel a little more comfortable with my job and the environment on the compound. I met several colleagues I liked and quickly tried to learn everyone's names. I learned the names of the other officers as well as the local staff who worked on the compound. I also tried to learn the first names of the Marine contingent providing the physical protection of the compound, rather than using rank or last names.

For me, it was a gesture of respect and kindness. Those men and women risked their lives for me, day in and day out, and the least I could do was learn their names. I'd learned long ago to treat the lowest with the same, if not more, kindness than the highest. They needed it more.

Our Marines were a unit from the Marine Corps Security Force, rather than the Marine Security Guards (MSG) usually placed at embassies. They were assigned to protect US officials in the area after the Benghazi attacks.

I figured most Americans didn't realize the administration assigned troops on the ground in Libya, since it ran counter to the "no boots on the ground" policy. I hated that expression and false claim—no boots on the ground. Even though our Marines were a small contingent, I believed one boot was just as important as 100,000 and by claiming or pretending otherwise dishonored our warfighters' sacrifice and service.

The majority of our Marine contingent protected the embassy, but some were also located on the residence compound. They manned several locations, including the Marine command room inside the main villa by the office, and what we referred to as Mike-3.

Mike-3 was the highest fortified position on the compound, armed with a fifty-caliber machine gun, reams of ammunition, and protected by huge mounds of sandbags. Mike-3 served as the compound's primary protection, in the event violence came to our front gate. I thought it resembled an improvised turret.

I didn't know much about our Marines, duties, and weapons. I thought it might help with my job to know and I was curious, so I went up to check out Mike-3 one morning. That's where I met Hunter. Hunter stood about my height with dark hair and eyes and had an extremely foul mouth around the Marines. Not so much around me.

"Hey, you're not allowed up here." He looked stern as he scowled at me.

"Oh, I'm sorry. I didn't realize." I blushed and turned to leave, thinking he was serious, and the area was off limits.

"Oh woah, wait, I'm just joking." Hunter was laughing. "Who are you? That's never worked with any officers here before."

"I'm an analyst."

"I'm the staff sergeant here."

"I heard this is where you keep the 50-cal and came to check it out," I said.

Hunter walked me over to Mike-3 and introduced me to everyone. They all seemed shocked to see me up there, but welcoming. Then they showed me the weapons and equipment and talked about their requirements for manning the post. They didn't get many visitors. I blamed Hunter for scaring them away. He laughed at my attempt to tease him and later walked back inside the Marine command room with me.

"How long are you here?"

"We're on six-month rotations, but I'll stay longer," he said. "The rest of the Marines will switch out in January, then the next crew will be here until early July."

"Well, let me know if you need any cutting-edge analysis up there at Mike-3." I smiled at my own attempt at a joke. I knew strategic analysis would not help them much, but I wanted to do something to help the Marines who protected us.

The Marines would handle any bad guys literally climbing over the walls or attacking the front gate, as happened in Benghazi, and everyone in the entire region remained concerned about another such attack. Therefore, I began writing tailored assessments for the Marines' situational awareness. I didn't believe the information was actually cutting-edge, but I tried to make it useful.

I wrote one-page updates on developments in Tripoli for them once a week, which Hunter put in the Marine command room for all the Marines to read. I hoped it helped them prepare for, or at least maintain awareness of, the wide variety of threats we faced in Tripoli. Little did I know it was only the beginning of what would become a long year of escalating threats and crises.

In Tripoli, there was limited violence between the time of the Benghazi attacks in September 2012 and August 2013. Several isolated incidents occurred during that time, such as a car-bomb explosion outside the French Embassy and the use of rocket propelled grenades (RPG) against the Corinthia Hotel and the United Arab Emirates Embassy and residence in downtown Tripoli in July. The attacks resulted in no casualties and limited damage.

That all changed with the end of Ramadan. The events unfolding that month would set the tone for the coming year.

The embassy closed along with multiple other US Embassies and Consulates in the region for nearly a week due to a regional al-Qa'ida threat timed for the end of Ramadan. The ambassador suspended all moves, although no major terrorist attack occurred.

On the evening of the Eid al-Fitr, or the holiday to end Ramadan, rumors emerged on social media and via embassy contacts that a large convoy was headed to Tripoli from Misrata. Initial information suggested the militia forces sought to conduct a coup against then Prime Minister Ali Zaydan. The militia's loyalties allegedly lay with the recently appointed General National Congress (GNC) President Nuri Abu Sahmayn.

I immediately passed word of the rumored coup to the security officers and they recalled all personnel to the compound. Several officers who returned from moves reported seeing a large increase in the number of 'technicals' on the streets. Technicals in Libya consisted of a flatbed truck, usually some type of pickup truck, with a heavy weapon permanently mounted in the back.

The convoy and technicals remained inside Tripoli that month and set up checkpoints at all major intersections and near government facilities.

I wanted to learn more from a source with political insight, not just locals posting to social media. I gained permission to invite Muhammad, the Libyan I met on my flight into Tripoli, to a meeting at the compound. I believed he'd have a unique perspective on the situation.

Muhammad met me and another officer on the compound that month. Muhammad looked every bit the Libyan Revolutionary hipster stereotype. He wore skinny jeans, pointy dress shoes, a leather jacket, too much cologne, and had perfectly styled hair. We greeted one another with a slight head nod rather than a handshake to respect his religious beliefs about not touching an unrelated female. Then we held a long discussion about the militias.

"The Misratan militia has no intention of overthrowing the government at this time," said Muhammad.

"How do you know?" I asked.

"The militia commanders from Misrata and GNC president said the convoy came here to protect the government. Why would they lie? I believe the president when he says he invited the militia forces to Tripoli to provide additional security."

"If their intentions are pure, then why not announce the movement beforehand? What did the prime minister know?"

"Then the Zintan would have tried to stop them," replied Muhammad. "The prime minister knew nothing, he would have told the Zintan."

"The Zintan alone could not stop them."

"No, but Zintan plus their allies could."

Despite Muhammad's belief the convoy came in peace, I remained skeptical about the Misratans immediate intentions.

31

I knew elements of the militia bloc from Misrata joined forces with others who shared their Islamist ideology and referred to themselves as the Libyan Revolutionary Operations Room (LROR) under the direct leadership of the president. The prime minister, however, seemed to have no prior knowledge of the convoy's movement, its formation, or its intent.

I briefed the ambassador and country team on the convoy's movement and possible intentions during the intelligence briefing. I said the intent remained obscured, detailed the mixed reporting, and explained how our officers worked to collect more information. I stated the LROR did not appear to be conducting a coup and joked that it was a faux coup, which the ambassador didn't find funny. At all.

I honestly thought she'd send me packing that night. I decided to maintain my highest level of formality with her in all future meetings and briefings. No more light-hearted moments or attempts at levity. Not that I was very funny, but I tried. I was usually the only one who laughed at my jokes anyway.

My attempted joke led to a lengthy discussion about what actually constituted a coup. I provided the terms and definitions established by the US government on the issue. The ambassador seemed to believe the militia bloc from Misrata was, in fact, in Tripoli to provide additional security and had no ill intent toward the prime minister. The ambassador's opinion matched Muhammad's.

The ambassador usually listened closely to me during the intelligence briefing but frequently disagreed with the information I provided. Although we maintained a courteous working relationship, the briefing occasionally became contentious and also frequently involved her dog, which I also thought odd.

The dog would bark during briefings and crawl into people's laps. I'd be in the middle of a thought and feel something rubbing against my leg, which freaked me out.

The ambassador also routinely met with Libyan government officials and was quite close to the prime minister, so when reporting sounded at odds with what the ambassador heard in an official capacity, she disagreed. I simply provided the latest assessments based on all the intelligence available, not just the views and opinions of Libyan political leaders and advisors. I also explained how those two perspectives differed.

I prayed for wisdom and patience. She listened to the facts, but I needed to find a way to effectively convey our assessments. The information was important and I needed to share it in a way that would get her to listen. I considered that my responsibility.

As a result of the militias' presence in Tripoli, inter-militia tensions and violence spiked. Tripoli's neighborhood militias, such as the Suq al-Juma and Abu Salim Brigades, appeared to align with the LROR and Misratan militia based on shared ideology and convenience.

Other nearby militias like the Warfali and Warshafana did not want the Misratans or the LROR near their territory. Therefore, they pushed back violently against any perceived infringement, as Muhammad speculated they would.

The LROR also functioned as an umbrella organization, or operations center, for the Libya Shield units that fell under the MoD. The MoD divided the Libya Shield into units based on geography and assigned each a name or number corresponding to location. Misratans formed the Central Shield, but the Shield units of most concern to me were Shields One and Two.

Libya Shield One, led by Wisam Bin Humayd, closely cooperated with the US and UN designated terrorist group Ansar al-Sharia, the terrorist group responsible for the Benghazi attacks. Wisam maintained close ties to Ansar al-Sharia leaders. Shield One and Ansar al-Sharia would later merge with other extremist groups to form the Benghazi Revolutionary Shura Council, which they announced on social media.

Libya Shield Two, led by Buka al-Uraybi, also maintained close ties to Shield One, Ansar al-Sharia, and other extremist groups. Libya Shield One, Two, and Central fell under the purview of the LROR, the MoD, and the president.

As a result of those relationships with the government and the increasingly apparent extremist tendencies of the Islamist leaning blocs, the Libyan public's wariness of Islamists also increased. Libyans were especially concerned with the Muslim Brotherhood's influence in their country.

As antagonism in Tripoli increased with the presence of the LROR and Misratan militia, one specific location under dispute was Camp Yunis, often referred to as Camp Twenty-Seven because it was twenty-seven kilometers west of downtown Tripoli. A Libyan military counterterrorism force used the camp for a training ground as part of a joint program with the US military called the 1208 program.

US military personnel frequently visited and provided training at the camp, but on the night a militia overran the camp, no US citizens were present.

In late August, tensions peaked and an opposing militia, believing another militia had gained the upper hand, overran Camp Twenty-Seven and looted all the weapons, vehicles, and supplies. The US provided most of the stolen weapons and vehicles to the Libyan government as part of the training agreement.

The Libyan government proved unable to recover Camp Twenty-Seven, the weapons, or the vehicles. The 1208 force guards did not defend the camp—they simply left when confronted. The 1208 force stored the weapons in a facility with a secure biometric entrance, which was opened. No attempt was made to retake the camp, either through Libyan diplomatic channels or through force. It remained vacant for months.

The ambassador called Libyan government officials and expressed the US' displeasure over the incident. She sent the 1208 trainers back to AFRICOM.

No one took concrete actions to recover the weapons or hold those responsible accountable.

But I believed, even if the Libyans knew the identities of the militia members, the Libyan government likely had them on the payroll, either through the MoD with the LROR and Misratans, or through the MoI with the Zintan and Warshafana. Therefore, the public and the militias themselves, often viewed militia members as operating under official authorities and for the greater good. Sort of a vigilante justice operation.

I briefed the incident to the security officers. I provided details on how a militia overran the camp, the Libyan security forces reactions, and the loss of numerous US-provided, high-tech, and sophisticated weapons and vehicles.

Those weapons and vehicles could now be used against us.

The militia could use similar tactics to overrun our compounds.

I worried, I researched more, and I prayed.

At the end of the month, Reebok, my new boss, and Captain arrived. I provided them both a briefing on their first evening in Tripoli.

I gave my then standard 'Libya Today' briefing that I provided to all newcomers.

The briefing changed based on current events, but the message remained essentially the same—the country was divided, and it would be really bad if that division grew worse. Although that summary doesn't sound very articulate, I provided more nuance in the actual briefings.

I focused on how the Libyan government struggled to remain cohesive. That a divide appeared to be forming in the country between the Islamist leaning and secular leaning groups, but it was difficult to determine with any certainty because alliances constantly shifted, and the vast majority of Libyans were conservative Muslims as a baseline.

At that time, a single militia could probably take power, but no single group could hold power. And that was key.

The powerful tribes and militias seemed to follow their own checks and balances, and the public held them accountable. I warned that as divisions deepened and goals aligned, the balance could shift dramatically one way or the other. The two key factors that could change the situation long term were oil and the terrorist groups.

I liked Reebok and Captain. They both struck me as capable. They listened attentively and asked intelligent questions, which I appreciated.

I liked intelligent people, which was one of the things I appreciated about my job. They surrounded me, but in a good way.

Reebok was extremely no-nonsense and liked to get straight to the point, he announced to all personnel he wouldn't tolerate any behavior on the compound he deemed even remotely inappropriate, with a heavy emphasis on sexual harassment. He had a zero-tolerance policy and made it known. He said if someone chose to harass others, his or her next choice would be chicken or beef. On the flight home.

In his first all-hands he also explained that he applied for the position in Libya for several professional and personal reasons.

He was injured in an operation several years prior but his dedication to the mission continued to compel him to serve in dangerous environments. In addition, he lived in the region before and wanted to return. He also loved to run.

Captain was intensely focused and told me he previously served as a Navy SEAL in Iraq and Afghanistan and wanted to continue to use his skills to serve his country in a different capacity, one that did not involve constantly fighting in wars. He said, standing in a war zone. Only I appreciated the irony.

Some of my colleagues met Captain before he departed the US for Libya and told me they thought he looked like Captain America. I agreed and felt incredibly thankful to have him with us on the compound in Libya. Even if he didn't have actual superhero powers, he was certainly someone I wanted on my side in a fight, or impending civil war.

I decided to begin sending weekly cable updates to the analysts back at CIA Headquarters. They all expressed interest in atmospherics, things that would not meet threshold for official reports, but would provide insight into the fast-paced developments and constantly changing environment in Libya.

In my first update back, I provided a general accounting of the faux coup—yes, I still called it that, just not to the ambassador—and the incident at Camp Twenty-Seven, reactions, and my take on potential fallout. I believed the incident would highlight the Libyan govern-ment's vulnerabilities, and its lack of control over any sort of military or law enforcement capacity.

I also privately believed the incident publicly demonstrated how the US government would, or in that case would not, respond to violent incidents against US interests in Tripoli in the future. It set a standard.

We wouldn't respond to a militia attack.

I continued to work long hours, every day of the week, with no days off. Reebok was also an early riser, so I tried to scan new informa-tion as quickly as possible every morning before he inevitably asked, "What's going on in Libya today?"

He asked me almost every morning, sometimes B.C.—before coffee, which kept me on my toes. I started brewing my coffee in my villa before going to the office, so I could sip it on my short walk to the main villa, and I'd have a couple minutes for the caffeine to kick in before I ran into him.

Reebok also expected me to know all the ins and outs of the country, just like the former chief. Sometimes I thought he enjoyed finding obscure articles on Libya to ask me about, just to catch me off guard. And he certainly found them.

No pressure, just read and know everything. I reminded myself as I shoved my nose further into my iPad to read the latest breaking news. But he came to me for information, and that meant I needed to know—it was my responsibility. I felt overwhelmed by it, which meant I worked harder and longer.

I carried my mini iPad with me everywhere, except into the classified areas. I read it while I ate, walked between buildings, as soon as I woke up, and before I went to sleep. I never stopped researching and analyzing information, not for a single second I was awake in the country.

I also tried to make more time for people, for my colleagues. I didn't actually enjoy feeling like an outsider. It was lonely. Plus, I wanted to know the people I spent every waking moment trying to protect, and who, in turn, protected me.

I still ate breakfast outside each day, right next to the front door, and made a point of saying good morning to each person as they went into work. Some would stop and chat with me for a moment before moving on.

One morning I met Flash and Arcade, new security officer arrivals. Both had dark hair and eyes, were slightly taller than me, with beards and tattoos, and built of solid muscle.

Arcade was quiet and observant, but I usually got a gruff good morning out of him. He stood and walked like a boxer, slightly hunched over and always on his toes. I wasn't surprised to learn he was extremely well educated and also had a gym he owned and ran on the side.

Flash always looked effortlessly cool. He was an artist and we frequently talked about drawing, lead, and ink. He brought some of his art supplies with him. I would later come to realize, despite his best efforts to conceal it, Flash had a strong sense of duty and was among those officers who cared most deeply about his job and the people he protected.

September was a somber month in Libya that year. Much of the month focused in some way on the terrorist attacks conducted against the US State Department Temporary Mission Facility and CIA Annex in Benghazi the year prior, which I usually referred to as the Benghazi attacks.

In early September, the lead FBI investigator and analyst flew to Tripoli to conduct interviews with potential local witnesses who couldn't leave the country. They conducted most of the interviews at the embassy. They met separately with me nearly every day they remained in country to discuss terrorism.

The FBI gathered information on the attacks as part of their investigation. The FBI, not the CIA, conducted the investigation. However, as a CIA counterterrorism analyst I knew a great deal about the terrorist networks, relationships, and key figures operating in eastern Libya. Thus, the FBI coordinated closely with me and other personnel in Tripoli.

We exchanged information on Ansar al-Sharia and how the group formed and evolved since 2012. I explained how organizations in Libya, be it terrorist or other, frequently changed names.

I believed Libyan organizations changed names to conceal their intentions or simply to accommodate new members. The groups placed much more value and importance on relationships than structure, which made it difficult at times to determine command and control.

Ansar al-Sharia in Libya, Tunisia, and elsewhere followed both of those basic principals. Ansar al-Sharia appeared willing to work with any extremist group in Libya that shared its ideology or had a personal connection on some level.

I believed Ansar al-Sharia would change its name in the future when it suited its purpose.

I also requested a briefing from the FBI on their assessment of the attack. I thought it would help for officers to know the FBI's priorities to further drive collection, cooperation, and sharing. The FBI provided a basic overview briefing and showed the surveillance camera footage of the attacks for the officers on the weekend before the one-year anniversary of the attacks.

Counterterrorism remained a top priority.

I became a counterterrorism analyst entirely because of the September 11, 2001 attacks. The attacks occurred near the end of my time at the University of Puget Sound, where I graduated with an English degree in Writing, Rhetoric, and Culture. My older brother graduated from college that year. My two younger brothers had already completed high school. We all still lived in the Pacific Northwest near our family.

Those attacks changed the courses of our lives. I thought I'd work for local emergency services, such as the police or fire, while I wrote books. At the time, I interned for a county government's Emergency Management division. On September 11, 2001, classes were cancelled, and I went to work instead, preparing an Urban Search and Rescue Team to deploy to the Pentagon and the World Trade Center.

My manager at the county was a retired Army colonel. I told him I wanted to do more after graduation, to serve at the national level. He recommended the Defense Intelligence Agency, which appealed to me because my brothers all signed up to serve in the Department of Defense as well.

My youngest brother enlisted first. He joined the Air Force.

My middle brother went next, he enlisted in the Army.

I received an offer from DIA and began the paperwork process.

There was no way my older brother was going to be left behind—he commissioned into the Army as an officer. They all chose the communications specialty.

We left home within months of each other in late 2002 and early 2003. By then, we knew the Iraq war was coming. And my mother, though proud, was distraught and her health not what it once was.

"I can't believe you're all leaving at the same time." Unshed tears filled my mother's eyes.

"I bet I deploy first." My baby brother towered over me by then. "First to enlist, first to deploy."

"Then I won't be far behind." My middle brother never was.

"I bet our sister goes first, wouldn't that be unexpected?" My oldest brother looked right into my eyes.

"Yeah, right." I laughed, mashed potatoes once again poised on my spoon. It was Thanksgiving, our last holiday together before my baby brother left home to attend basic training.

"Remember I'll be praying for you every day. Hold your faith close, keep God in your heart, and listen to the still small voice he sends you," said my mother.

"That's His Holy Spirit," said my brother.

"Yes, some call it intuition or a gut feeling, but that is God guiding you. Listen to it and He'll keep you safe."

"We'll come home from the war, mom. And then you'll have your chance to cry like a baby when we're back at this table," he said.

We stopped to pray right then, food left for the moment, but our thoughts on the current and coming wars. We held hands and bowed our heads together, one last time over Thanksgiving dinner, which remains my favorite holiday, mostly because of that day.

In the end, I was the first to deploy, which definitely surprised everyone, but believe me, I rubbed it in as any competitive sister would with her beloved siblings. My father was the most displeased. I remember calling to tell him and he said, "they're sending my baby girl to Iraq?"

I started with DIA in the spring of 2003 and by November I was on a plane to Baghdad. I first attended a course on driving and shooting, DIA decided that was enough training for a civilian going to Iraq and sent me off.

To this day, the only pictures I have of myself posing with a weapon are from that deployment. I had my friend take a photo of me holding my M-4 on Camp Slayer in Baghdad before we drove to the Green Zone, which I sent my mother, and asked her to mail a copy to each of my brothers.

That's how I told them I'd deployed. That picture.

They were still in various stages of training.

On the anniversary of the attacks, in Libya, the ambassador closed the embassy and Reebok halted moves for the day. Instead, all officers remained on the compounds. Reebok and Captain coordinated issues with Washington D.C. while I analyzed information and provided briefings but the significance of the day was not far from anyone's thoughts.

Despite the extreme heat that September, on the evening of the 11th we built a large bonfire on the compound to commemorate those who died in the attacks in 2001 and in 2012.

A security officer, who served in Benghazi the night of the attacks, served as team lead with us in Tripoli again that year and led the ceremony. I liked him a great deal and thought he was an exceptional officer. He briefly talked about what happened that night, the extraordinary actions of all the personnel in Benghazi, and honored the officers who died.

He called for a moment of silence. Then an officer played *Amazing Grace*. I, along with the rest of the officers, listened and stared into the fire. We stayed at the bonfire for quite a while that night. No one spoke much. One by one we departed to our rooms.

For me, September 11th became a day to reflect on the lives of those we lost, to say a prayer of thanks for the sacrifices they made, and to renew my determination to ensure my own life made a difference.

I was in Arabic language training September 11—12, 2012 when the Benghazi attacks occurred. I served with, and knew well, the CIA analysts who drafted those now infamous talking points. I watched from afar, consumed with Arabic, as they toiled to answer the stream of requests for information, congressional inquiries, senate testimonies, intelligence products, and numerous other tasks in response to the attacks and those talking points. It continued for years. It's probably still happening.

There's been much written on what happened that night, from the CIA security officers' firsthand account, to a former diplomatic security officer's State Department take, to the account of the former acting director of the CIA that night. There's even more information in the media—everyone it seems, has an opinion.

So, here's what I knew at the time:

I knew the only people who truly knew what happened on the ground that night were the people on the ground that night. End of story. In addition to the CIA security officers' firsthand account, there was a detailed senate report and trial testimony that provided additional firsthand information.

As a career counterterrorism analyst, I knew a multi-phase, coordinated attack with precision fire required planning and experience.

Those responsible for the attack used some rudimentary tactics, but rudimentary did not equal untrained, nonthreatening, or nonlethal.

It's easy to second guess decisions, hindsight's twenty-twenty, there's the fog of war, and all the other clichés. In the end, brave people saved lives, and other people caused the loss of life. Those responsible for the loss of life need to be held accountable.

Here's what concerned me in Tripoli one year later:

In Benghazi, there was no specific warning about that attack despite the fact CIA officers met with sources and collected information about terrorist plans and intentions in the city. One year later in Tripoli, we had even less information, especially because there was no longer a US presence in Benghazi, which meant we'd have even less warning about Ansar al-Sharia plans and intentions throughout the entire region.

In Benghazi, local terrorists pulled off a major attack against a hugely popular and well-loved ambassador in a city where the US was celebrated. In Tripoli, the new ambassador was not well liked and the US presence was not particularly welcome.

In Benghazi, they used a local militia for outer security, which caused significant problems the night of the attack. In Tripoli, we used a local militia for outer security.

In Benghazi, there wasn't enough internal security. In Tripoli, we had more officers and a larger footprint. There still wasn't enough internal security.

What I believed:

I believed a similar attack could easily happen in Tripoli. It seemed the only pre-attack indicators in Benghazi were the series of security incidents against Western diplomatic targets. So, for my corner of Libya, I'd monitor security incidents against Western targets and if we didn't receive specific threat information, at least we'd have that as a warning mechanism.

I also believed that my faith would help guide me, maybe not in the way I wanted, but maybe in the way we needed. I remember attending a brown-bag lunch session at CIA Headquarters given by a CIA operations officer who was in Benghazi during the attacks. At the end of his briefing, he talked about how he believed the attacks could've been even worse, but for the difference of a few important things. Days before the attacks, officers conducted emergency medical training, enhanced a small security measure, and other similar things. He said whether we believed that to be luck, fortune, providence, or God's intervention, it saved lives. He said he wouldn't be there speaking to us that day, but for the grace of God.

I prayed for that same grace.

CHAPTER FIVE

EVACUATION: WEAPONS ISSUED

(JULY 24, 2014)

The night of the evacuation announcement on July 24th, 2014, the fighting between the Zintan and Operation Dawn continued to rage. While the major focus of the fighting centered on Tripoli International Airport, the small arms fire moved closer to the compound. In addition, the direction of the sound suggested the heaviest clashes remained to the northeast, closer to the embassy, and moving into Zintan territory from downtown Tripoli.

The Zintan continued to launch GRAD rockets and anti-aircraft artillery—which isn't restricted to use on airborne targets—from the vicinity of the compound toward the militia forces fighting around the embassy and the Qasr Bin Gashr neighborhood next to the airport, which was overtaken by Operation Dawn forces earlier in the week. They used rockets and anti-aircraft artillery because there was an abundance left over in the country from the former regime which was now in the hands of the militia forces. Body armor remained mandatory for all personnel moving about outside.

I turned my radio back to the main channel. I'd been listening to updates from the Marines on the locations of weapons fire and impacts after I finished checking the Chalk list. Explosions rattled the windows and flashed in the dark night sky.

The militias hadn't slowed combat all day, which was unusual. Fighting up until that point was intense but didn't last throughout every hour of the entire day.

I turned to go back downstairs. Dinner was long over and Gambler announced that the issuance of rifles, Glocks, and extra magazines would begin in ten minutes.

"Hey, you pick up your rifle yet?" Stitch, the driver of my vehicle, walked in the front door and saw me by the warrior table.

"No, I was just on my way there now," I said. "Should I put it in the vehicle tonight or keep it in my room?"

"I'd keep it with me, but that's up to you."

"Okay, I'll wait until tomorrow. Then maybe we could review procedure, what you need from me as right seat?"

"Absolutely, just let me know when you're ready."

Together we walked downstairs. Stitch was new and I didn't know him as well as the others. He served as the Special Operations Forces (SOF) Command representative assigned to work in close cooperation with us.

As we entered the basement, we saw almost all personnel waiting in line to receive weapons and ammunition. The security officers had their own stash, so Stitch broke off to join them out back. I guessed Nomad was already back there by then too.

I walked over to get in line. Otter stood ahead of me in line chatting with Blue. I said hello and they quickly moved to include me and then Belle walked over to join us. We often spent time together and the current situation only made us closer.

They talked about seating assignments. I should've known.

"I'm with Triage!" said Belle. She had a natural affinity for him too, since they were both from the same state. They had a lot in common.

"What Chalk?" I asked.

"Four," she replied.

"I'm Chalk three, with Stitch."

"I'm bringing up the rear. Totally stoked. I hope I get to set this place up in flames once and for all. Throw on a few grenades," said Otter. "Chalk five, with Gambler."

"Aw, man. I want to be with Gambler. No fair. You're going to have so much fun," joked Blue. "I'm Chalk two, Arcade's right seat."

"With Arcade? Good, I'm glad we're spreading the Arabic speakers out. That puts one of us in most chalks," said Belle. She, Blue, and I all knew Arabic.

"Plus, it makes sense they'd put you with him, loudest with the quietest," I teased Blue.

He was known for being a talker and was by far the most social of our group.

"Hah. Touché," said Blue. "I saw they split you up from Nomad."

"Oh my goodness, hush."

"Oh come on, we already know."

"Yeah, yeah, and I know it actually doesn't matter, but it's private. Even if it was against the rules, what're they going to do, send us home?" I said with a healthy dose of sarcasm. They couldn't send us home. We were trapped. That was the point. But they also needed Nomad and me to help get everyone else out.

Otter, Belle, and Blue laughed lightly, but they also all felt the pain behind those words. After the fighting began, we were stuck in Libya, and everyone felt trapped and on edge because of it. We made jokes off and on about the situation, one officer even started a game with a reward for who could best substitute the five stages of grief for the five stages of being trapped in Tripoli. Dark humor, but it helped some people deal with the situation.

I didn't participate. I didn't think it was funny.

While we talked, the line moved forward and Blue, a former Marine, moved first to accept his weapons from Gambler. He handed Blue an extra Glock, two extra magazines, a rifle, and magazines for that. Otter and Belle accepted a rifle and two magazines. When I stepped forward, I relayed that I was designated tactical commander like Blue. Gambler gave me even more weapons—a rifle, five extra magazines, an extra Glock, and more magazines for the Glock. I was loaded down.

"Wow. You're packing heat," said Blue. "What's up with that?"

"I am Stitch's right seat on the ride out,"

"Woah," said Belle, "Be careful—seriously."

"I'll try, but that goes for you too. If we encounter something, I have a feeling we'll all be in it together."

Otter, Blue, and Belle looked concerned, but no one said anything further about the drive out. They knew I closely monitored intelligence for threats and security information. And they collected much of the threat information themselves from their contacts.

"Well—what's next?" asked Blue, changing the topic.

"I need to set these down in my room, then I'll be back to help more with destruction," I said.

"Me too. Looks like there's a sledgehammer party starting out back." Belle walked out back to the housing in the rear with Otter, while Blue and I strode toward the villas out front.

"Dang, it's still hot out." Blue wiped his brow.

It was well past sunset, and the air felt heavy with heat, humidity, and smoke. Explosions continued to echo in the dark and we could hear heavy and light weapons fire all around us. Blue strode by my side until we reached my villa.

"You need help with those?"

I knew he'd drop everything to help me with the weapons if I asked. I shifted them in my arms but shook my head no.

"I'm good, but thanks."

"Suit yourself," he said and continued to his villa.

I actually did want a refresher on the rifle and help oiling it, since it looked like it'd been on the shelf for quite a long time, but I planned to ask Nomad. I knew he wouldn't judge or tease me at all for asking for help. Blue wouldn't judge, but he'd certainly tease, and I wasn't in the mood for it.

I hustled back up to my villa and felt more than a little disappointed Nomad wasn't there. Even though I figured he remained busy with destruction, I always hoped to see him there. He made me feel safer.

I laid out all the weapons and ammo on the spare bed in my room and debated what to do next. Normally, we wouldn't leave weapons out and unattended, but circumstances change.

The rifle needed oil, but I thought it'd be better to wait for Nomad. Even though I felt confident the training would come back to me once I started, I thought it wiser to wait for help. And faster. I didn't have time to look it up or try to figure it out on my own. There was a lot of work to do yet.

Although I didn't find Nomad, I did find the gear he left behind. Clearly the security officers were preparing for the worst on the drive out, and there was quite a stash. I saw a large rifle with a grenade launcher on it, extra grenades, night vision goggles, and other things I couldn't as easily identify, but definitely all weapons.

My stomach turned in knots, I knew I had to hold it together for just a little while longer. A few more days. I'd make it. The other officers and I were prepared, we'd get to the border, and we'd be safe.

Just a little bit longer.

I tried to convince myself not to worry, but it didn't work. My prayer for protection became a constant mantra in the back my mind and I fought to keep my doubts from outweighing my hope.

I forced myself to focus on other things instead of the looming evacuation, like the massive destruction currently underway.

I left my room and went back to the rear of the main villa to join the sledgehammer group. We usually blacked-out the compound, but they kept some dim lights on behind the office area that night to enable destruction. It looked like Gambler organized that area. He swung his sledgehammer with a fury and electronic parts went flying all over. It was the most disheveled I'd ever seen him.

I joined the group of personnel sweeping up the parts and putting them, with the larger chunks, into the back of the truck that would take them to the fire. Moe sat in the vehicle preparing to take the load out to the fire, it was almost full. No one said much and we all focused on working as quickly as possible.

The fighting around our compound intensified. The artillery sounded loud and close, combined with the sound of the hammers. It was almost impossible to hear anything else.

When Moe started the engine and drove the load out, another vehicle backed into the spot. Nomad drove that one and when he saw me he nodded and stared at me for a moment. I stared back and then nodded slightly, an unspoken encouragement, and we both went back to work. It was nice to have him there. I always felt safer when he was near, even though logically I knew that it was impossible to protect against an incoming rocket.

We continued to work for several more hours. I thought we'd easily destroyed millions of dollars that day and there was so much more to do. We destroyed most of the electronics though, and that was the priority. The only electronic equipment left operational were two classified computers reserved for Harbor, Captain, myself, and a few other officers to send updates and reports back to Washington D.C. and to organize the evacuation.

I figured it was around 0200 by that time and I felt exhausted. Everyone looked tired. Officers started peeling off one by one to return to the villas, and when there were only a handful of people left, I found Nomad by his truck.

"I'm headed back to my villa now," I whispered.

He looked at me and whispered back, "I'll be right behind you."

"Alright."

"Soon."

I decided to walk through the main villa to exit the front door before walking to my own villa and the relative safety of my room. Artillery fire resounded all around me. I felt concerned about indirect rounds landing on the compound again.

The fighting always intensified in those early morning hours between 0200 and 0600. I still had on my vest, but it wasn't really enough, not against rockets. It was like trying to block the sun with a piece of glass.

Once I left the front door, I walked as quickly as possible to my villa, then up the stairs beside the floor-to-ceiling windows. Normally, I loved those windows and the sunlight they let in, but lately they were just another threat. They weren't bullet proof. Any bomb or rocket that exploded close enough would break those windows and send shards of glass flying.

As soon as I got to my room, I took off my heavy body armor. I really wanted to take a shower. I was covered in sweat and dirt and who knew what other foul junk from the fire, but my bathroom window faced east toward most of the fighting. I decided to take a quick shower anyway and get ready for bed as fast as I possibly could.

I also turned on some music. Not so loud I couldn't hear the radios, but just enough to drown out the sound of some distant artillery.

I sat on the couch, near the stairwell and as far from the windows as possible and waited for Nomad. He also quickly showered after he returned to the villa and then joined me. We sat there for a while, not saying much, and I think he knew how apprehensive I felt. My mind raced, but I refused to let fear take hold. I'd deal with it later, if or when we made it to safety.

Then Nomad whispered, "Have I told you yet today how beautiful you are?"

"Not yet," I whispered back.

"You are beautiful," he said as he hugged me close.

I didn't sleep much that night, but I did try to at least rest a little. The sound of bombs and rockets sounded so loud and didn't let up— not once. I learned to excel at distinguishing the outgoing from the incoming and tensed whenever I heard incoming.

The radio also squawked all night, which wasn't normal either. It sounded like Gambler stayed up the entire night working on various aspects of destruction. Gambler was in charge of that and took the responsibility seriously. He knew, as well as I, the chances of the compound falling into enemy hands after we left were high. He wanted to be prepared for that, leaving nothing behind, especially any trace of officers' personal information.

Captain and Robin also made radio calls throughout the short night. It seemed as though they remained busy coordinating the evacuation route and the associated logistics. Captain worked to ensure AFRICOM and the US military were fully integrated into our planning process.

Ultimately, no one slept much that night.

I woke up with the dawn sun streaming in through my east-facing windows and the exchange of renewed weapons fire. It seemed like Operation Dawn forces gained more ground, because the fighting sounded even closer than the day before. I lay there listening for a few minutes. I could also hear increased small arms fire. It sounded like it was extremely close, possibly at Army Command and Staff College off Airport Road, near our location and the airport.

The sound of heavy artillery also continued in the direction of the airport. The Zintan sounded like they launched on offensive against the opposing forces occupying the Qasr Bin Gashr neighborhood. The opposing forces sounded like they were firing back, with more accuracy than the days before.

I felt exhausted but summoned the will to get up and face the day. Just as I was sitting up, I heard Harbor call out for me on the radio.

"A-lyst. A-lyst. Harbor."

I leaned over and grabbed the radio sitting on the nightstand. "Send it."

"I need to see you in the office."

"I'll be there in fifteen minutes."

I hustled to get ready. I put on the same clothes I wore the previous day. I was in for another long, grueling, and filthy day. I put on my body armor and weapons. I placed my Glock on my hip, knife in my boot. I pulled my hair back into a ponytail and put on my compass necklace.

The sight of my arms gave me pause, black and blue bruises dotted the length of them and I ached everywhere.

Nomad found me and walked me to the back door of our villa.

"Ready?" I stared into his eyes for a moment, mentally preparing myself to walk outside into the ongoing light and heavy weapons fire—the explosions of the larger rockets and artillery continued to echo around us and reverberate through the compound.

"I'm always ready. Are you?"

"Will you help me oil my rifle today?" I ignored his question to buy myself a little more time to prepare.

"Yes, I took a look at it yesterday and it definitely needs some. It'd still fire but would be better to get it in the best condition possible to avoid jams."

"I'll find you later then. Thanks."

"You're very welcome."

Nomad and I left together to walk to the main villa. We walked as quickly as possible again and as we entered the front door another barrage of nearby rockets launched.

"When will they run out?" asked Nomad.

"Probably not for a very long time. I desperately need coffee. Immediately. You want one too?"

"Yeah, today I'll take the caffeine. Thanks."

I prepared myself a triple espresso and made Nomad a double. I passed it to him before hurrying down to the office. I saw Harbor in the back corner and walked straight to him.

"That was fast, thanks. I know it's still early," said Harbor, "but I need to send another update to Washington. Would you mind logging on and sending me the latest on the fighting and threats?"

"Right away, sir."

"That coffee smells great. I'm going to go get a cup myself, grab some food. Please call me when you're done."

"Yes, sir," I responded as I settled in to write.

CHAPTER SIX

FLASHBACK: POWERFUL TRIBES

(FALL 2013)

In the weeks following the Benghazi anniversary, work continued as usual. Captain, and his new deputy, Robin, organized and conducted a trip to southwest Libya. They held meetings with local councils and border officials in Nalut and Wazin. They gathered details on the route, potential pitfalls, and established contacts.

Some security officers helped conduct the trip and provided protection. Some of those same officers would ultimately remain in Tripoli and assist in the evacuation, while some later rotated out.

We believed the route was a viable last resort in an emergency, but not ideal given the length, mountain pass, and number of tribes and groups the route would necessitate coordination with before use.

The route went through some treacherous terrain. We resided at the edge of a vast desert, after all. The route cut through at least one hostile area and it contained switchbacks with blind corners, which was never good when ambush was a concern—which it was.

One tribe along the route was the Amizegh, ethnically Berber, and one of the largest minority groups in Libya along with the Toubou and the Taureg.

That September, the minority groups shut down an oil field in southern Libya in protest against their treatment by the new Libyan Government. The minority groups demanded equal representation and wanted their languages included in the new constitution.

As a result of the shutdown, along with the continued shutdown of the fields in eastern Libya by the Federalists, oil production plummeted.

The oil shortages caused second order effects on the population. Gas shortages spread through the country and gas lines at stations in Tripoli stretched for miles. Electrical plants requiring oil or gas for production stopped functioning, and blackouts swept through the capital for hours a day during one of the hottest months of the year.

When Muhammad came to the compound that month to meet with us, we discussed the oil shutdowns. Muhammad wore a black fedora during that visit, continuing to embrace the role of the Libyan hipster.

"We will send delegations to meet with the minority leaders," said Muhammad. "The government wants the shutdowns to end as quickly as possible."

"To what demands will they capitulate?" I asked.

"All of them."

"Won't that embolden other groups to carry out similar tactics in the future?"

"Perhaps, but the government needs the oil to flow. We cannot have gas lines and blackouts. Public opinion is of utmost importance."

The Libyan leaders did as Muhammad said they would. They sent delegations to meet with the minority leaders and negotiate an end to the shutdowns. The oil started flowing again from the south.

Another tribe saw the effectiveness of such tactics and it shut down the manmade river in anger over the arrest of a tribal member. The Ghadafi regime built the manmade river decades prior, it carried water from the oases of southern Libya up to the capital. The manmade river provided almost all of the drinking water for Tripoli.

The faucets in the city ran dry. Hawkers sold bottled water on street corners for many times the normal price.

The Libyan government quickly negotiated another settlement.

The blackouts and water shortages, however, did not affect US personnel. The embassy had a few pallets of extra bottled water in reserve. The compound was far more prepared. We had a generator on site—which fortunately had been full to capacity when the incident began—large underground fuel reserves, and similarly large water reserves for such emergency situations.

Every time I read a social media post about the lack of water, I felt parched and took a sip of water. I drank a great deal of water that month. I felt extremely grateful for the support officers' foresight to plan well for such emergencies.

I saw cases of Meals Ready to Eat (MRE) in the basement next to the cases of water stacked floor to ceiling and hoped we'd never be in a situation where we'd have to eat MREs in Libya. That would be a dark day. They had to eat MREs in Iraq soon after I redeployed from there and I was grateful I had escaped that.

When I was a kid, I thought MREs were so cool. My grandfather would sometimes bring a couple home and my brothers and I would take them on "camping" trips in the backyard or on daring expeditions into the unknown of the neighbor's yard. Those MREs sustained us and fueled my imagination. Then I ate one as an adult in a training course and hoped I'd never have to again.

Still, it was better than starving and I'd take what I could get in an emergency.

Meanwhile, the fuel, electrical, and water shortages had no impact on the operations of Ansar al-Sharia groups in eastern Libya. They continued to expand their assassination campaign against security and former government officials.

Improvised explosive device (IED) attacks also increased. Extremists placed most IEDs in the front driver's side wheel well of vehicles in order to assassinate the driver. However, they also carried out several vehicle-borne IED attacks against the remaining foreign and Libyan government buildings in Benghazi and Darnah.

Although Ansar al-Sharia never claimed attacks, all signs indicated the group was culpable. I believed its intent was to anonymously sow discord and instability through attacks—then offer to provide that security in lieu of a capable government force. The group frequently publicly displayed their 'peace keeping' and humanitarian operations. They never claimed terrorist operations.

I wasn't fooled.

In late September, a new tranche of officers arrived on the compound, including Belle, Otter, and Blue. I knew upon meeting her Belle and I would become close friends.

Belle was incredibly smart and looked like one of those vintage bombshells that aircrews used to paint on warplanes during World War Two. She spoke Arabic, was an excellent officer, and far more outgoing than me. The most critical element for our future friendship was we didn't feel threatened by each other. Instead we supported each other and enjoyed having intellectual conversations. In the years since we met, we've solved nearly all the world's problems during late night chats over a warm drink.

Otter and I could've been brother and sister, we were about the same height and Otter also had blonde hair and blue eyes. He was much bubblier than me though, and not a typical officer. He was kind and friendly without expecting anything but friendship in return, except maybe my brain. We ended up sharing a desk space for most of the year.

Blue was a natural leader. He was a former Marine, funny, also spoke Arabic, a bit older than me, and had a family at home. Blue liked to crack jokes most of the time, especially at inopportune moments, but he was also genuinely funny, unlike me. People almost always laughed at his jokes, even when told in a foreign language to foreign nationals.

"Are you ready for your 'welcome to Libya, it's a hot mess' briefing?" I asked them post-breakfast soon after they arrived.

"Definitely." Otter led the group as and we walked toward the office.

I continued to give all newcomers an overview briefing and I had a whiteboard set up in the office to walk them through the key points.

"Wow." Blue looked over at the whiteboard covered in marker. "That's some serious *Beautiful Mind* chaos going on there. How do you make sense of that?"

"Don't worry. I'll walk everyone through it," I said. "This is what I do here. This is all I do. Live and breathe Libya. Plus, the board's meant to demonstrate how messy the situation is."

"It certainly does that," said Belle. "What do the colors represent?"

"Well, I wrote down all the key players and groups in black. Green boxes indicate more secular-aligned, blue boxes indicate Islamist-aligned, and the red indicate straight up terrorist ties. The first thing you need to know is I've made sweeping generalizations on alignment, secular versus Islamist, with the color coding. In reality it's much more nuanced than that, but as groups become more polarized that nuance will likely dissipate and morph into the generalizations I've drawn here, which I'll explain in detail."

"Not enough colors?" asked Belle.

"Well, it's easier to wrap my head around looking at it like this," added Otter.

"Exactly, that's the intent. There's a spectrum of beliefs, particularly within the Islamist-aligned groups. Not all Islamist groups are extremists and not all individuals in the groups share the same beliefs or goals," I said. It was an important distinction, but for an introductory briefing, the generalizations worked best.

"Is there a similar concept in the US to compare the generalizations with?" asked Otter.

"It's sort of, kind of, like the terms liberal and conservative in the US. Most people don't entirely fall into only one category or the other, but it's still a useful framework."

"And a deepening divide at that," said Blue.

"Yes, but hopefully our belief systems and political landscape won't grow as divided as they are here."

Then I talked them through the whiteboard. I explained how people, groups, and organizations aligned at that moment in Libya, how they changed alliances based on their own interests, and how extremists were spreading through the country and quickly turning Libya into a terrorist safe haven.

I realized the longer I spent in the country, the more the threat turned inward, the closer I grew to my colleagues, the more focused I became with warning about, and helping prevent, another terrorist attack against our own officers.

A congressional delegation was visiting Tripoli and part of my duties as CIA analyst there included providing briefings to all congressional or staff delegations. I always focused on the current state of Libya and I never discussed the Benghazi attacks, because I couldn't comment on the FBI's investigation.

The congressman, however, wanted to discuss the attacks and it was his key agenda item. The intelligence briefing on Libya also included the ambassador and Reebok.

The meeting grew tense as it became clear we could not divulge information related in any way to the FBI's investigation. It was not a pleasant experience. I wanted to point out I didn't make the rules, but I think on some level, he was fully aware of the legalities about active investigations.

The congressman told the ambassador the State Department failed in Benghazi. It was their lack of security and preparedness that led to the death of Ambassador Stevens. The ambassador countered that perhaps it was because the department was so good they had not lost an ambassador in decades.

As the conversation continued and became more heated, the congressman brought up the political controversy surrounding the attacks and further stated no one would have even cared about what happened during the attacks had it only been CIA officers who died that night. He believed the attack only mattered as much as it did because an ambassador was killed.

I felt shocked and it must have shown on my face.

He quickly explained what he intended to say was because one of the victims was high profile, the ambassador, it raised the profile of the incident overall.

I didn't think it made his statement any more acceptable. My shock quickly turned to fury. I was livid. As a CIA officer serving in Libya, I took that personally. My life had value. All our lives had value.

I was not expendable. I didn't appreciate the implication that somehow, I was, that I'd be an acceptable—overlooked even—loss to my government.

My fury then turned to doubt, doubt about my purpose, my service, and my continued presence in the country. I prayed for wisdom, and for the grace to remain silent, when all I wanted to do was lash out at the congressman which wouldn't end well anyway.

October 2013 didn't make me feel less expendable or more valued. The month began with sequestration and the furlough of the US federal government. That meant while serving in Libya and working extensive overtime, the other officers and I didn't receive our salaries for more than a week. Not that I could spend the money in Tripoli, but it was the principle of the thing.

The month also began with an attack on the Russian Embassy in downtown Tripoli.

Assailants from the Suq al-Juma neighborhood, most likely members of the neighborhood militia, attacked the Russian Embassy in early October. Earlier the same week, a Russian woman stabbed a former Libyan military officer and his mother in the Suq al-Juma neighborhood, resulting in his death. Assailants responded by tracking down the Russian woman, incapacitating her, and taking her to a private militia prison at Mitiga Airbase.

Members of the militia thought the woman might be associated with the Russian Embassy or harbored nefarious intent against their government. In a further retaliatory measure, assailants associated with the militia set off a car bomb in front of the Russian Embassy, overran the walls, tore down the Russian flag, and set the building on fire.

Russian diplomatic security eventually fought off the attackers and then evacuated their embassy staff overland to Tunisia using the coastal road and Ras Ajdir border crossing.

We closely monitored the attack given the parallels to the Benghazi attacks and concern a similar event could happen to our facilities in Tripoli. The coastal road also topped our list of potential emergency evacuations routes, so we discussed the viability of using the same route in the future after the Russians used it for an evacuation.

I researched the attack and provided a briefing to all personnel on the mechanics of it and indicators for a future scenario.

It didn't bode well for how Libyans would treat diplomats in Tripoli.

Not at all.

Once again, the Libyan government didn't intervene. Other militias remained silent. Security forces stayed at home. No one helped the Russians.

I added another attack to my lengthening list of security incidents in Tripoli.

During that same time, the US Military and FBI were also in the final stages of planning an operation to capture one of the FBI's Most Wanted in Tripoli, Libya—Abu Anas al-Libi, whose true name was Nazih Abdul-Hamed Nabih al-Ruqai'i. Abu Anas helped plan the 1998 East Africa Embassy bombings and the US president recently approved a concept of operations that would allow US Special Operations Forces to enter Tripoli, capture Abu Anas, and hand him over to the FBI for extradition to the United States and prosecution for his crimes.

I paid close attention to the operation, because a raid against a prominent terrorist in Tripoli would affect us. I knew for every action there would be a reaction. I wanted to be prepared for the inevitable backlash.

The US Mission hosted the US Special Operations Forces officers for the operation but didn't have a direct role in the raid. For my part, I primarily focused on potential repercussions of the operation. I assessed possible fallout for the Libyan government, impact on public opinion, and reactions of terrorist groups.

I figured the terrorist groups wouldn't like the US to swoop in and arrest a prominent terrorist on their turf. They'd probably be angry and seek to retaliate. And since we sat on their turf, it stood to reason they'd come after us following the operation.

During the pre-dawn hours of October 5, 2013, US Special Operations Forces conducted the raid and successfully captured Abu Anas in downtown Tripoli. News of his capture quickly spread and the US Special Operations Forces officers scrambled to get Abu Anas, and themselves, out of Libya.

The Libyan Prime Minister publicly denied knowledge of the operation, which led many to view him as weak.

The Libyan president claimed the capture violated Libyan sovereignty and demanded the US return Abu Anas for prosecution in Libya.

The Libyan public seemed to understand the US' decision to capture Abu Anas to some degree and sympathized with the desire for justice. However, Libyans also wondered why the US, and not their own government, had the capacity to remove a world-renowned terrorist from the streets of downtown Tripoli.

I thought that a legitimate question. Why didn't the local government arrest a world-renowned terrorist openly living in their capital?

Then in rolled the threats. I focused on those. I researched each threat to determine which appeared credible and required further attention, and which seemed unreliable or fragmentary. Most threats fell into the latter category, like an angry call-in who threatened to 'do something bad' in response to the operation.

I looked at them all, categorized the threats, and cabled back to CIA Headquarters each day with a summary of reactions to the operation. I included notes on any research I completed.

There were a lot of threats.

Most of the threats sounded vague, but several seemed credible. Almost all threatened to attack US facilities or kidnap the ambassador or any US personnel in the country.

I believed each should be taken seriously and thoroughly researched, but with the understanding most sources obtained the information indirectly from unknown sub sources or via a lengthy chain of acquisition. It was my job as an analyst to coordinate with the other analysts at CIA Headquarters to differentiate the credible from the non credible.

I invited Muhammad to the compound once again to discuss the reaction to the operation and threats. Otter joined us during our meeting that month.

"Congratulations on the capture of Abu Anas," said Muhammad, "But why didn't someone tell our government? You violated our sovereignty. I thought we were friends."

"It wasn't my decision," I said.

"You could have told me."

"Are Libyans angry about it?" asked Otter.

"Some, but most understand. I understand, but you could have told me."

"Who is angry?" asked Otter.

"Ansar al-Sharia wants revenge, as you must know. The group announced that on social media."

"Knowing is half the battle. That's their intent, but do you think they have the capability?" I asked.

"Maybe. The group is not strong in Tripoli, but one cannot rule out the possibility of an attack. Look what just happened to the Russians. These things happen. Especially when beliefs are violated," said Muhammad. "You must know there will be consequences to what you have done here."

"What do you think will happen?" I asked.

"Only God knows."

Yes indeed, only God knew. And I prayed he'd keep us safe. But I also kept my Glock close in my go-bag and my knife tucked securely in my boot at all times.

I studied Arabic full time for a year before my arrival in Libya. It's a notoriously tough language to learn, and for good reason. There are five levels to the US government's scale for language proficiency; level zero is no proficiency and level five is considered the native speaker level. In the romance languages like Spanish and French, a few months(ish) of full-time study resulted in a level three proficiency. In Arabic, the full year resulted in a level two and it required a second full year to reach level three. I hit the mark and obtained my level two, with a plus in reading comprehension, which I spent the most time studying.

I carried flashcards with me everywhere I went that year.

I kept color-coded vocabulary, verb conjugations, and grammar rules in my handbag at all times, replacing my usual book. I pulled them out while waiting in lines, between meetings, during meals, and even in the bathtub.

I discarded the daily-life vocabulary, like words for food and clothing, and instead focused on military and geo-political words. I couldn't order a meal at a restaurant, but I could carry on a basic conversation about the tactics used by terrorists in the Middle East.

I obsessed over it, worried if I didn't learn a particular word or phrase it could result in my death or the deaths of my colleagues. During one training session, my instructor led me through a scenario.

My instructor pretended to stop me at a checkpoint as I drove to a meeting. He pulled out a fake pistol, pointed it at me, and screamed in Arabic that he was going to kill me.

Being screamed at in Arabic was not awesome. Having a fake weapon pointed at me wasn't great either. Even though it wasn't real, it was intense.

I froze.

He demanded to know my response, what would I do? Kill him first or die? Kill or die. Kill or die, he demanded again.

I was glad when that scenario ended. I chose not to die. He spoke to me for a long time afterward about the scenario. He recommended I think about that and other similar scenarios I might encounter in Libya, practice the vocabulary, and pretend to respond. He reminded me I was going to a hostile area and I might one day have to make such a choice. I prayed it would never come to that.

When the year ended, my colleagues and I prepared to depart for our various assignments. A fellow CIA analyst friend of mine was going to another unstable North African country.

On our last day at CIA Headquarters, we stared at the television monitors and watched as hostile forces breached the outer perimeter of a US Embassy in the region.

"Here's to poor life choices," he said as he turned to me with a grimace.

I shook my head.

"To surviving," I countered. I stood by my choices and prayed I was right.

The week after the operation to capture Abu Anas, I provided an intelligence briefing to the security officers on the numerous threats. I gave separate briefings to the ambassador, Reebok, and the country team on reactions to the operation, provided succinct summaries of the reporting, and finished with my assessments of the threat.

"As an analyst, aren't you supposed to connect the dots?" the ambassador asked after one such intelligence briefing. I figured the ambassador was annoyed I couldn't provide a specific time and place of an intended attack, but I bristled.

"Yes, ma'am." I hated the expression "connect the dots" with a passion.

Policy makers like to use that expression when making accusations of intelligence failures. Policy failures didn't exist in our world. If a policy prevented the collection of intelligence information, it was never the policy that failed. It was the intelligence analysts who failed to connect information no one obtained. If a policy maker ignored, failed to read, or failed to act on the analysts' warnings, they believed the blame still lay with the intelligence analysts, not with the policy maker. An analyst could write article after article warning the sky was falling, but if the policy maker ignored or refused to listen, it was a huge shock when the sky fell. And they always blamed the analysts.

"The problem is there are many dots," I said. "I could make any picture I want. The goal is not to connect the dots, but to make sense of the dots."

"What do you mean?"

I grabbed a piece of paper and pencil and sat next to the ambassador while everyone else listened. I drew dots all over the paper as I tried to think of the best way to explain.

"So, each dot here represents a possible threat. We know they want to attack us, that much is clear, but what we need to know is who, what, when, where, why, and how. The first thing we do is look at credibility of the information and weigh each dot accordingly."

I darkened some of the dots and partially erased others.

"And while this information might be more credible, it's often fragmentary," I said pointing at the darkened dots. Then I started drawing lines between some.

"We know this terrorist trained with this one or this one knew that one in the past or this group trained as suicide bombers or these are particularly interested in attacking during Ramadan, and this threat is to attack your vehicle.

"And we can connect all of those but that doesn't mean these specific terrorists will conduct a suicide attack during Ramadan against your vehicle.

"So, then we incorporate the less credible, looking for patterns. Judging the likelihood certain training did or did not take place. Whether terrorist leaders with a proclivity for suicide attacks live in Libya. Things like that.

"The biggest challenge in putting together the picture are these blank spaces," I said, pointing to the empty areas on the paper.

"These are the intelligence gaps. The things we don't know. For example, the CIA no longer has a presence in Benghazi, so that is a challenge for the entire country," I said. And that was putting it lightly. I really did try to be tactful and objective, even when riled.

"The empty spaces are sometimes the greatest threat, the things we don't see coming, and that's why we warn and explain gaps," I added.

"So how do you make an assessment? And what is the CIA's assessment?" asked the ambassador.

"Assessments are made by thoroughly researching the available information, from all sources. Then one extrapolates likely possibilities based on one's knowledge and experience following terrorist groups. Probabilistic language and confidence levels in assessments are added, and there are many layers of vetting."

Then I reviewed the CIA's assessment again. The ambassador still seemed frustrated.

Everyone felt on edge, waiting to see if there would be an attack or some kind of response. A response eventually came, but not in the way anyone expected, certainly not in the way I expected.

Was that a policy failure or an intelligence failure?

At the time, it didn't matter, we just had to deal with it.

CHAPTER SEVEN

EVACUATION: DESTROY EVERYTHING

(JULY 25, 2014)

Later that morning on July 25th, 2014, I sat down at the last remaining computer in the office to write the update for Harbor. Sound echoed strangely around the empty room. There wasn't much left other than this sole terminal. It made me feel hallow to see the room like that, just a shell. I turned back to the monitor and started the log on process.

While I waited, I went to check social media on my iPad for updates on the fighting directly from Tripolitanians. I sipped my coffee and read through the latest postings. It always surprised me so many Libyan groups, including Operation Dawn forces, announced their plans and intentions on social media.

Based on recent postings and my own observations, it seemed the fighting moved significantly closer. The fighting near our location appeared to be at the Command and Staff College, as I thought. Near the embassy, Operation Dawn forced the Zintan out of the Islamic Call Center, one of their strongholds, and the fighters fled to the neighborhoods surrounding the embassy. From their locations, the Zintan continued to launch artillery and small arms fire toward the Islamic Call Center, and Dawn forces returned fire.

I needed to compare that data to the intelligence information as well, but it seemed accurate based on past information of Operation Dawn's intent. The computer was still booting up, so I walked over to the Marine command room to check in with Hunter.

I found Hunter looking more exhausted and frazzled than I'd ever seen him. I hated to bother him, but I needed to write the daily update on the militia fighting.

"Hey Hunter, I'm seeing lots of chatter about fighting near the college and the Islamic Call Center, is that consistent with what your Marines have seen and heard this morning?" I asked.

"Yeah. Exactly. It was a bad night. Marines at the embassy said they're getting sprayed with indirect. Most of them had to stay hunkered down in their positions all night. All we can do is watch."

Hunter looked exhausted and frustrated. He then dropped an f-bomb and quickly apologized for it, but then dropped another one.

"Hell, I'm sorry, shouldn't say that in front of you."

"Well, Hicks, you could always try harsh language," I joked, hoping he'd seen *Aliens*.

"That didn't work in the movie, and it hasn't been effective here either. Trust me. I've tried," said Hunter, clearly understanding.

"You need anything?"

"Sleep. We're already well past our turnover date."

"I know, I'm sorry."

The radio squawked on the Marine channel with another round of artillery reported, this time only half a klick away. We could hear and feel the impact from those rockets even more strongly than previous volleys.

"I need to write the update. Thanks for the information and let me know if I can help with anything. Stay frosty," I said, quoting the movie again.

"You too. And alert."

I returned to my desk and saw my email finally opened. I first checked through all the latest intelligence reports. Then I wrote my update for Harbor. The classified information was also largely consistent, although there was a lag time in reporting, so I summarized what I read from social media, learned from the Marines, read in intelligence, and what our sources reported.

The only information that struck me as odd was the report of rocket impact on our location. I thought about it for a few minutes, analyzing the possible causes, and realized it must be the destruction fires that led people to believe a rocket hit our compound.

I typed a quick note to analysts at CIA Headquarters letting them know the postings were inaccurate. The compound had not taken a large direct hit and the report was most likely based on false assumptions about the causes of the destruction fires. Once I finished, I hit send, provided Harbor the full update, and started the log off process.

"Harbor. Harbor," I called out on the radio.

"Go for Harbor."

"I finished the update, it's with you now." I left the office and walked upstairs in search of food. I passed Harbor in the stairwell and he thanked me again for the update.

Upstairs, I saw day two of destruction in full swing, so I hurried over to the food cart. Not much food remained by that time, but I took a couple pieces of cold bacon and made another triple espresso. I didn't even bother sitting down for breakfast, my meal quickly consumed. The main floor was in chaos as officers moved around in their destruction activities and the Marines ran back and forth in their security duties.

Belle walked in and saw me as I finished my bacon.

"You done? We need help clearing out the office in the front villa, I thought you and I could handle that," said Belle.

"Sure, just one second," I said as I gulped my last bite and then put my dishes in the sink. I didn't bother to wash them since it was our last day.

"What's in that villa?" I asked.

"I'm actually not entirely sure. It's the office Ali uses and apparently he has a lot of administrative type paperwork. Unclassified personnel information we need to destroy."

"Let's go."

"How are you holding up?"

"Hanging in there. I'm worried but trying to stay focused. I give myself periodic pep talks, like 'Keep it together!'"

"I know what you mean."

"You doing okay?"

"As well as can be expected. I'm trying to stay busy so I don't think about being scared."

"Same here. I haven't really had time to process feeling scared yet."

We continued chatting as we walked to the front villa. We found the office inside. The front villas housed the Marines and the designated common areas and neither Belle nor I had been in the office before.

She and I went to work pulling paperwork down off the walls. There was a huge bulletin board with documents all over it. As we started pulling down layers, we found passport photos. There were a lot of them and most of them were of Belle and me. Sometimes being one of only a handful of women was less than ideal. Belle seemed to think the same.

"Um…creepy," said Belle.

"Yeah," I replied. "Why would they need so many copies?"

"I don't even want to know."

"Gross."

"Yeah. Let's burn this stuff as quickly as possible."

We started shoving all the documents into large garbage bags and took turns dragging them out to the curb to be taken to the fire. We emptied the filing cabinet, but the drawers on the desk were locked.

"Is there a key?" I asked.

"No idea, let me check," replied Belle pulling her radio from where it was clipped on her pocket. "Gambler. Gambler. Belle."

"Come back for Gambler."

"We're in the front villa office. Is there a key for the desk drawers?"

"Ali has it, you'll have to force them open."

"Roger that," said Belle into the radio, then turned to me. "Well, do you have a hammer, crowbar, or any tool we can use to bust this open?"

"Nope and to be honest, I'm a little worried about what we're going to find."

As we stood there debating how best to force open the drawers, Nomad walked in with Arcade, carrying large sledgehammers.

"We heard the call of women in need," teased Nomad, "And we men are useful for carrying heavy things."

"And destroying stuff," said Arcade in his gruff way.

With that, Arcade walked over to the desk and began wailing on the drawers. Nomad walked around the entire bottom floor from room to room, smashing every television and computer screen he saw. He said he didn't want the bad guys getting nice televisions. He said the screens belonged to America and wouldn't be fully appreciated anyway. None of us argued his point. It was better to destroy everything.

Arcade ripped the desk drawers out and inside we found more copies of passports. The copies included notes written in Arabic.

"What does this stuff say? Anything important?" asked Arcade.

Belle and I looked over his shoulder, reading the Arabic. Each copy included what appeared to be notes about the individual.

"This doesn't look good," said Belle.

"I'm not sure, but I think we need to verify no one's mentioned the evacuation to Ali. I'm going to run to the office and let Gambler know. Can you all finish up here?" I asked.

"Absolutely. Call us if you need anything," said Nomad.

I left to inform Gambler about what we found. It could mean nothing, but I figured it was worth sharing. The other three quickly bagged the rest of the documents and took the load directly to the destruction fire. The villa was completely cleaned out once they finished.

After speaking with Gambler about the documents, he left to talk to Harbor about Ali. I stepped out of the back of the main villa and jumped when I heard a series of loud, sharp, and extremely close explosions. Not rockets, but something else.

My stomach clenched and lodged somewhere in my throat, while I simultaneously broke out in a cold sweat. Had the compound been breached? I feared the worst and quickly jumped back in the doorway where I saw Triage.

"Hey, it's okay, just blasting caps," said Triage.

"That sounded close," I replied, still recovering. My breath came in gasps.

"It is. Moe and Stitch just took the entire stock back to the fire. We have to destroy those."

"Are they going to destroy any more of the explosives?"

"No, destroying the blasting caps should cover our bases. As much as possible anyway."

"Okay. Do you know where I can find some oil for my rifle?"

"Nomad already grabbed some for you."

"Awesome. Thanks."

"Anytime. Don't forget to sanitize your room. Gambler wants everything we're not taking with us put on the fire, except maybe clothes."

"I'll go do that now."

I smiled my thanks to Triage and started walking toward my room. I moved quickly since the militias still battled outside.

Once I reached my villa, I ran inside and up the stairs to my room, grabbing several large garbage bags from the kitchen along the way. I didn't bother putting my clothes in the fire, since I figured it wouldn't really matter or identify me anyway. I threw out anything that had my name on it, pictures of my family, of my hometown, anything that might in anyway give a clue about my personal life or me.

I felt saddest about throwing away my bow and arrows. I loved my bow and there were so many positive memories tied to it.

I held the bow close for a moment, thinking back to my first time shooting it with Nomad and our subsequent bet, which led to our first coffee date. I gave myself a moment to feel sad, took a deep breath, shoved the bow in the garbage bag, and with a heavy heart took the bags out to the truck collecting personal belongings for the fire. I threw everything into the back of the truck and then stepped back onto the sidewalk.

"Boo," I quietly said using one of Nomad's favorite words. It was simple, but so expressive.

Nomad saw me standing by the truck looking forlorn and joined me.

"Bow?" he asked.

"Yeah."

I hated Libya so much in that moment.

I looked up and saw Flash on the other side of the truck with a similar expression. I figured he had just thrown on his art supplies. He probably felt the same way I did.

"You ready to oil the—" asked Nomad.

A loud explosion nearby cut off his last word. I flinched, nodded in spite of it, and we hurried back inside.

Once inside, Nomad rested his hand on my back as we walked, trying to comfort me. Inside my room, Nomad gave me a quick refresher on the rifle. I knew how to use it, I qualified on one several times, but it was nice to get a one-on-one refresher before a major operation. Especially from a warrior and especially from one who specialized in weapons.

I then fit the stock to my shoulder. I spent a few minutes going through the motions of taking off the safety, taking aim, lining up the sites, and loading and unloading the rifle. For good measure, we oiled all our other weapons as well, just in case.

"I'm going to go put the extra ammo in the vehicle now," I said.

"Don't forget a scarf to cover the rifle."

"Really, even for this?"

"Yes, it's mostly for the border crossing and transit to Tunis. We're not supposed to have weapons there."

"Oh, got it. I think the only one I have big enough is this sparkly blue one from my mother."

"Well, you'll have the prettiest rifle around," said Nomad.

"Right? If only people knew," I said.

"Here, I'll help you carry the magazines over."

I needed Stitch to meet us. He had the key. I pulled my radio from my pocket then called out, "Stitch. Stitch."

"Go for Stitch."

"Can I meet you at our vehicle?"

"Be right there."

Nomad and I exited the back door of the villa and walked around to the vehicle staging area. Each vehicle was armored and had diplomatic plates identifying us as American. Not ideal in Libya, but in theory it should help in Tunisia. Stitch met us at the Hilux. Stitch had already filled the gas and diesel canisters in the back of the truck and a strong gas odor emanated from them.

"You'll definitely want to wrap your backpack in a garbage bag in the morning. Otherwise, your bag and everything you own will reek like gas," said Stitch. "I'll leave some extras in the back."

"Will do. Where do you want these?" I gestured toward the magazines and scarf.

"Well, the rifle you'll want in the right seat by your legs, covered with the scarf, preferably nestled up next to the center console. You'll see where mine will go on the left side. Mags and extra Glock under your legs in front of your seat."

I opened the door of the Hilux and took the magazines from Nomad. I thanked him for his help and he winked at me, which still made me blush, despite everything going on around us. Then he returned toward the main villa.

I placed my blue scarf where my rifle would go in the morning and draped it to cover the magazines I put on the floor next to where the rifle would rest.

"Looks like it's going to be tight in there," I said to Stitch.

"Yep, not a comfy ride," said Stitch.

"Can you walk me through what you need from me tomorrow?"

"Yes, ma'am. The main thing is to be vigilant and call out any threats, anything unusual," he said.

He went on to explain I was responsible for the safety and well being of the occupants of the vehicle which centered on telling him about any concerns, which he would handle for the vehicle, as the security officer in charge. I preferred to defer to him on any vehicle concerns or issues, since he was the trained and experienced warrior.

I wanted to feel prepared and for me that meant knowledge of what was to come.

He said if we came under fire, we would first evade. If the vehicle became inoperable, he would coordinate any defense, and I would move the other two officers in our vehicle to safety.

I'd also help navigate if the need arose but we had a navigation system and if all went well we'd simply follow the vehicle in front of us.

"That's basically it," said Stitch. "Think you can handle that?"

"Yes," I said, "No big deal."

Except it was a huge deal, a huge responsibility and we both knew it. The frequent explosions and gunfire around us, even then, was a reminder of that.

I looked down at my seat in the vehicle, then up at the dark smoke blackening the sky, and asked the time.

"It's 1600 now," Stitch told me.

"Just twelve more hours then," I said, thinking about what lay ahead and about all the things that could go wrong.

CHAPTER EIGHT

FLASHBACK: MAYHEM DOWNTOWN

(LATE FALL 2013)

During the early morning hours of October 10, 2013, just five days after the capture of Abu Anas, the LROR (Libyan Revolutionary Operations Room) kidnapped the prime minister from his room at the Corinthia Hotel in downtown Tripoli.

I was sound asleep when a knock on my door woke me that morning. Reebok didn't want to use the radio and wake everyone, so he sent someone to get me. I rushed to prepare and spent a long day in the office attempting to make sense of the situation.

At first, no one seemed to know who took the prime minister, where they took him, or whether he remained alive and well. Information was difficult to come by in those early hours.

The LROR later claimed they kidnapped the PM in response to the Libyan Government's involvement in Abu Anas' capture. The Libyan president visited the prime minister in LROR's custody. What did that mean? And how did it impact the deepening divide between the two?

While both later denied the Libyan president's involvement in the kidnapping, the president did not secure the PM's release, did not leave the room with him, and previously gave himself official commander-in-chief authority over the LROR.

That suggested to me it occurred with the president's knowledge.

I believed the LROR's kidnapping of the prime minister, possibly with the president's knowledge, deepened the political and religious divide in the Libyan government. Members of the GNC appeared to side with either the PM or the president—few remained neutral. Most believed they acted in Libya's best interest.

After he was released, the prime minister changed his security posture. He increased the number of his personal security guards and leaned on the MOI for support in that endeavor, deepening the divide just a little bit further.

It deepened in increments then, little by little, but soon it would reach a tipping point and then I feared it would happen all at once.

I briefed the response and the signs of a deepening divide to the Ambassador and Reebok.

Reebok and I also engaged in several long discussions about the Libyan Muslim Brotherhood. Belle, Blue, and Otter often participated and added their thoughts.

The Libyan Muslim Brotherhood during that timeframe pushed for recognition and greater prominence in the government. They portrayed themselves as fundamentally different from the Egyptian Muslim Brotherhood, focused instead on equality, peace, and governance.

After the events in Egypt, however, there was widespread public concern about the Libyan Muslim Brotherhood's prominence and position in Libyan politics. The public seemed to want to limit the group's power.

One officer wondered if the Libyan Muslim Brotherhood really was extreme, or more focused on equitable governance. He asked how Libyans would react if they gained power. We discussed the fallout on the Zintan, since the Zintan controlled the territory on which we lived. The boss and I also debated how an Islamist government could impact, positively or negatively, terrorist groups already operating in the country.

I speculated that a future scenario with Libya returning as a state sponsor of terrorism was not outside the realm of possibility. Particularly given the current trajectory of the country and fringe players involved, primarily the former LIFG (Libyan Islamic Fighting Group) members who now held senior political or government positions in

Libya and maintained close connections with the Brotherhood, terrorists in the east, and al-Qa'ida members.

I felt tired from all the long days and greatly appreciated having Belle, Otter, and Blue as friends. They'd started joining me for breakfast at the table outside.

The four of us frequently talked about any new work-related developments and soon began discussing our lives outside of work and outside of Libya in greater detail. Others occasionally joined our small breakfast club. Blue began calling the table inside where the security officers sat the 'warrior table,' and it caught on throughout the compound.

During meals I'd sometimes hear the local staff humming as they worked around the compound. I realized one afternoon one man hummed hymns. Church hymns, like the ones I'd sung in my youth. I sat stunned for a moment and then hummed along, a huge smile on my face.

He was a Christian from Nigeria who, like many Sub-Saharan Africans, traveled north in the hope of a better life, opportunity for work, or passage to Europe. His wife and many other Sub-Saharan Africans worked on the compound as well. She sang hymns in my villa as she cleaned. He wrote a Bible verse on the outside of his office door in permanent marker.

In general, the locals didn't treat migrants well. It was a country steeped in prejudice.

Most of the workers on our compound were migrants. One of the kitchen staff came from elsewhere in the region but the others came from farther away. I practiced my Arabic with the one, chatted with the others, and most of the other officers on the compound gave them additional tips or gifts on the side.

When I told my mother about them, she began adding extra gifts in my care packages for me to hand out.

The staff was kind and friendly, and they risked their lives to work for the Americans. I worried what might happen to them if we were attacked. Where would they go? What would become of them?

I said a prayer for them too, and I like to think some of them also said one for me.

I still worry about them.

Then, one night at the end of October 2013, as I left the office to return to my villa, I saw Nomad for the first time.

He must have arrived earlier that day or the previous night. I saw him sitting at the warrior table, laughing with Moe and Triage. His laugh caught my attention first and I thought it was a positive sign he had already gravitated toward two of my favorite security officers. I paused for a moment to really look.

Nomad had his longer-than-average hair pulled back, was clean shaven, wore a plain t-shirt and jeans, and seemed comfortable in his own skin. Not arrogant, but confident. He was tall, muscular, and ridiculously good-looking.

I tried not to stare.

I kept walking and opened the front door to leave. I breathed a silent sigh of relief I did not smack into the door in my distraction. As I opened it, the door squeaked, and they looked over at me. I smiled their way, said goodnight, and walked out without running into anything. I thought that was a win under the circumstances.

I could feel Nomad's eyes on me and I took one ever-so-brief glance back.

November in Libya began with a focus on the General Purpose Force (GPF). In theory, the GPF would serve as the new Libyan military. Recruitment and retention into the Libyan armed forces stagnated after the Revolution, and the public was wary of its ties to the former regime. Concurrently, the Revolution saw the rise of militias.

After the Revolution, the Libyan government brought militias under the control of the MoI and MoD, they brought the militias in wholesale, without separating members into different units. As a result, the militias never fully integrated into a government structure and the members' loyalties remained with their militias and tribes.

Militia members also remained higher paid than their military and law enforcement counterparts. The government better funded, uniformed, and trained the militia members. There was very little incentive for young Libyan men seeking work to join official law enforcement or military instead of their local militia, which technically fell under the MoI or MoD anyway. The women could do neither in Libya.

Therefore, the new effort became the GPF. The prime minister mentioned early on how he needed a better security force. The US Administration, seemingly feeling responsible to help, came up with the idea of a GPF, which the ambassador proposed to the PM. He agreed, but there was no broad support for the GPF, and it appeared as though the Libyan government did not have a vested interest in its creation.

They seemed to think the militias worked out just fine. When there was a crisis, they called on the militias for help. Not the military or law enforcement.

The GPF program involved the recruitment of thousands of young Libyan men under the auspices of the MoD, who would undergo initial training in Libya, then continue their training under the leadership and direction of foreign military experts in a foreign country. Upon their return they would be integrated into the Libyan military and serve their country in the same capacity as, but instead of, the militias.

The GPF program until that date was an unmitigated disaster. Some recruits completed the initial stage of training and moved on to the second phase in locations like Turkey and Jordan. In almost every instance, the majority of recruits were sent home for poor behavior. In the worst cases some recruits committed crimes, such as sexual assaults against their host country nationals. In addition, the Libyan government never paid the foreign military for the training, as was previously agreed upon.

For the US effort, the US military required the names of recruits prior to leaving Libya in order to fully vet the names and weed out any with terrorist ties. In addition, the US required partial payment of the sum total in advance. The training would occur in a third country, not in the US, but be conducted by US military personnel.

Despite months of requests, the Minister of Defense would not sign the final agreement for the US-GPF training program. The MoD never provided names of recruits for the required vetting effort.

The country wasted the opportunity.

The ambassador, Reebok, the rest of the country team, and I discussed the GPF on multiple occasions during the weekly intelligence briefing. The country team couldn't understand why there was never any progress on the effort.

The program was approved on both sides beforehand and now simply required a signature, a nominal amount of money, and list of names. Reebok repeatedly referred to the situation using the metaphor "you can lead a horse to water but you can't make him drink." Someone else claimed local militia fighters only excelled at two things, setting things on fire and forming committees, and were doomed to fail.

The ambassador continued to push the program since it was the administration's primary, or only, policy effort to help Libya build capacity and stabilize.

It was frustrating, to say the least. Libyans begged for help. They pleaded. And then the men chosen to represent their country squandered the opportunity by getting drunk, setting things on fire, and trying to rape or assault the men and women in the host country trying to help them.

During my meeting that month with Muhammad and Otter, I focused on the GPF and asked Muhammad for his thoughts on the program and why it failed.

"How could it possibly succeed?" asked Muhammad. "No one wants the new system except the Americans."

"The prime minister asked for a military force. In addition, capacity building is an extremely important component of stabilizing a country," I said.

"Capacity building?"

"Establishing a secure environment in which the country can grow and prosper. A law enforcement or military capability is necessary for that."

"We have the militias. Why not help us train our militias?"

"They are not integrated into the government. We provide assistance to government forces, not militia forces," I countered. He didn't seem to appreciate the difference.

"We need America's help, not its judgment. You led this war and now you have left us to flounder on our own. We are doing the best we can, but we need American assistance. We need concrete help, not to be talked down to, not to be bossed around."

"What assistance?" I asked, but Muhammad went on, full of anger.

"Our government has stagnated under the pressure to recruit and train thousands of men and provide millions of dollars for a program we do not believe in, do not want, and have been given no real choice in."

"What do you want then?"

"Public recognition. Your ambassador does not publicly support our elected leaders and their decisions. Why? And what happens when circumstances change or worsen? Will the US condemn us and create its own puppet government in Libya that it can more easily control?"

I decided then I needed a vacation. I was already overdue.

I couldn't relate to that willingness to give up or settle for half measures. I grew up playing to win. My older brother and I were the most competitive of all, perhaps because we were only thirteen months apart in age. I was a surprise pregnancy for my parents, my mother went to see the doctor for the flu and the nurse came in singing happy birthday.

She wanted us to be close in age, although probably not that close, because she wanted us to be friends. And we were. My brothers were my close friends. We played together when we were little, my friends were their friends and vice versa.

By the time we reached high school, my brother asked my best friend to his senior prom and I went with his. We spent weekends hiking together. Most summers my father took us camping. I grew up watching far more *G.I. Joe* and *Transformers* cartoons than *Care Bears* and *My Little Pony*. I can still quote the opening to *Star Trek* from memory.

But one thing we really loved was game nights.

We played long board games like *Monopoly* and *Risk* with ardent passion. *Risk* was our favorite, obviously. Many a night we stayed awake until the wee hours of the morning, unwilling to surrender or concede defeat. We'd play until the other sibling conquered the last country and lost the final soldier.

As we grew up, we all remained close and most of our friends came from our church youth group. We then learned strategy focused card games like *Rook* and *Euchre*, and we'd have tournaments and stay up all evening for game nights my mother almost always hosted at our house.

It also kept us entertained during the nine months of the year it rained in the Pacific Northwest. The other three months we spent outside in the forests, mountains, islands, and ocean, although none of us really minded hiking in the rain either.

My mother kept an open-door policy and said she'd rather have everyone at our house than wonder where we were, who we were with, and what we were up to. She also provided food and snacks and made our house festive, since we didn't have much money and couldn't afford things like fancy vacations, restaurants, or activities. We lived below the poverty line.

But I was given what I needed, even if it wasn't always exactly what I thought I wanted. The games sharpened my memory, taught me strategy and geography, and to avoid expensive New York City hotels at all costs. My brothers taught me about loyalty, the perks of being a girl while also relating to boys, and the awesomeness of first-person shooter video games.

Instead of complaining about what we didn't have, I learned to make the most of what we did.

I learned to never, ever give up, even when facing overwhelming odds.

And I'd need almost all those skills in Libya.

Meanwhile, the violence in eastern Libya continued unabated. Ansar al-Sharia's propaganda campaign churned on and it conducted multiple assassinations and low-level attacks in Benghazi. The Libyan Special Operations Forces (LSOF) in Benghazi, led by Wanis Bukhamada, began to fight back even harder against Ansar al-Sharia.

The LSOF had a small contingent of men, but they were highly trained, and the only effective fighting force in the country. Muhammad asked for US assistance to LSOF. He pointed out that LSOF was, after all, a legitimate part of the Libyan government fighting against a terrorist group.

The MoD would not consider LSOF for the GPF effort given the MoD's Islamist leaning tendencies, which were wholly opposed to LSOF's fight against Islamic extremists.

The LSOF on multiple occasions requested help or assistance of any kind from the MoD, the Libyan government, and other foreign neighbors and governments. They received none.

In mid-November 2013, I focused the intelligence briefings on the spread of Ansar al-Sharia, the flow of foreign fighters to Syria and Iraq, and the establishment of training camps in Libya.

Sightings of black flags and the Ansar al-Sharia logo began to spread throughout Libya. Rumors increased that Ansar al-Sharia had a presence in cities and towns beyond Benghazi and Darnah, such as in Sirte and Sabratha. Information on terrorist activities in eastern Libya consisted of rumors and the occasional social media posting depicting a blurry photo of a black flag in an unidentifiable location.

However, an attempted double suicide attack in Sousse and Monastir, Tunisia, late the previous month changed all that. One suicide bomber died in his attempt, the other did not, and news soon began to circulate that the bombers attended a training camp in western Libya, somewhere near Sabratha.

I knew many fighters from North Africa traveled to Libya to receive training. Ansar al-Sharia conducted most, if not all, of its training in the group's stronghold in and around Darnah.

Many of those same fighters also left Libya to participate in the fighting in Syria. Much like the decade before, North Africans continued to make up the bulk of foreign fighters in Syria and Iraq. The fighters went for a variety of reasons. Some claimed they wanted to help their brothers in Syria continue the Arab Spring and gain their independence, others just wanted to fight.

The North African fighters frequently trained in Libya first, traveled via air to Turkey, and then made their way across the border into Syria.

I researched the transit routes in an effort to determine from where in Libya they flew, who was helping them, and how they made it work. I analyzed data on the training camps, their locations, and the tactics in which the fighters trained.

I coordinated with analysts at CIA Headquarters and briefed the results to the ambassador and Reebok. We believed most of the fighters left Libya from Tripoli, often from Mitiga Airbase, located on the eastern outskirts of Tripoli. Former LIFG members probably controlled Mitiga and maintained offices there, it appeared they sent fighters and weapons to Syria.

I began to research the local airbase and the "former" extremists who controlled it.

The Misratan forces, which remained in Tripoli, began attempts to coordinate with those same elements, LROR, and other Islamist-aligned militias. The Misratans, however, would not be in Tripoli much longer. On 15 November 2013 Tripolitanians held a peaceful protest against militias in the neighborhood of Gharghour. The Misratan militia opened fire on the unarmed public using machine guns and heavy weapons. Some fought back. In the end, they killed forty-three people and wounded an estimated 400 more.

Backlash against the so-called "Gharghour Massacre" was immediate. The Libyan government ordered the Misratan militia to return to their city and the militia complied.

When news of the fighting broke on social media, I notified Reebok and the security officers, who in turn recalled all personnel. Several officers had moves in the city that day, some close to the neighborhood. Although I notified the security officers of the planned protest in advance, no one expected it to turn violent.

Flash was in the security officers' team room that day with Arcade and another officer. The new security officer was all about his hair. I thought it was a lovely Elvis-esque bouffant and believed his hair probably couldn't be moved, even in a hurricane.

After I notified them about the violence and they put out the recall order, I stayed to chat for a minute as they monitored the radios and moves.

"So, why are you guys here?" I asked, "Why choose to be security officers?"

"Well," started Flash, "I don't exactly like military authority."

"Doesn't agree with us at all," echoed the new officer, "But we have special skills."

"Highly sought-after, well-paid skills," added Flash.

"What about your families?" I asked. "Don't you miss them?"

"Are you joking? I see them more now than when I was active duty," said Flash.

"This actually provides more stability in a way, we have a schedule, guaranteed time off," added Arcade.

"But there's no job security, that doesn't bother you?" I asked. I also didn't buy the whole schedule excuse. I knew many of them extended, often despite their personal desire to the contrary, and were required to complete extensive training during their time off. Training was a huge time suck they rarely mentioned.

"Who has real job security?" asked Flash. "Didn't you just work for your government for free in a war zone during the furlough? We got paid."

"I might receive my salary one day. There must be another reason you're here."

"We all have friends who have died in the line of duty. That's hard to leave. Hard to walk away from. This is a way to stay in the fight, do something that matters," said Flash.

"We have each other's backs," added Arcade.

We chatted a while longer before I went back to the office and finished my work for the day.

I felt exhausted and desperately needed a break. I'd been working at least twelve hours a day, often more, seven days a week, for four months by that time. I had leave scheduled for the last two weeks of November and was excited to see my mother and spend Thanksgiving with my family.

My temporary backfill arrived and I prepared to leave. On my last night before vacation I saw Nomad sitting with Moe, eating a late dinner. I grabbed my own food and joined them.

I properly introduced myself to Nomad and the three of us began to chat. They asked where I was going on vacation and I told them the Pacific Northwest. Nomad shared details of his last time along the coast, how he took a road trip from Oregon to Canada with his friend. Moe had never traveled there.

I talked at length about my beloved Northwest. I described my favorite hiking spots and how much I missed trees and mountains.

I always made a point of hugging at least one tree whenever I went home. I was a literal tree hugger, which Nomad and Moe found hilarious. I rented a cabin in the forest, and I was looking forward to spending some time alone, with no gunfire or explosions.

I planned to hike all day and spend the evenings with some good books, music, and a warm fire.

"It sounds like you're an action nerd," teased Moe.

"Analyst by day, tree-hugger by night," said Nomad.

"A hippie in disguise," I agreed, with a smile.

Nomad was also outdoorsy and loved to travel, so we talked for a while about our favorite hiking spots in the world. I'd hiked all over the Pacific Northwest, of course, and spent my first summer in Washington D.C. going to the Shenandoah National Park every free weekend. I'd hiked all around the world too, from Alaska's Arctic National Wildlife Refuge to Scotland's Great Glen Way to Israel's

Ein Gedi Nature Preserve to Vietnam's Halong Bay Islands to Japan's Fushimi Inari Shrine.

"Have you hiked the Alps?" asked Nomad.

"No, most of my travel to Europe has been work related," I said *of course he'd pick the one place I hadn't visited.* "They all want to talk about terrorism."

"Too bad. I think you'd like the Alps. The mountains are tame but beautiful."

"Now I feel like the mountains are calling me home."

"They are," agreed Nomad and Moe.

As I walked back to my room that night, I realized I felt a little less eager to leave than I was that morning. Nomad intrigued me and I decided I wanted to get to know him better in the future.

CHAPTER NINE

EVACUATION: BRIEFING THE ROUTE

(JULY 25, 2014)

The evening of July 25th, 2014, it sounded as though enemy forces surrounded the compound. The Islamist forces were trying to surround the Zintan militias in reality, but since the compound was located on Zintan territory we were, by default, probably being surrounded.

I knew there was a great deal of resistance by US policy makers to calling the tribal and militia fighting a civil war, but I also knew just by being there in Libya it was an existential fight, where both sides felt threatened to the core of their beliefs. It wasn't going to end anytime soon.

Ultimately, I didn't feel as though the definition mattered a great deal in our current situation, since it certainly felt as though we were caught in the middle of a civil war, and we needed to operate as though we were in one.

Captain planned to give the briefing on the evacuation route after dinner, followed by Obi's briefing on security and contingencies. In order to prepare for my part, I decided to take some time out of destruction and review the latest intelligence reporting one last time before our departure early the next morning.

During dinner, while the others ate, I logged on to the sole remaining computer on the classified system. I didn't want to eat dinner and decided to stop drinking anything because I was concerned about needing to stop along the evacuation route. There was nowhere to use the bathroom along the way. I'd drive out in the middle of a flat desert with truckloads of men and the US government watching overhead. Not a chance I would use the side of the road—there weren't many trees or bushes in the desert to offer concealment.

I'd need some espresso in the morning, however. It'd been weeks since I had more than a few hours sleep per night and more than a year since I slept through the night.

I realized the computer booted up as I sat lost in thought and started sifting through the day's intelligence reports. I took about an hour to read through everything then jotted down a few notes on a card for the intelligence briefing I'd give to start the evacuation discussion.

By that time it was almost 1800, so I logged off and walked upstairs. The main floor was already full. All the officers crowded into the living room of the main villa. I scanned the room for Nomad and saw him on the other side of the room by Moe and Triage. He looked at me for a moment and then turned his attention as Harbor stepped forward to speak.

"Good evening everyone," said Harbor. "I know it's been a very busy couple of days and you're all very tired. Unfortunately, the most difficult part is yet to come, and a time when every single person will need to be as alert as possible. As you can each hear and see, the fighting has not subsided. We expect when we leave tomorrow the fighting will be ongoing and we will be traveling through some hostile territory."

Harbor turned to me.

"Could you give a short summary on the status of enemy forces and threats?"

"Yes, sir," I said as I stepped forward. "As I'm sure you've all heard, the fighting has moved closer and intensified, and that's because Operation Dawn gained ground.

"Directly to our south, Dawn forces control Qasr Bin Gashr, al-Afiya clinic, and the areas immediately east of Tripoli International Airport.

"To our west, Dawn controls Janzur, Camp Twenty-Seven, and areas further out but they are pushing their way closer. There is some unconfirmed information they may've attacked Libya International TV Station just to our west.

"To our north, Dawn gained significant territory. They took over the Islamic Call Center, the 7 April Camp, the Hamza Barracks, the racetrack, and are now extremely close to the main embassy compound.

"To our east, Dawn forces are fully entrenched in the Wadi Rabi'a area," I took a deep breath then continued.

"Our route goes south, which will be explained further in a moment, but in addition to Dawn forces, we will also pass through Warshafana territory. Libyans view the Warshafana tribe as Qadhafi loyalists. As a result of US involvement in the Revolution and Qadhafi's death, they don't particularly like us, although they are aligned with the Zintan.

"In addition, Dawn forces recently used new tactics to include car bombs and suicide attacks, in addition to the heavy artillery and small arms we're constantly hearing. The Zintan claimed they found several unexploded car bombs within a mile of our location. We also know they have several tanks and we may see them on the road as we go south.

"The kidnapping threat also remains a significant concern. Our information indicates extremist elements inside Operation Dawn desperately want to kidnap a US diplomat to use as a bargaining chip, as we've seen done repeatedly to diplomats in Libya since the beginning of the year.

"Some of you have also already heard that we know they're stopping other convoys departing Libya specifically looking for Americans.

"As Harbor mentioned, we expect fighting will continue through the night and during the evacuation," I finished.

I stopped talking then and stepped back into the crowd as Captain stepped forward. I looked at Nomad. He looked grim, but stayed focused on Captain.

"Thanks," said Captain. "As she indicated, the evacuation route will take us south.

"We'll meet at the vehicles at 0400. Drivers will go over any last-minute vehicle instructions with our chalk members and prepare for the drive. The embassy convoys will arrive at 0500 and integrate their vehicles into the chalk order.

"Our Zintan escorts will arrive by 0515 to lead the convoy through the first half of the route, up to Nalut and the beginning of Amizegh tribal land. Our Amizegh escorts will meet us there and take us to the border.

"We will encounter at least five checkpoints, all of which we anticipate will be guarded with multiple militia members and heavy artillery. The first is the one we're most concerned about, that one is Warshafana controlled, and we're depending on our Zintan escorts to help us obtain passage.

"I'll be in the first vehicle with Nomad and Dolby. Robin will be in the second with Moe. After we arrive at the first checkpoint, Nomad, Dolby, and I will stay behind until every vehicle obtains passage.

"Robin will continue out ahead to meet our Amizegh contacts in advance of the convoy's arrival. There they'll arrange passage through the border village.

"That's the general plan, but I'd like to speak to all drivers and tactical commanders after this briefing to further discuss specifics of the route and navigation."

Captain finished and stepped to the side to make room for Obi by the board that was set up with the Chalk list.

"I believe you know what Chalk and vehicle you are in, but if not, you can find your name on this board," said Obi. "The board sketches out each Chalk, each vehicle in the Chalk, and the positions of each person in that vehicle.

"You'll see the Arabic speakers are spread out with at least one in each Chalk. The medics are also separated in different Chalks, although there aren't enough for each vehicle. Two Chalks also have a Hilux carrying extra fuel.

"There are multiple Chalks and each one is led and trailed with vehicles driven by security officers. Note the VIPs. Harbor is in the lead vehicle of Chalk three, and the ambassador in another. I'll be leading Chalk three, vehicle one with Flash and Harbor. Diplomatic Security will be taking care of the ambassador's vehicle. Gambler is bringing up the rear until Nomad, Dolby, and Captain fall back.

"In total, there will be multiple vehicles in every Chalk with every vehicle full. I've divided the security officers up so all our vehicles will have one driving. A security officer or other officer with relevant experience fills the right seat position, or tactical commander. The security officer driving the lead vehicle is the designated Chalk leader and makes all final decisions for the Chalk.

"Tactical commanders are responsible for the protection of all vehicle occupants, navigation as required, and communication via radio with the Chalk leaders.

"Now, as we've just heard, a lot could go wrong. Here's the plan if something does—"

Obi cleared his throat, slightly shifted, and continued to describe the response plans to various scenarios. Most involved getting off the "X" as quickly as possible, which meant swiftly moving away from the immediate threat or point of hostile contact with all due haste.

If a vehicle encounters a serious mechanical problem negatively impacting movement, such as a flat tire, we should seek to fix that problem as quickly as possible as long as there is no immediate threat in the vicinity.

If the mechanical problem is unfixable, we should transfer all personnel, weapons, and gear to the other vehicles in the Chalk. We should not only abandon the vehicle, but also destroy it. Each vehicle would have an incendiary device should it be required for vehicle destruction. If a vehicle stops, all other vehicles in that Chalk should stay together, but all other Chalks should continue.

If a vehicle encounters indirect fire, we should notify the Chalk and leave the vicinity with all due haste.

If a vehicle encounters direct fire and becomes inoperable, we should engage the enemy from a defensive posture only, while the occupants of the vehicle move as quickly as possible to the other Chalk vehicles, taking only our go-bags. We should destroy the abandoned vehicle if possible.

If we were ambushed, we should push through the ambush.

If we were stopped for any reason and a Chalk can't continue, we should immediately notify the other Chalks for relay to the mobile communications vehicle in Chalk one. The senior Marine officer will be in that vehicle and will notify AFRICOM that immediate assistance is required.

There would be three F-16s, two Osprey, and ISR flying overhead monitoring the convoy until we successfully crossed the Tunisian border, but they cannot fly in Tripoli airspace due to the heavy use of anti-aircraft artillery by the militias. They would be close, there to respond in an emergency, but too far to avert an attack should it come.

"In summary," said Obi, "We'll be moving as quickly as possible, Chalks should stay together and report everything to the Chalk leader, and if a threat is encountered get the hell out of there.

"Make sure you have your passports on your person. Not in your backpack, not in an extra jacket pocket, not even in a go-bag. Keep it on your person at all times. Double check, then triple check you have your passport. Tactical commanders, before departure, ensure all occupants of your vehicle have their passports," then he asked, "Any questions?"

Everyone had tons of questions, there were so many what-ifs, but no one said a word. We were all thinking through the scenarios and how we should or would react. I hadn't realized I'd be responsible for radio communications. I also didn't realize Nomad would be responsible for the most dangerous parts of the evacuation. First, leading us out through hostile territory to the initial checkpoint, then shifting to bring up the rear.

I knew as we left the compound and moved through Libya, word of our departure would spread like wildfire, and the last vehicle would be the most vulnerable.

Captain then gathered all the drivers and tactical commanders for a detailed discussion on the route. Gambler led the remaining personnel back downstairs to continue destruction.

Nomad sat near Captain at the main table and the other men were all crowded around to listen. I hung back against the far wall, close enough I could hear. Captain went through the specific route, when and how the Zintan contacts would arrive, how they would assist the convoy, how we would obtain passage at various points. He spent most of the time discussing radios, contingencies, and specific operational responses.

After the discussion ended, I went downstairs to help the others finish cleaning out the office. I passed Belle and Blue loading scraps into the back of the truck outside. I passed the Marine command room where Hunter and the Marines were shutting down the last of their equipment. I heard Flash somewhere behind me.

As I walked into the room, I saw everything was cleared out except the huge American flag hung on the far wall. I strode over to the flag and stood there staring at it. I considered for a moment the sacrifices we'd made in Libya. The lives lost. The tears shed. The sleepless nights, the pain, and the suffering of loved ones left behind. In that moment, it felt like it had all been in vain—we were giving up.

I felt the presence of someone behind me. I turned and saw Flash. "Will you help me?" I asked.

Together we took the flag down from the wall. Flash and I carefully folded the flag. Flash was responsible for raising funds for the families of the CIA security officers who died in Benghazi, he was the one who had made stars to put on the wall in the main villa to honor them.

"I already grabbed the other flag from the team room," Flash said, "I plan to give these to their families. Along with the stars."

I nodded. I knew he'd try. I hadn't heard whether or not Reebok wanted the flags for some other purpose, but he wasn't there and I thought giving them to the families was the right thing to do.

I continued to help with destruction for several more hours. I helped Tunes, the National Security Agency (NSA) officer assigned to the compound, empty his storage container with all the technical and communication equipment. Emptying his container required numerous trips to the destruction fire. By the time we finished, my arms ached and I had bruises everywhere. Explosions continued to echo in the night.

I also answered several urgent messages from the ambassador. She seemed to worry more as the time drew nearer. She and Harbor spoke regularly on the phone, but cell service was intermittent, probably due to the fighting, and whenever the ambassador couldn't reach Harbor she tried me.

The ambassador wanted the makes and models of our vehicles, even though AFRICOM and Washington already had that information. She asked for plate numbers, names, other information we sent up earlier. I heard rumors from my counterparts that news of the evacuation leaked on social media and caused some panic. I scanned social media in English and Arabic and couldn't confirm the information leaked.

Harbor finally told me not to check my messages anymore, to go to bed, and try to sleep. I thanked him and returned to my room. I stopped to put my body armor back on and walked as quickly as possible.

I could still hear the fighting rage as I returned to my villa that last night. It was still focused to our northeast and south by Tripoli International Airport. In the night, tracer rounds streaked red across the sky and the air smelled heavily of artillery.

I ran up the stairs of my villa and entered my room. Nomad heard me and joined me there.

"Can't you sleep?" I whispered.

"In a bit," he replied, "Let's talk about tomorrow."

I took off my body armor and set it on the floor next to my go-bag I packed earlier. I took off my Glock and set it by the body armor. Then I sat next to Nomad.

"You doing okay?" asked Nomad.

"My mind is busy, thinking about tomorrow. Why am I a tactical commander?" I asked. The very idea of it terrified me. Why was I chosen? What if something happened and I didn't know how to respond? I wasn't former Special Operations, like the others, or even former military. I was an analyst. I wasn't trained for combat.

"I'm not happy about that, but there's nothing I can do. But you know why, you know you are capable. I'm confident you can do it. I have faith in you and so do they. Stitch is a good officer, stick close to him and listen to what he says. He asked for you to be his right seat, so he wants you there."

"But why me?"

"Why not you? You have proven repeatedly you remain calm in a crisis. You think things through, and make sound, practical decisions. Everyone here also knows you know how to shoot well. Even though it's your bow, you're the only one who's been able to target shoot at all here."

I considered what he said, but I still felt nervous. I didn't feel prepared to serve as right seat, but I'd do it and I'd do it to the best of my ability. I'd be the only woman to serve in such a position. And although I was nervous, I thought it noteworthy they didn't assign roles based on gender, but on capability.

I took a deep, calming breath.

"It's interesting how people react under extreme pressure. Some people rise to the occasion, are capable of more than they ever thought possible, and far exceed everyone's expectations, like you and the other warriors. And others—do not," I said.

"You mean Whirlwind?"

"And another officer. I don't think she could be more fake enthusiastic. Her smile has become even more maniacal than usual."

"Yeah. I noticed. Try to stay away from her tomorrow."

"I will, but sometimes she follows me around," I said with a shudder. "Tomorrow, the first thing I'm going to do in the vehicle is remind Whirlwind not to touch his weapon unless told to do so."

Nomad smiled, "And that's why you're tactical commander. You don't take crap from anyone."

I tried to smile back, "You okay?"

"Yeah, I need sleep."

"So say we all," I muttered and nodded in agreement, my mind turning to his role during the evacuation. "You're leading the convoy."

It wasn't really a question, but Nomad nodded. He knew I was worried.

"What do you think are our chances of making it to Tunis without incident?"

"Well, they don't know we're leaving, right? That matters."

"Yes, we do have the element of surprise—for now," I said, trying not to sound too worried. I thought it'd be a miracle if we made it without any casualties or incident.

Then he stared deep into my eyes and slowly, emphatically said, "Hang on a little longer. Tomorrow, stay alert. Move with purpose. You got this. I believe in you."

I stared into his eyes and tried to keep the panic at bay.

He was right. I could do this. We stopped talking and just sat for a few moments. Neither saying a word but thinking through the next day. It was already well past midnight and we had to meet at the vehicles at 0400, and although sleep was necessary, it seemed impossible as well.

He gave me the encouragement I needed.

I firmly believed he was sent to me and the other security officers to our compound, to lead us out and help us survive.

CHAPTER TEN

FLASHBACK: TERRORISM SPREADS

(EARLY WINTER 2013)

December 2013 began with escalating violence in eastern Libya. Ansar al-Sharia led the spate of violence in Benghazi. Almost all sources pointed to the group's responsibility, although Ansar al-Sharia still refrained from claiming attacks. When the other officers asked their contacts to provide concrete evidence or examples, the response was generally some form of "it is known."

On December 5, 2013, unknown assailants, most likely associated with Ansar al-Sharia, assassinated an American schoolteacher while he was on his morning run in the city of Benghazi. His death led to an uproar among residents who demanded justice. The American's death was the latest in a long series of assassinations and the public had grown weary of the violence.

They called on the Libyan government to support them. They wanted law enforcement and a sense of security in the city.

The LSOF (Libyan Special Operations Forces) responded with renewed counter attacks on Ansar al-Sharia. They set up roadblocks and established neighborhood watch type programs. Bukhamada led his forces in numerous assaults against Ansar al-Sharia strongholds.

I believed LSOF probably also suffered as a result of the assassination campaign against military and security forces with ties to the
former regime in Benghazi. Although the LSOF fell under the chain
of command of the MoD, the MoD maintained close ties to the LROR
(Libyan Revolutionary Operations Room) and Islamist-aligned figures,
and refrained from providing direct support to Bukhamada. In addition, the Shield Forces in Benghazi, including Libya Shields One and
Two, which also fell under the chain of command of the MoD, sympathized more with Ansar al-Sharia and the terrorist group's fight against
the LSOF.

I believed as a result the LSOF would likely seek help from outside
entities in its fight against terrorism.

I briefed the information to the ambassador during the weekly
intelligence briefing and she informed the group that some of the LSOF
members reached out to her. A lengthy discussion ensued on whether
or how the US government might provide support to capable forces
in Libya.

I believed LSOF to be a capable force in Benghazi and they fought
against terrorists associated with Ansar al-Sharia. The US would also
be publicly demonstrating support to the legitimately elected government, preventing the spread of terrorism, and possibly stopping future
attacks. It would further signal to the Islamist-aligned bloc the US
would not sit idly by while the extremists fomented dissent and unrest.
The decision was not up to me.

The FBI expressed a desire to support the request for help. The US
military agreed. The CIA was ready. The State Department weighed
options. Ultimately bureaucracy kept the administration from
providing the needed assistance.

Some believed it didn't matter, that LSOF would obtain assistance
from another source or another country and would continue to fight
another day. One US military officer claimed US support didn't matter.

I disagreed and the officer attempted to downplay the importance
of the LSOF and patronize my knowledge by calling me "young lady"
during an intelligence briefing. I saw red, but Reebok backed me up
and I used logic and reason to calmly point out how very wrong that
officer was.

I believed the lack of support sent a message, a strong one. It made
clear to the Islamist-aligned groups and militias they had nothing to

fear from the US. It made clear to the secular-aligned groups and militias they could not rely on the US for support.

The ambassador then stated US policy dictated we would not choose a side. We held discussions with everyone but supported no one. The US would not "interfere." We would watch and wait. I thought that would've been a far better policy decision in March 2011, less so at the end of 2013.

I felt frustrated to learn we could not or would not intervene. Muhammad refused to meet with us that month, stating he was giving up hope in the US and if the Americans would not help his country, then he would no longer meet with Otter and me.

The month also witnessed the divide between secular and Islamist-aligned elements deepen. It became clear to me burgeoning alliances grew stronger with each passing day.

In addition, the public grew more discontent as days, weeks, and months passed without any concrete evidence of change in their country. A draft constitution should've been completed. Basic services should function. They should be able to walk down the street without fear of being robbed, kidnapped, or shot. They hadn't given up, but they wanted help. Explosions and gunfire could be heard every night and there was no end in sight.

The month passed quickly and I continued to eat breakfast outside with Belle, Blue, and Otter. December brought colder weather to Libya and I often wore my hat and gloves outside. I traded my t-shirts for flannel and fleece.

Dolby arrived that month and I met him as Belle, Otter, Blue, and I sat on the porch eating breakfast. Dolby was shorter than all of the other security officers, covered in tattoos, and had a ginormous beard and even bigger ego. By the end of the week, Blue decided enough was enough and started to give him a hard time.

At breakfast one morning, as Dolby walked by, Blue called out to him.

"Yo, Dolby. What's up with your rifle?"

"Dude, what do you mean? It's fine," said Dolby, looking down at his MP5 rifle.

"It looks like a little toy rifle. Miniature. Is that thing real?"

"Not cool, dude, not cool," Dolby looked and sounded like he wanted to rip Blue's limbs from his body, but that didn't stop Blue from prodding further.

"How do you even shoot that thing?" Blue added in a high-pitched voice, "Pew...pew, pew...pew, pew, pew...."

Dolby was not amused and went inside to eat at the warrior table. Belle, Otter, and I tried to muffle our laughter.

"Bold move, Blue," said Arcade, who walked inside behind Dolby, "Making fun of a trained killer holding a submachine gun."

"Pew...pew, pew...." was Blue's only response.

Christmas came and went. Our cook went all out on dinner that evening and Reebok gave us some time off. Most people stayed in their rooms, missing their families.

My mother sent me a tiny Christmas tree with ornaments. Belle's friend sent her a gingerbread house kit. We met up with Otter and Blue and took the supplies to the Marines' villa. There we watched *Home Alone*, decorated the tiny tree, and put together the gingerbread house with the Marines.

I also took out my recurve bow for the first time. I brought it back with me from home and it took some time to set up an archery range. I received permission from Reebok to set it up at the back of our compound and worked with another officer to buy hay bails. Obi, our new lead security officer who'd just arrived in Tripoli, also provided his assistance.

Obi was an older, experienced officer. He kept to himself, but led with authority, and everyone held him in great esteem. He seemed intrigued and at a loss for words when I requested the targets for my improvised archery range, but he handed some over. His officers couldn't use them at that time anyway. He joked, if I scored the first bow kill his security officers would be jealous, so to stick to the range. That left me at a loss for words.

I took my bow and arrows to the back and spent an hour shooting targets. Several people stopped by to watch. Since I am left handed and no one else was, they couldn't properly use my bow, although several tried. Otter was the most determined and wanted to learn how to shoot with his opposite hand.

Nomad returned the next day from his leave. I was happy to see him again and tried not to smile the entire day whenever I saw him. We didn't have time to speak again that day, but I could tell he was interested in getting to know me better too. I looked for him whenever I left the office for meals, on my runs, or to check social media.

Near the end of high school, I transitioned into an outdoor adventuress with a healthy dose of wanderlust, which begins to explain the bow and my travels. My brothers and I always were active outdoors, especially hiking and camping in the summers, but I really embraced the adventures toward the end of my childhood.

I made the choice to start seeking out the extraordinary.

I started rock climbing, snowshoeing, kayaking, and backpacking. I went on my first backpacking trip with my older brother and his best friend in the Olympic National Park out on the peninsula, which is in fact, a rainforest. It rained nearly the entire time. And it was fantastic. We went on many trips with many friends after that.

My brother and I helped plan, organize, and lead backpacking, hiking, and rock-climbing trips for our church.

During spring break our sophomore year of college, we drove from our home down to San Diego and back, stopping at the national parks to camp, hike, and climb along the way.

My senior year of high school, I visited Vancouver British Columbia and loved the experience of going to another country. That was my first trip out of the country. I wanted more. I applied for my first passport and vowed to fill it with visa stamps. My first trip overseas ended up being to Iraq, with a days-long stop in Qatar along the way.

Although I worked throughout college to help pay for it, I still used my spare time to learn other important outdoor skills. In my free time, I obtained my Emergency Medical Technician-Basic certification. I also volunteered with the local Explorer Search and Rescue program, where I learned navigation, taught basic first aid, and did things like sleep under a tarp in the snow.

My mother married my stepfather my freshman year of college as well. He was an avid hunter and archery enthusiast. He preferred a longbow and made his own arrows. He also practiced with throwing knives, throwing hatchet, slingshot, and other such things. He taught anyone in our family who wanted to learn. We all did. He helped me pick out my first recurve bow.

My stepfather remains madly in love with my mother and they're the happiest couple I know. He's now retired after forty-one years three months and one day of government service—not that he counted—some if it was active duty but most in the reserves and civil service. He spent the bulk of his career at Joint Base Lewis McChord, from where my grandfather also retired.

That's how I learned archery.

I haven't stopped adventuring and traveling since.

And those were all experiences that helped me in Libya. Except the snow tarp night, I could've lived without that one.

A few days after Christmas in Libya, the month took a steep turn for the worse.

Four US military personnel stationed at the embassy coordinated a trip. They planned to conduct reconnaissance of possible evacuation routes in western Libya, near Sabratha. Although some officers previously conducted a trip on that route, the four wanted to review the route for AFRICOM's awareness and recon potential side roads that could be used in an emergency.

The four left in two vehicles mid-morning on December 27, 2013. Later that afternoon, as they began their return to the embassy, they encountered a checkpoint. The first vehicle passed through without incident. However, the heavily armed militia guards at the checkpoint stopped the second vehicle.

The militia removed the US military personnel from the vehicle and held them at gunpoint on the side of the road while other militia members ran to the second vehicle, which had stopped. The second vehicle called QRF (Quick Reaction Force) for help.

The security officers hustled to respond. Moe and Obi hastily called in Nomad, Triage, Flash, and several other security officers and put together a comprehensive plan of approach. By then, they didn't know the current situation on the ground because communication had ceased. They prepared for the worst.

Within fifteen minutes, several armored vehicles loaded with weapons and the security officers departed en route to Sabratha. Moe remained behind in the team room to coordinate the response from there and to prepare additional resources with AFRICOM if needed.

I refused to compare it to the Benghazi attacks and prayed for their safety.

I didn't see it coming. There was no additional warning, but we assessed terrorists trained in that area. I'd warned about it several times.

Otter, Blue, Belle and other officers began calling their contacts in an attempt to gather additional information. Otter tried calling Muhammad to see if he could help. Muhammad promised he would provide assistance.

I scanned social media for any references to the incident. All personnel on the compound crowded around the warrior table, trying to help in any way we could, worried about the safety of our friends. My prayers became a sort of incoherent mumbling in the back of my mind as I researched information.

I thought if word of their detention passed to Ansar al-Sharia they'd be in serious trouble. I was concerned the US military personnel were already in terrorist hands or soon would be, given the rumors Ansar al-Sharia operated in that same area and possibly maintained ties to the local militias.

It took Nomad and the rest of the security officers over an hour to drive to the Sabratha. They relayed information to Moe as it happened. They arrived at the checkpoint after darkness had already fallen to find the two US military personnel who were in the second vehicle forcefully held on the side of the road by the militia. Flames engulfed their vehicle behind them. The security officers and linguist negotiated their return from the militia and then tried to learn the location of the other two military personnel.

The guards claimed their fellow militia members took the other two to the prison in Sabratha. The militia leader said they were carrying illegal weapons. Nomad pointed out that all US personnel carried papers issued by the Libyan government authorizing us to carry weapons.

The militia leader said the Libyan government had no authority there.

The security officers quickly departed to find the other two US military personnel. Upon receiving word of their possible location, I looked up the prison in the Sabratha and passed the coordinates to Moe, who passed them on to the team driving there. The other team held back and staged for a response if needed.

The security officers found the prison and attempted to gain the release of the two. The militia refused. They claimed an official in the MoI ordered the militia to take the two US military personnel to their headquarters in Tripoli.

The heavily armed militia members placed the two US military personnel in a technical—a flatbed truck, usually some type of pickup truck, with a heavy weapon permanently mounted in the back—and began the long drive back to Tripoli. Both of the teams' vehicles closely followed. They didn't want to escalate the situation, but they wouldn't let fellow Americans out of their sight.

As they departed Sabratha, news of their detention broke on social media. It was the middle of the night by then, but I passed information to Moe and Reebok as locals posted it. First there were pictures of the checkpoint, then the burned-out vehicle, and then passport photos and identification cards of the US military personnel.

Upon arrival in Tripoli, the militia forced all four US military personnel and the security officers to stay at the MoI facility. It took the ambassador's charge d'affaires going down to the facility in the early hours of December 28, 2013, to secure their release.

The ambassador ordered all four of the US military personnel to leave Libya later that morning. They did not return to the embassy and instead went to the international airport for the next available flight out.

What worried me was the MoI held them, not the MoD. I knew the MoD didn't care for our presence, but the MoI was new.

The security officers returned as the sun began to rise. I stayed up all night, monitoring the situation on social media. I waited to sleep until all the officers were safely inside the compound. Then I logged off and walked to my room as they unloaded their vehicles.

On the way, I saw Nomad and I stopped to talk to him for a moment.

"I'm glad you made it back safely. We were all worried," I said.

"I heard you helped from here. Thank you," he said, "And thanks for staying up until we made it 'home' safely."

"I'm just glad everyone's okay."

"Me too. When I saw that vehicle engulfed in flames, I thought the worst. I wasn't sure we'd all make it back."

"I'm really glad you did," I said with a relieved smile. "Belle told me you were the source of her most surreal moment yet." The relief and exhaustion made me feel a bit giddy and detached, like I watched the conversation instead of participated in it.

Either way, it helped me come down from the adrenaline rush and I wanted to prolong the conversation if only for a moment. I enjoyed talking to him and he must have enjoyed talking to me too, since he remained there with me after a long and dangerous operation.

"This should be a good story. Why's that?" asked Nomad.

"Belle said before you left you grabbed the grenade launcher from the team room, passed her on your way out, and casually asked her to let Moe know you had the grenade launcher. She said you asked her like it was no big deal."

"I guess maybe it was for her?" he asked with a small chuckle.

"I think so. It would've been for me too. Belle told me she was sure you were talking to someone else until she looked around behind her and realized she was the only person in the room," I said.

"I'll remember that for next time," said Nomad with a smile of his own.

"Hopefully there won't be a next time. It's been a long night. I'll need to write this up later this morning. Can I talk to you more then?"

"Definitely. Get some sleep."

"You too. Sleep well."

I returned to my room and fell into an exhausted sleep for a few hours before going back into the office to write up the incident and cable the information back to analysts and officers at CIA Headquarters.

The need to uncover threats, identify possible attacks, and protect my friends in Libya began to consume me.

I started the New Year by watching the sunrise. It's something I tried to do every year, no matter where I traveled in the world—my own personal tradition. I'd found a spot outside, facing east, where I could watch the sunrise in silence and contemplate the year I'd left behind and the one ahead.

That year was no exception. I woke before dawn on the first day of 2014. I brewed hot coffee, ensconced myself in warm clothes, and carried a small throw blanket.

I wandered up to one of the villa balconies that faced east, sat in the chair I placed there the night before, and watched the sunrise in silence. I thanked God for surviving another year and asked for wisdom and courage in the days to come.

I thought the best thing about Libya was the sky. That morning was no exception, the sunrise looked beautiful, and I hoped it bode well for the year to come.

Two days later, however, a British man and a woman from New Zealand were found dead on a beach in Sabratha, unknown assailants attacked the couple on the beach where they apparently had a picnic. The assailants shot them execution style in the back of the head and left their bodies and belongings on the beach.

There were no credible claims for the attack. There was widespread speculation terrorists associated with Ansar al-Sharia conducted the execution, possibly in retaliation for the late December incident in Sabratha involving the US Military members. Ansar al-Sharia, it seemed, felt unhappy with the loss of potential hostages and took out its anger on the first Western foreigners the group found.

January also came with an increased focus on the oil crisis. The Federalists continued their blockade of the oil fields and all oil production had been on hold since July. That led to increasing concerns about the viability of the infrastructure. Italy, as the primary importer of Libya's oil, seemed the most concerned.

Winter fell on Europe and people needed fuel to warm their homes. Demand for oil significantly increased.

Libyans also continued to suffer from lack of gas for their vehicles and occasionally from electricity due to the ongoing blockades.

Libya's finances took a plunge deep into the red, primarily from a lack of consistent revenue. The loss of regular oil production and sales negatively impacted the overall budget. The government also continued to subsidize gas, bread, and other basic needs at an exorbitant cost. Most citizens also received a paycheck from the government, simply for being a citizen. They didn't pay taxes. It was an oil rich country, they hadn't needed the added revenue.

Pay for militia members increased after militias staged another armed sit-in of the GNC's assembly building, demanding higher wages. That meant Ansar al-Sharia associated militia members also received a pay raise.

Then fighting broke out in Sabha, the capital of Fezzan in southern Libya. The fighting occurred between the Awlad Sulayman tribe and the Toubou minority group. Otter and I called Muhammad to set up a meeting. Muhammad agreed and met us on the compound that same week.

"I can't figure out the reason for the fighting in Sabha," I said, "Do you know what's going on?"

"It's the tribes. There have always been tensions in that region between the Awlad Sulayman and the Toubou. The Awlad Sulayman tribe is Arab and Islamic. The Toubou are not Arab and more secular—they're not even really Libyan."

"The Toubou have lived in Libya for hundreds of years. Why fight now?"

"It doesn't matter how long they've lived here. They are from Chad, you know this. Plus, why not fight now? They don't need a reason. Next I believe the Alwad Sulayman will call on the Misratans for help."

"Which means the Toubou will call on the Zintan, yes?"

"Yes, and even though the fighting shut down the airport in Sabha, they will find a way to travel to Sabha."

"Right, probably overland," I agreed.

That same week, the president and MoD requested the Misratan militia travel to Sabha to implement a ceasefire. The prime minister and MoI asked the Zintan to do the same.

In a show of considerable posturing, the Zintan began preparations for their peacekeeping role by setting up at the MoD facility near the compound where they fired seemingly ceaseless rounds of heavy artillery for apparent "target practice."

I'd been on my daily run around the inside of the compound when it started. I was on lap ten or so when the heavy weapons fire began and the code red alert sounded. Marines began yelling at me to take cover. I ran straight to the nearest villa, which happened to be my own, grabbed my radio, and took cover with the others in our bunker area.

The bunker area was under the fortified stairwell, surrounded by sandbags, with a small walkway inside. I'd been slightly claustrophobic before my arrival in Libya, preferring nature and open spaces, but that experience took it to a whole new level.

Gambler, who arrived that month, gave the all clear once he determined the Zintan fired their heavy artillery at targets, not enemy forces, and in the opposite direction of our location.

After that incident, I offered to give Gambler my introductory intelligence briefing, and Obi joined us as well. Gambler, a former military officer, reminded me of a mix between western cowboy and old-fashioned southern gentleman. He was quieter than most but exuded confidence and authority.

I gave my usual briefing, with the latest updated intelligence and asked if they had any questions.

"I've noticed they like to shoot their weapons at each other quite a lot," said Obi, "but there are not many casualties. Do you know why?"

"I don't think there's one specific reason. It appears as though Libyans, even militia members, don't truly want to kill each other," I said. "The only exception seems to be terrorists and even then they tend to conduct bombings against empty buildings sometimes, rather than engage in direct combat."

"So they're just trying to scare each other?" asked Gambler.

"Basically, yes, it seems that way. It's primarily posturing. One side trying to gain ground by presenting a stronger show of force," I said. "Most of it, so far, is for show."

"Are there any casualties?" asked Gambler.

"Sometimes 'fighting' will continue all night and by morning there may be one or two killed, one or two injured, on the opposing side. Usually casualties are very low considering the magnitude and length of the engagement."

"Why?" asked Gambler.

"Part of the reason is the low population. The country has a vast territory with a small population, only a few million total although Tripoli is also the largest city."

"So, there's no direct threat to us then?" asked Obi.

"For now, not from the posturing—it's not directed against us. There's definitely a threat from indirect fire. As you know, everything they're firing hits something, somewhere. Casualties are limited among the opposing force, but higher among bystanders and civilians. Plus, as things continue, the opposing forces will eventually realize posturing isn't working and start shooting or bombing each other with the intent to kill," I said.

"Eventually," agreed Gambler.

"Exactly, do or do not, there is no try."

The militia posturing continued in Tripoli unabated. One side or the other would occasionally fire heavy weaponry in the general direction of the other. Usually high enough they did not hit anyone. Casualties were rare. Rounds falling from the sky were not. We often took cover during times of heavy weapons fire. Reebok ordered some officers to build more heavily fortified concrete bunkers, buried in the earth, near the villas.

I researched the fighting in Sabha for the next intelligence briefing. News and reporting on southern Libya remained sparse, but I put together the information I had and presented it to the Ambassador and Reebok. Even though we couldn't make sense of why the fighting started, both sides felt passionately about the fight, and it continued for weeks.

CHAPTER ELEVEN

EVACUATION: PREPPING THE CONVOY

(JULY 26, 2014)

I woke with a start the morning of the evacuation, July 26th, 2014. I'd actually fallen asleep beside Nomad, but the sound of a large explosion near the compound jolted me awake. It shook the room, rattled the windows, and reverberated in my chest. It felt close. I looked at Nomad, my heart pounding, but he remained fast asleep. That amazed me. I looked at the clock and it was just over half an hour until the 0400 meeting time so I turned off the alarm and woke Nomad.

"You didn't hear that explosion?" I whispered.

"What explosion?" he yawned back with a slight smile. Then he turned serious, "Let's get moving."

I quickly showered, dressed, donned my gear, and prepared to leave our villa with Nomad.

I wore jeans, black t-shirt, and boots. I added my compass necklace around my neck. I put one pocketknife in my back pocket and another into my left boot. I then put on my belt with magazine pouch and holster attached, to which I added my two full magazines and loaded Glock. After that, I lifted my body armor over my head and tightened it into place with the Velcro. Then put a long sleeve black jacket over that with a scarf around my neck. Finally, I picked up my go-bag and rifle.

Nomad had already finished gearing up and waited for me. As an experienced warrior, he could get ready much faster than I. He had on light colored pants and shirt, boots, multiple knives, Glock with extra ammo, and his body armor.

In addition to those 'normal' things I was used to seeing, he also wore his helmet with night vision goggles attached. Depending on our exact departure time, it may be necessary to leave the compound without headlights and drive out under darkness. He had his rifle and grenade launcher combo in one hand, a large container with ammo for the rifle in the other, his go-bag over his shoulder, and a sling full of grenades across his chest.

He certainly looked like a warrior.

Nomad hurried to the front door and I followed behind more slowly, looking around the villa one last time.

He stopped by the door, a few feet from me, with a serious look on his face. He frowned as he stared at me for several seconds.

"Thank you," he said, "For everything."

He leaned down and quickly kissed me. He looked at me for a moment longer, as if trying to memorize the moment, and he exited without another word.

I stood still, shocked, and trying not to panic. I knew, without him saying it, he was telling me goodbye in case we didn't see each other again in private. In case we didn't both make it to Tunis. My heart started hammering in my chest and I tried to force myself to focus. It was not the time or the place to succumb to emotion of any sort. I had a job to do and needed to focus. My life depended on it. All our lives did.

I took a few long, shuddering breaths. Looked around one last time. I then squared my shoulders, strode through the doorway, and toward my vehicle. I could hear heavy artillery and small arms fire close by, but as long as it wasn't literally at the front gate, we were still rolling out in just over an hour.

I arrived first at the vehicle. I had an extra set of keys from Stitch, in case we needed to flee during the night and he was waylayed. I unlocked the vehicle and opened the right front door. I already placed the extra ammo in front of the right seat the day before, so I only needed to add my rifle and extra Glock. I tucked my M4 between the center console of the Hilux and the right seat and covered it with the scarf. I next set the extra Glock on the floor under the scarf and put my go-bag in front of the magazines.

I sat down in the vehicle to make sure I still fit in the space with all the weapons and my gear. I did. It would be an uncomfortable ride, with the body armor especially, but it'd do.

"G'morning," mumbled Tunes. He looked sleepy and I knew he was up late into the night finishing the destruction of his office too.

"Hey, you ready?" I asked.

"Ready to throw it on the ground," he joked.

I smiled slightly. I liked Tunes a great deal. He was quiet but funny and also loved music, which would give us something in common to chat about during the coming drive.

"Sweet. You get much sleep?"

"Nah."

"Me neither. At least the drive is only supposed to take nine or so hours, we'll be in Tunis for dinner," I said.

"I may skip dinner and go straight to my luxurious hotel bed. With high thread count sheets, delightful down comforter, and soft mattress and pillows."

We both smiled and felt a little more relaxed just thinking about it. Then the relative silence broke with a shuffling gate and small voice.

"What're we supposed to do now?" asked Whirlwind.

"For now, set up your stuff in the back seat. There are extra trash bags here in which to put our backpacks. Stitch left them for us last night. We've got the extra diesel and gas in the back of the truck, so this should help the smell and any leaks from getting on our last few belongings," I said.

While we put our weapons and gear in the back seats, I wrapped my backpack in a trash bag and tucked it between the back window and the gas cans in the truck bed. I had my clothes and personal emergency essentials I packed the day before in it. However, I also knew if we abandoned the vehicle, it was gone.

I handed Tunes and Whirlwind the last two garbage bags.

"I'm going to the main villa to make an espresso and grab a small bite to eat. I'll also bring back some extra water bottles and box of granola bars," I said.

"Sweet," said Tunes, "I'll join you."

As we started to walk away Whirlwind asked again, "What do I do now?"

"Finish putting your gear away, then eat some breakfast. Don't forget there's nowhere to stop for the bathroom, your only option will be the side of the road," I replied.

"Okay," said Whirlwind and turned back to his garbage bag.

Our radios squawked and interrupted our conversation.

"We have a problem with the embassy convoy," came Hunter's voice over the radios.

"Repeat last transmission," the voice was Captain's and he didn't sound happy.

"Problem with the embassy convoy," Hunter repeated.

"Roger," said Captain, "I'm on my way. Have your guys let them in the side entrance."

"Roger that, solid copy," came Hunter's reply.

Tunes and I paused to listen. We both felt surprised.

"They're early," I said.

Tunes and I continued to the main villa. It sounded like the militias' weapons fire was moving closer to the compound, so we instinctively stepped up our pace. People crowded the villa while darting about making last minute preparations. The Marines who'd remained on duty at Mike-3 manning the 50-cal throughout the night were taking down the last of their gear for departure.

As Tunes and I reached the front steps, we could see and hear the embassy vehicles driving onto the compound. The radio squawked again. Captain called Harbor on the radio.

"Go for Harbor."

"This'll take a while to sort out," said Captain, sounding very frustrated, "The embassy vehicles came in the wrong order. We need to rearrange them. And the ambassador would like to see you in the main villa."

"Got it," said Harbor, sounding equally annoyed.

Tunes and I looked at each other again, his face mirroring my own surprise.

"Holy crap," said Tunes, "How could they screw that up?"

"So ridiculous," I replied, "I really shouldn't be surprised considering everything else, but I bet this'll delay us."

We hurried inside.

I went straight to the espresso machine. I stuck with a double espresso and planned to savor every last sip. I also made one for Nomad and took it to him out by the vehicles, going out the side entrance to avoid the chaos. We frequently made each other coffee and I knew he wouldn't have time with the vehicle rearrangement. I also wanted to see the status of the vehicles for myself.

I didn't say anything, simply handed the coffee to him, and he nodded his thanks as he ordered people about. He helped the others set up the vehicles into the proper Chalk alignment. I sipped my hot coffee in the pre-dawn darkness and watched for a moment. The vehicle drivers used parking lights instead of headlights to contain the brightness, but the flash of numerous brake lights looked blinding in the dark. It was like watching a complex game of Tetris.

I watched the madness until I finished my coffee and then went in search of food. I didn't want to eat much but knew I needed something. My stomach twisted in knots. My favorite snack in the whole world was banana and peanut butter so I decided to force that down. I cut up a banana, then loaded it with peanut butter, and savored every bite.

The ambassador walked in as I finished my small meal.

"Can you believe how unorganized they are?" the ambassador asked me, "They made us wait out on the road. On the road. For five minutes."

"I think they were expecting you to arrive at 0500 as planned," I replied trying to maintain my calm.

"Well that just wouldn't do. There was heavy weapons fire near us. Heavy weapons fire! I could not in good conscious have anyone stay there a second longer."

She paused waiting for me to reply, but I remained silent.

"I told everyone to leave as quickly as possible and we also need to leave here right now. Right now! I told Harbor that. I don't care why he's not ready. I'm in charge here."

"I believe Harbor is waiting for our local guards to arrive to escort us to the border. He also doesn't want to depart until we have all local and AFRICOM assets in place."

"This is my decision. We need to leave. Now. We've been here too long already. News of the evacuation will leak any moment. We must go."

"We've been stuck in this civil war for nearly two weeks. Why the urgency now?"

"I don't care how long it's been, we need to leave. Now."

"I'll go find Harbor for you."

I grabbed a half dozen large water bottles and a box of granola bars to take to the Hilux, the other staff had gone through our travel provisions and there wasn't much left.

On my way out I ran into a Foreign Service Officer. We always got along fairly well and I paused when he said hello.

"Sounds like the ambassador is a bit—on edge." I whispered.

"More than a little," he quietly replied, "We sustained several rocket impacts yesterday, including on my front porch. At least it wasn't my room."

"Oh, I didn't realize you'd actually been hit yesterday. We had some indirect fire too, but no heavy weapons."

"Minimal damage, but certainly disconcerting. Then someone, and I cannot confirm or deny who, decided to have the Marines complete the destruction, while some of the embassy staff drank the last of the 'diplomatic' alcohol."

"Are you serious? Oh my goodness. That's horrible! Are they still drunk? Is that what this 'problem' is about?"

"No idea, but at the very least hung-over. There was a lot of booze they were hoarding for a rainy day. Apparently yesterday was their rainy day."

I was furious and felt my face turn red with anger. My voice and hands trembled.

"That puts all our lives at risk! Plus, those Marines are not MSG, they're a combat unit. Are they trained on how to conduct proper destruction on an embassy?"

He just shrugged. I shifted the water and bars in my arms.

"I need to put this in the truck. I'll be back soon."

I hurried to the vehicle, put things away, and went in search of Harbor. I didn't want to call him on the radio and interrupt what sounded like a complete cluster of organizing the embassy convoy. One embassy driver had already rammed into another vehicle.

I saw Harbor on the corner, near the gate to the main villa. I walked over and said good morning.

"Sir, the ambassador is upset and pushing for an early departure. Did she speak with you?"

"Yes," Harbor sighed, "But unfortunately now we'll have a late departure. Our local guards and escorts should arrive momentarily, AFRICOM assets are in place, but then there are the vehicles to deal with."

"Yes, sir."

"Is she giving you a hard time?"

"She's making her feelings known, sir."

"Okay, I'll finish up here and make sure she's not causing problems with our officers."

"Sir, I also need to warn you that their early departure from the embassy probably didn't go unnoticed. I'd expect it to hit social media very soon. I'll be monitoring for that and any threats, but it'll significantly heighten the threat if it becomes public knowledge we're evacuating before we actually leave."

"Understood. Ultimately, it's lucky for them they made it here at all. If we'd been cut off from each other, they'd never make it out of the city, much less the country, on their own."

The radio squawked then, "Harbor, Harbor, Obi."

"Go for Harbor," he said.

"The ambassador would like to see you again inside."

"On my way."

Harbor let out a frustrated breath and put his radio back on his belt. We both saw Obi quick-stepping toward us.

"Good luck," I said as Harbor moved to close the distance from Obi. I knew he provided a great deal of top cover for us all and would continue to try to shield us all from the politics and the politicians' games.

CHAPTER TWELVE

FLASHBACK: KIDNAPPINGS SPIKE

(WINTER 2014)

The kidnappings of diplomats and foreign officials was the next major threat to spike in Tripoli at the beginning of 2014. It significantly lengthened the list of security incidents I maintained, a long series, already more than they'd witnessed in Benghazi before the September 2012 attacks.

The new spike tripped all the wires. Crossed every red line. Checked off all the warnings. Instead of heeding the warnings, the embassy pushed the line farther to the right. It meant that more would have to happen before action could be taken—the threat would have to become much worse before we could respond.

Kidnappings for ransom, or for other criminal intent, occurred frequently in Benghazi and Darnah, but spread to Tripoli over the few months prior. Most of the violence up to that point was Libyan on Libyan.

Carjackings were also a real concern. Carjackings occurred every day in Tripoli and were rampant. Many targeted foreign diplomats, but it seemed as though the intent remained criminal. Diplomats tended to drive nicer vehicles than the locals.

That changed in January 2014 when unknown assailants kidnapped a South Korean trade official. The assailants stopped his diplomatically plated vehicle, forcibly removed him from the vehicle, and held him hostage.

The assailants released the trade official to the South Korean government several days later. I never knew if a ransom was paid or not, but that was standard operating procedure for Libyan kidnappings.

Less than a week later, Egyptians arrested the leader of the LROR in Alexandria, Egypt. In response, the LROR laid siege to the Egyptian Embassy in Tripoli and held at least six Egyptian employees hostage. The LROR took several technicals on a rampage through the Janzur neighborhood of Tripoli, where foreign diplomats lived, looking for the Egyptian ambassador to Libya.

The LROR demanded the release of their leader in exchange for the release of the Egyptian diplomats. Several days later, the LROR released the Egyptian hostages, and Egypt released their leader.

That night, the LROR leader returned to Tripoli via the Tripoli International Airport. The LROR went in a group to meet his plane. The Zintan, who controlled the airport and opposed the LROR, tried to block their entry. Shots were exchanged inside the airport, but the LROR eventually left and the airport remained open.

In response, the LROR formed a kidnapping element under the leadership of a former LIFG member.

The assault on Tripoli International Airport prompted no official response. The Libyan government did nothing.

Our ambassador also gave no official response, but Reebok ensured even more security officers went on every airport move.

I stayed busy with work but tried to practice with my bow at least one day a week. It was my one hobby. That and running. We didn't have much free time, but even if we did there wasn't much to do on a small compound in Libya.

I noticed Nomad started running outside around the same time I did every day. Once he asked if he could run a lap with me. I didn't mind, but I could tell I ran a bit faster pace than him over distance. He could definitely out-lift, out-swim, and out-sprint me, but I could run distance well.

He occasionally joined our group outside for breakfast or other meals. We talked about our recent vacations and what we planned next. He wanted to visit Argentina and I mentioned how I'd always wanted to go there. He said I was welcome to tag along, but our dates didn't match up, so he said maybe next time.

I noticed immediately he was left-handed and worked my nerve up to invite him to join me at the archery range sometime.

"Absolutely I will," he said. "When a beautiful CIA officer asks you to join her at the archery range in a war zone to shoot her bow and arrows, you don't say no. That's a once in a lifetime opportunity."

I smiled at his teasing, "Well I'll let you know next time I go shoot."

"And I'll be there with bells on." He paused for a moment, seeming to debate his next words. "I noticed you don't ever swim."

"I don't know how," I said with an embarrassed smile.

"You never learned?"

"Well, I can tread water, but I can't swim very well. The ocean's much too cold where I'm from."

"Would you like a lesson?"

I looked at him for a moment, briefly pausing as I debated my words, trying to be bold. I still blushed slightly as I responded.

"Absolutely I would. When a handsome Navy SEAL offers to give you private swimming lessons while living on the edge of the Sahara Desert, you don't say no. That's a once in a lifetime opportunity," I replied.

He smiled back, "Indeed."

There were many different points of view on social activities and relationships overseas, deployed, and in war zones. Some people had the mentality "what happens overseas, stays overseas," but it wasn't Vegas. It never stayed there.

That was important, because it was also a work environment, and a much smaller world than some people thought.

I knew a few women who eagerly sampled every person willing, I knew a few men who did the same, all regardless of marital status, and I figured there was more of which I wasn't aware. They grasped at any moment of happiness they could find in the midst of fear, war, and death. I tried not to judge, because that was God's job, not mine, plus, no one could really understand how soul-crushingly lonely it was until they'd been there.

And it was profoundly lonely at times.

There was also the other extreme. Some people kept their heads down, didn't do anything but work, and hid alone in their rooms whenever they weren't in the office. There were many reasons for that, but I think they missed out on some of the best parts of serving overseas.

I treated it like a continuation of my life, because for me it was. I didn't stop living, and I didn't start playing the field. I stood by my morals and Christian convictions. And I lived. I worked hard, but I also enjoyed the few social activities, and when a handsome and intelligent former Navy SEAL caught my eye, I wasn't about to let that opportunity pass me by. I hadn't expected him at all.

But once again, I wasn't provided what I thought I wanted, I was given who I needed. I just didn't know it yet.

In February 2014, the political situation in Libya took a dramatic turn for the worse. The public believed the GNC had been hijacked by the Islamists, specifically by the Libyan president, who they felt obstructed progress.

The public believed he did so in coordination with the Muslim Brotherhood associated political party The Justice and Construction Party (JCP). The opposing party, the National Forces Alliance (NFA) supported the prime minister, and called for protests against the current course of the government. The JCP and the NFA were the two major political parties in Libya, which were banned under the Ghadafi regime.

The JCP was Islamist-aligned and the NFA more secular-aligned. They, along with independents, made up the GNC.

Libyans believed the GNC's mandate to govern expired on February 7, 2014. The ambassador, Reebok, and I discussed the date several times and the ambassador stated that even though Libyans held widespread conviction that February 7th was the specific date the government should dissolve according to the original mandate, she could find no such records or confirmation. The ambassador remained silent in the ongoing debate. She watched and waited. She did not intervene.

Various elements of the Libyan government sought public support for their causes. The prime minister called for international support to his government. The NFA claimed to best represent Libyan interests. The Zintan opposed the JCP and also boasted of their intent to correct the course of their revolution.

Muhammad called me on multiple occasions demanding to know why the US abandoned Libya. He accused us of supporting the Islamists and the Muslim Brotherhood as the US did in Egypt. Muhammad claimed the US only cared about Libya's oil, but begged for more help.

The GNC voted to give themselves an extension on their electoral mandate and to remain in power through the end of the year. The president approved the extension.

Anger swelled in Libya over the perceived abuse of power and on February 7, 2014 the people took to the streets. A massive protest began centering in Martyr's Square in downtown Tripoli. People held up signs demanding "no to extension" and "no to the brotherhood roadmap."

Nomad and Blue, who were out on a move that day, avoided Martyr's Square but drove nearby and saw signs in Arabic for sale. They bought several and brought them back to the compound for me to analyze. They tried to determine the size of the crowd and noted general atmospherics they later relayed to me. In turn, I passed the information to analysts at CIA Headquarters.

Protests in Tripoli were not uncommon, but I hadn't heard of one so large since the Revolution. My major concern centered on the fact the protests contained strong anti-Brotherhood, anti-Islamist, rhetoric. I believed that was another strong indicator of the deepening divide, and shared that belief in cables to CIA Headquarters.

I walked up to the team room later that month to notify the security officers of another possible protest and found Nomad, Belle, Blue, Dolby, and several others chatting at the warrior table. I stopped to listen. They discussed US policy.

"We're here for freedom and democracy," insisted Dolby, "That's what America fights for."

"Those may be our principles," said Belle, "But that's not why we're here in Libya. We're here because it is in our national security interests to be here. Our administration sets our national priorities and strategy. We then respond to collect against those priorities."

"And what are US interests in Libya then?" asked Dolby, "I mean, the whole point of the US intervention was to give people their freedom. They should be thanking us."

"Well, I think everyone agrees counterterrorism and counter-proliferation are key US policies. Those are some reasons we're here," said Belle.

"But it seems like US policy is not actually doing all that much. Saying a lot, but not doing a lot," chimed in Otter.

"It's like the administration is trying to get everyone to be our best friend," said Blue, "So worried about upsetting one side or the other and being seen as the big bad super power, so we do nothing."

"But not everyone wants to be our friend," added Nomad, "terrorists will be terrorists."

"You'd think someone would realize that. Instead we try to placate, compromise. We're the United States of America. We don't need to compromise," said Captain.

"'Merica," said Arcade as he joined the conversation. It was a common toast, parting shot, or filler word.

"I think our administration is attempting to implement a policy of neutrality here," I said, "And they seem to believe by taking no strong action, they make no enemies, but they also make no friends."

"Do the bare minimum?" asked Nomad.

"Seems that way, but what no one seems to be considering is that inaction is an action. There is no neutral. By not taking action, sometimes by default you are picking a side," I said, "And we seriously need to finish what we've started before initiating new wars."

"Like that saying, with great power comes great responsibility," said Belle.

"I wish we would go all in, but in specific locations. I think the administration is spreading our military and security forces too thin, in too many conflicts covering too much geographic area," said Blue.

"True and if we went all in, instead of doing things halfway, maybe we wouldn't be repeatedly going back to the same hell holes," said Dolby.

"But instead the administration just sits back and hopes everything works out the way they want," said Captain.

"A policy of hope," mused Belle.

"Hope is not a foreign policy," said Arcade, ending the foreign policy discussion. He then added to Captain, "You're slipping on rule number one, bro."

"I know. I need a haircut," said Captain, running his hand through his hair.

"What's rule number one?" I asked.

"Always look good," Nomad, Captain, and Arcade said in unison.

Dolby responded with a string of profanities about Navy SEALs, book deals, and arrogance with a fierce scowl in their direction. Nomad, Captain, and Arcade all served as SEALs, Dolby however was a former Army Ranger.

"Don't be jealous, Ranger," said Arcade with a smirk.

I smiled and shook my head in mock disapproval. I loved hearing the banter between the military branches. It reminded me of when I visited my brothers during their training with different services.

My three brothers attended training for their occupation specialty on Ft. Gordon in Augusta, Georgia, within driving distance of Washington D.C. They never overlapped all three at the same time, but one or two were there at a time, and I was eventually able to visit all my brothers there.

Each time, we met at the Waffle House off post. I will love the Waffle House until my dying day for that reason alone.

I drove down once to visit my two younger brothers, one Army and one Air Force, on the same Army base. The airman received a food stipend, because their dining facility was closed for renovations although the airmen claimed it was because the food in the Army chow hall was sub par and he complained about having only one pool table, not enough time for video games, and had the soldiers convinced the airmen had a swimming pool and movie theatre in their building.

The soldiers had the chow hall, no video games, limited free time, and no entertainment. It was quite the contrast.

My youngest brother remains active duty Air Force. He has deployed in support of Operation Enduring Freedom, Operation Iraqi Freedom, and Operation New Dawn. He spent more than six years on various bases overseas. He's now married to a devout Christian, has six children and counting, and regularly attends church.

My middle brother was injured in training and medically discharged from the Army. He never deployed, which I think was quite hard for him. I know I would've been devastated and my family is incredibly proud of his service and sacrifice. He used the VA vocational rehabilitation program to obtain an engineering degree and works as a mechanical engineer. He's now divorced and the full-time custodial parent of three amazing little girls he's raising in faith.

My older brother deployed in support of Operation Iraqi Freedom twice, once for nine months and once for fifteen. He married one of our childhood friends from church, and he missed the entire first year of his firstborn's life. He left the Army soon after and served in the National Guard for a time. He and his wife have two biological children and two adopted, they're also raising them in the church.

The banter between us has faded, replaced by many years of war, distance, and hardships. But my love for them, and pride in their service, remains.

Meanwhile, the divide in Libya became even more apparent on February 14, 2014 when former Libyan General Khalifa Haftar made a statement on national television calling for the government to dissolve according to their mandate. Or else.

The president and JCP claimed it was a coup attempt and called for Haftar's arrest.

Another massive protest took place that day in Martyr's Square and every Friday for the rest of the month.

Then nothing happened. Haftar remained in the shadows. He took no action. There were no arrests.

The next week, militias under the Zintan umbrella stormed the GNC. The Zintan's Qaqa and Sawa'iq brigades forcibly halted the session of congress. Two militia leaders made a joint statement on Libyan national television calling for the dissolution of the GNC. They threatened to detain any GNC members who did not step down.

The president and JCP claimed it was a coup and called for their arrest. Again, no one conducted arrests or detentions. Another massive protest took place that Friday, calling for the dissolution of the GNC.

While the public spectacle and rhetoric continued, Islamist-aligned forces began to plot their revenge.

Muhammad called Otter and me to discuss the fallout.

"Former LIFG members can see the power vacuum. They are increasing efforts to forge alliances. They have consolidated leadership and are considering candidates for a new Libyan government. Why don't you do something?" asked Muhammad.

"Where are they, do they have a headquarters? Where can we find them?" asked Otter.

"The LROR moved into Camp Twenty-Seven. It is now their headquarters. I have even seen black flags flying at the camp. Terrorists are in Tripoli! Bomb the camp. It would be easy. Destroy the threat."

"It's not that simple," I said, "We can't bomb your country."

"You have before and I bet you will again. You have betrayed us."

I bet we would again too, but I couldn't tell him that.

I briefed the ambassador and Reebok on the developments every week. I highlighted the fact the LROR could train and stage for attacks at Camp Twenty-Seven. Kidnapping victims could be held there without any hope of rescue. The threat was at our doorstep.

In response, the ambassador began to meet with leadership figures on both sides of the spectrum. She met with the prime minister and NFA and someone posted pictures on social media. She met with the Zintan tribal council and someone posted pictures. She met with former LIFG, JCP, and Libyan Muslim Brotherhood members and someone posted pictures. She met with Misrata local council and more pictures.

All sides were outraged.

I didn't think it prudent for an ambassador to publicly meet with rebel forces or former terrorists, especially in the country where my life was on the line.

It would destroy the public's hope and would not end well for anyone.

I needed an outlet to vent my frustration. I ran more and I shot my bow more. One afternoon toward the end of February I decided to take a break early and visit the archery range. As I headed out the front door to my villa to get my bow I ran into Nomad just getting back from a move.

I told him I was going to shoot my bow and he was welcome to join me if he wanted target practice. He said that in fact he did have some free time and would meet me at the range.

I smiled to myself as I grabbed my bow and arrows and dashed out to the range. I arrived there first and started warming up. Nomad joined me a few minutes later and I felt of rush of happiness I tried to hide. We each took turns shooting for a while. Nomad proposed placing a bet, to make things more interesting.

I readily agreed. I thought I was a much better shot than he was with my recurve bow. After all, I'd been shooting it every week for months. I had learned from my stepfather years before.

In hindsight, I should've never underestimated a Navy SEAL.

For his bet, Nomad proposed a coffee date at a time and place of the winner's choosing. Loser had to serve the coffee. I agreed and we set up to shoot again, best two out of three, one after the other.

He hit the center of the bullseye every single time.

"Seriously?" I teased, "How can you be good at literally everything? Is that a prerequisite for Navy SEALs?"

"I'm just really excited to try your snobby Pacific Northwest coffee. You've been bragging about it for months."

"Well, that's understandable then. It's good coffee," I smiled back at him. Little did he know it was seriously good coffee, but I also knew that wasn't what held his interest.

"How about Friday morning? I don't have any moves scheduled mid-morning and it's our weekend. That's worth celebrating."

"Alright. Where?"

"The kitchen in our villa. Less questions that way," said Nomad.

"Okay. It's a date," I said, blushing as my smile widened.

That Friday morning, as another mass anti-GNC protest churned in the city shutting down moves, I prepared for our coffee date. I snuck some sugar from the main kitchen, brewed my specialty-roasted coffee in my villa, and played my favorite West Coast band on my iPad.

Nomad met me there and we talked for an hour. We had a lot of common interests and values, even though we were different in so many ways.

After an hour, we both had to leave. I needed to get back to the office and Nomad had to prepare for a move. He helped me clean up and I walked him to the back door to leave.

I stood close to him. When I looked up to say goodbye, Nomad leaned down very slowly, probably in case I wanted to stop him. Instead, I leaned up to meet him. He kissed me once, thanked me for the coffee, and he left discreetly.

I remained by the back door for several more minutes, smiling to myself and lost in thought about Nomad.

I felt completely, utterly twitterpated. It was a perfect morning, one of my happiest in a long time. I couldn't believe I met someone in Libya of all places. It was totally unexpected, but extraordinary.

CHAPTER THIRTEEN

EVACUATION: MOVING INTO POSITION

(JULY 26, 2014)

I watched Harbor and Obi talk for a moment on the morning of July 26th, 2014. It looked like a heated conversation. I felt bad for them. I knew they hadn't slept in days and then had to deal with the ambassador and the problematic convoy on top of the huge risk we were all about to take in evacuating overland during a bombing campaign. I marched back to my vehicle, scowling in annoyance. Stitch stood by the driver's door, putting his gear into position.

"I thought you were going to sleep through the evacuation," I joked.

"Yes, ma'am. I gave it some thought," he replied, "Come here a second, I'd like to show you a few things."

"Sure."

"First up, the medical kit," he said, moving toward the back of the truck.

"This is the primary medical kit for the convoy. If we have to abandon the vehicle, you or I should grab this bag if time and the situation permits. I wrapped it in a garbage bag already, but it's this first bag behind the back truck windows on my side. The kit is fairly robust and should take care of most emergency medical needs and basic trauma care. Anything beyond that and we'll need medevac and that is why the Osprey are flying with us. Nomad tells me you were an EMT?"

"Yes, but that was a while ago. I got my certification in college."

"In an emergency, that knowledge will come back. I'm glad you're with me."

"Thanks," I said, but I certainly didn't feel better, "What else?"

"Next are the grenades in the glove box," said Stitch as he moved around the vehicle to my seat and opened the glove box.

Obviously, the grenades in the glove box, I thought. *Of course, that's up next, totally normal.* I felt my eyes widen in surprise and tried to pay closer attention. I didn't know how to use a grenade.

"Six?" I asked.

"Yes, two of each type. The ones marked red are incendiary. Use them to destroy the vehicle if I'm not able to. The gray ones are flash bangs. Use those if you need to pop smoke, as they say in the movies. Last are the plain grenades, those are the fragmentary grenades you're probably used to."

"Stitch, you know I'm not used to any kind of grenade, right? How do I use them?"

"A figure of speech," he laughed. I didn't laugh. Not a single part of me found anything about it funny.

Then he showed me how to properly use the grenades, reminded me they were for emergencies only, and only if he became unable to use them himself, then he carefully placed them back in the glove box.

"Finally..." started Stitch.

"There's more?" I asked in disbelief. I wondered what other weapons I'd be responsible for using. RPG? Sniper rifle? I hoped not and Stitch laughed in response. I wanted to scream that I wasn't a warrior. I didn't know any of this. I remained silent, however, and paid attention.

"Hah, don't worry. Food and water. I put a case of water in the far back of the truck bed and there's food under all the seats. We need provisions in case we get stuck out there overnight."

"Yeah, I threw a fleece into my backpack and strapped a sleeping mat to the outside for the same reason. The Sahara gets cold at night, even in the summer."

"Yes ma'am."

We stood there quietly waiting for a while, me trying not to panic, when Tunes and Triage walked over to join us.

"Sounds like the embassy folks didn't have enough up-armored vehicles, but we'll make do with what we have," said Triage.

"They mentioned they didn't have enough weeks ago," I said, "I wondered what they planned to do. Are they using any thin skin?"

"Only the box truck over there. They said it's for the Marines' weapons. They have to take all the weapons with them."

"Marines driving?" I asked.

"Yes, but I also heard a rumor the weapons only account for a small portion of that space. The rest allegedly is filled with the ambassador's luggage," said Triage.

"Putting Marine's lives at risk for Gucci shoes and Prada handbags that shouldn't even be in a war zone in the first place?" I felt my face flush with anger.

"That's the rumor. And don't forget about her dog."

"So egregious, and they kept it all for themselves, of course."

"Of course."

"Did you bring your bow?" asked Stitch.

"No, I didn't think there'd be room," I said.

"Makes more sense to bring that along than designer handbags or a pet. Technically it's a weapon," said Triage.

"Technically, your mom's a weapon," joked Tunes, trying to lighten the mood.

"Nice try, but I still miss my bow," I said to Tunes.

We all shook our heads in disgust. The embassy staff was so ill prepared. The State Department learned nothing from the Benghazi attacks.

Triage looked at his watch and I guessed it was getting close to 0600. The sky had a pre-dawn glow and was starting to lighten.

"I am going to the bathroom one last time before we depart." I'd been going at every opportunity all morning.

I left the others and hustled to the main villa. I went straight to the bathroom, splashed some water on my face, and stood still for a moment taking deep breaths. I felt angry and frightened and I tried not to let it show with every ounce of my being.

I realized I hadn't prayed all morning in my deepening panic and said a quick one then. It was more like desperately begging for help, but I think I was understood.

I next walked to the espresso machine, figuring it would help to have one more shot before hitting the road, if there was any coffee left. The machine was a mess, but enough coffee remained for one last espresso. I sipped on it slowly as I started walking back toward the front door.

When I reached the front door, I heard the ambassador calling me and stopped with my hand on the doorknob.

"Yes, ma'am?" I asked.

"Did you speak to Harbor? I called for him again and he has not responded."

"Yes, I relayed your desire to leave early."

"Well it's already been an hour and now we're running late."

"Yes, ma'am. I believe we've nearly finished arranging the vehicles into the correct Chalk order. Security officers lead each Chalk for safety-related purposes. I believe your vehicle will be located in the center where it's safest...."

"Yes, yes, I already know that. I was right to send those eleven out through Mitiga Airbase. We wouldn't have enough vehicles otherwise."

I remained silent. I didn't agree and believed it was an unnecessary risk. I also thought the ambassador was only trying to defend a bad decision, so there was no point arguing now. It was in the past. I also didn't agree, however, that driving the long route overland to Tunis was the best course of action.

"You chose this evacuation route we're taking today too?" I asked.

"Of course. The Marine captain and AFRICOM didn't agree with the route, but I have ground truth knowledge they don't."

"Why not the southern airfield officers carried out reconnaissance on?"

"It was too late to change plans at that point."

That confirmed to me the ambassador selected the evacuation route before our officers even conducted the trip to the southern airfield. There was so much unnecessary risk. They took great personal risk to drive through heavy fighting and hostile territory to investigate the feasibility of using the airfield, the viability of the runway, and whether or not a US military aircraft could land there. In doing so, they took half of the security officers with them, which left me and the other officers more vulnerable.

All of it was worth the risk if it would save us in the end, but if the decision was already made, it was pointless. Unnecessary. In addition, all of that occurred after the fighting started. After the administration left us stuck for nearly two weeks in the middle of a civil war without sending us any kind of assistance or allowing anyone to take action.

I opened my mouth to respond but was cut off by the radio before I could say a word. I decided it was probably for the best. Nothing I had to say in response would've been appropriate.

"Net call, net call, net call. All personnel report to your vehicles. Repeat, all personnel report to your vehicles."

I opened the door then, and the ambassador stepped in front of me and out the door without another word. I tried not to glare, took yet another deep, steadying breath and strode straight to my vehicle. I tossed my empty coffee cup over my shoulder and onto the ground behind me.

Stitch sat in the driver's seat as I walked up to the vehicle. He had already moved it into Chalk order position, but I noticed our fuel-laden Hilux right away. Tunes stood by the open door on his side behind Stitch and I saw Whirlwind stumbling over to join them. I opened my vehicle door, made sure my rifle and pistol were properly positioned, and sat down. I didn't fasten my seat belt. At a minimum we'd wait another half hour before departing, since Chalks one and two would depart first at fifteen-minute intervals.

Once we were all inside the vehicle, Stitch turned to us.

"Any last-minute questions or comments?" he asked.

"I, uh, I have the money for our Chalk," said Whirlwind, "It's all in this bag here."

He held up a plain black backpack.

"How much?" asked Tunes.

"What's the purpose?" I asked at the same time.

"It's ten thousand dollars. Harbor divided up the remaining cash between Chalks. I have the cash for our Chalk. It's for use in an emergency, in case we need to buy our way out of a bad situation. We couldn't leave it behind."

"Well," said Stitch, "Why don't you keep that safely on your person at all times and hopefully we won't need it."

I felt thankful we had some cash reserves and I appreciated Stitch's handling of the announcement. He had a way of putting people at ease and that was certainly needed with Whirlwind. The money would be useful if we had to abandon the vehicle or became stuck in the desert—it'd help us buy an escape. Smuggling was big business in Libya, but it was all for a price.

"Do you have anything to add as tactical commander?" Stitch asked me.

As a SOF representative, I thought he'd give us orders. Obviously, if things went south and lives were on the line everyone would follow Stitch's commands without hesitation. But if he was asking me, I wouldn't hold back.

"Whirlwind and Tunes, I have just a few things to review before we roll out," I began.

I really liked Tunes and hoped he knew I was reviewing precautions for everyone's safety. I felt truly concerned about Whirlwind.

"Don't draw your weapons inside the vehicle under any circumstances unless there is an imminent threat and or Stitch directs us to do so."

I felt more than a little worried Whirlwind would fumble with his weapon and accidentally shoot me in the back since he was sitting right behind me in the vehicle.

"Keep your doors locked at all times. Stay alert. We're responsible for our own safety. If you see a threat call it out."

"Call it out loudly," inserted Stitch in agreement.

"Whirlwind, you watch our right side, Tunes our left. Don't forget to look behind you as well. You already know the major threats—getting caught in the crossfire, direct assault, ambush, kidnapping, and so on. Those will all look fairly similar in execution. Anything that looks suspicious, call out a warning. Now, passports. Everyone have theirs?" I asked.

Tunes, Whirlwind, Stitch, and I all held up our passports for everyone to see and then put them safely back on our persons.

"What does everyone have in their go-bags?" Tunes asked. "I'd like to know what we're working with."

We each quickly outlined what we packed in our go-bags. Extra ammunition, medical kits, flashlights, identification, knives, water, and the list went on. Most of us also carried some Libyan dinar and I had some Tunisian dinar left from a previous trip there.

I also carried gummy bears in my go-bag at all times. I didn't mention that though. I didn't think the others would fully appreciate gummy bears as my life-sustaining-food-in-a-dire-emergency-situation selection.

Stitch also went over the medical supplies in his go-bag and mentioned the larger medical kit in the back of the truck. He didn't mention the six grenades in the glove box.

After we finished reviewing our assets, we all sat quietly and waited. Stitch seemed as calm as ever. I tried to appear calm, as always, but inside I felt worried. I'd looked for Nomad as I walked to the vehicle earlier but didn't see him. I knew he was up in the first vehicle and would soon be the first to pull out.

CHAPTER FOURTEEN

FLASHBACK: MANDATE EXPIRES

(EARLY SPRING 2014)

March 2014 began with the continuation of large anti-GNC protests on Friday mornings that continued throughout the day. The people protested the extension of the GNC. They contested the authority of the Muslim Brotherhood and Islamist-aligned blocs in the government.

Early in the month, after much vacillation and negotiation, the GNC announced new elections would be held in June. Once the new government was elected, the GNC would dissolve, and a new congress would take its place.

The secularists cheered, the Islamists plotted, and the people remained discontent.

Meanwhile, the country continued to suffer from a massive budget deficit that seemed to get worse with each passing day. Oil production remained around one hundred thousand barrels per day, compared to over a million per day before the Revolution.

The Federalists maintained control of the oil fields, but they too needed money to fund their cause. Rumors began to circulate that the Federalists tried to make deals to sell the oil on the black market, on their own terms.

In mid-March a ship called the M.V. Morning Glory docked in eastern Libya and rebels—probably associated with the Federalists—off-loaded oil onto the tanker.

The prime minister responded on March 11th with an attempted naval blockade in Libyan waters, but not quickly or strongly enough. In response, the GNC placed a vote of no confidence in the prime minister. His government collapsed. Fearing for his life, he fled the country.

The GNC appointed an interim prime minister, Abdullah al-Thini, who would lead the government until the elections scheduled for June.

The GNC then requested US assistance in stopping the tanker. The US administration agreed to help that time. On March 16th, a team of Navy SEALs authorized by the US president stopped the tanker in international waters and returned the ship to a port near Tripoli where the GNC arranged for offloading the oil.

The event caused further unrest. Many Libyans believed the US shouldn't have intervened in the tanker incident, still more felt frustrated their government couldn't do more to protect Libya's interests. Muhammad called Otter and me exasperated.

"The US intervenes now for the oil? Do you have any idea what kind of message that sends?" asked Muhammad.

"The GNC asked the US to intervene," I countered.

"We asked for a lot of things. Why now?"

I didn't have an answer. I didn't understand why the administration would intervene at that moment for an oil tanker, but would not intervene to secure our officers in Benghazi the year prior, or target the terrorists involved in that attack, or to save us from the looming descent into civil war. I wondered why the administration would care more about stopping an illicit oil sale than about my life, which I'd spent in service to my country.

That was the moment I began to really doubt what I was doing there. My faith wavered.

That was the second time I'd been made to feel expendable.

That month Flash also began to organize morning 'run-swim-runs' for all officers on the compound, although only security officers participated. We each tried as a group to find ways to bond, to strengthen relationships, and blow off steam. Organized physical activities were Flash's favorite way. Flash asked me to join them.

"What does the run-swim-run entail?" I asked Flash.

"One mile at an all-out sprint, then swim laps for thirty minutes, then another mile sprint," said Flash.

"And it's open to everyone?"

"Yep, are you going to join us?"

"But it's only been security officers all week."

"Maybe, but it's open to everyone."

"How fast are you doing the miles? And I'm just learning to swim properly, so I might not be fast enough."

"The miles are about seven minutes. Don't worry about the swimming, that's just ten minutes flat, as many laps as you can do or just tread water."

"Alright. I think I can do a seven-minute mile. What time tomorrow?"

"0600, before the day gets going."

"I'll see you then."

I met them by the pool the next morning ready to go. Or so I thought. They actually ran a sub-six-minute mile and I couldn't keep up. I ran a few seconds over seven minutes and they all waited for me at the end, cheering me on.

I continued to join them, not every day, but as often as my work allowed. Some people believed MWR, or morale welfare and recreation programs, were designed for personnel to have fun with the side benefit of building camaraderie among a group of people whose lives depended on each other. I thought the opposite. MWR activities were critical for our survival and built trust, with the side benefit of occasionally being fun.

I also appreciated the men's adherence to boundaries and no harassment policy. I'd heard horror stories about sexual harassment, especially in war zones. I'd worried about what I'd encounter in Libya. I also had my past experience with someone else's sexual misconduct in Iraq, which didn't help.

In Iraq, my roommate was a prostitute. I mean that in the literal sense. And it wasn't an abstract, "oh I knew a guy who knew a guy who told me that." No. My roommate, a National Guard member, literally had sex with men and women for money with nothing separating me from them except a sheet in a small converted shipping container. I reported it, but they didn't take action until she redeployed. Her chain of command had also been involved. I heard she was later court martialed—they found video evidence and two footlockers full of cash. I worried every night someone would go to the wrong bunk. My bunk. I made it clear to the men their attention was unwanted, especially the more aggressive ones, but I also slept with my pistol on my nightstand.

So, I had cause for concern.

In Libya, I received more attention than normal, but the men steered well clear of harassment. They never acted aggressively toward me, but they also knew it'd ruin their careers if I reported it. And I would have.

I think Reebok's leadership was the main reason for those boundaries. Leaders set the tone and enforce the rules, and Reebok took accusations of harassment seriously. He made it clear all violators would be disciplined. I believe that helped protect me from harassment. I knew without a doubt Reebok would listen to me and everyone else knew it too.

Meanwhile, in eastern Libya, terrorism also continued to spread. In December, Ansar al-Sharia conducted the first suicide attack in Libya, killing several LSOF members. In January, the US State Department designated Ansar al-Sharia a terrorist organization and the UN later imposed sanctions against the group for their cooperation with al-Qa'ida and the Islamic State.

Those events served to increase the group's notoriety and recruitment efforts. Eastern Libya quickly became a safe haven for multiple terrorist groups seeking to train fighters. Al-Qa'ida's branch in North Africa increased cooperation with Ansar al-Sharia, which had already begun with the attack in Algeria the prior year against the oil refinery in In-Amenas. More than half the operatives used in the attacks trained in Libya.

Rumors began that Islamic State fighters had returned to Libya and established a presence in Darnah. Ansar al-Sharia spread to Ajdabiya and continued to operate in Sirte.

I briefed Libya's devolution into a terrorist safe haven. I believed there was a strong possibility terrorists would conduct external attacks in the future, using Libya as a base to train and plan the attacks.

The ambassador didn't think the terrorists were that organized. Reebok asked if there were any examples. I explained that the attacks in Algeria in January 2013 and in Tunisia in October 2013 were examples of external attacks that already occurred and detailed how both attacks used fighters trained in Libya. I reviewed intelligence on other threat streams we currently followed.

I then reviewed the numerous attack plans directed against us in Libya. I also reminded them about the threats to kidnap US personnel. I briefed information on how extremists were particularly interested in foreign diplomats.

On March 21, 2014, unidentified assailants kidnapped a Tunisian diplomat in Tripoli. They stopped his vehicle, forcibly removed him from it, and he was not heard from until many weeks later.

Also, on March 21st, militia posturing and increased threats between the various groups resulted in the first attack on Tripoli International Airport. One morning, members of an opposing militia placed improvised explosive devices at the end of the main runway. The devices exploded causing minor damage to the runway. Fortunately, there were no planes using the runway at the time.

The Zintan shut down the airport to investigate the explosions. The airport re-opened the following day. However, European air carriers cancelled all flights into Tripoli for the foreseeable future.

The Zintan blamed the Misratans and threatened to attack Mitiga Airbase, which they viewed as an Islamist stronghold and staging area. The Misratans in turn increased their rhetoric and threatened to liberate Tripoli International Airport from Zintan control.

The ambassador continued to meet with all Libyan leaders, both official and nonofficial, both secular-aligned and Islamist-aligned. I thought she wanted to demonstrate the US would not pick a side, would remain neutral in any conflict, and sought only to support the people.

The people, on all sides, were outraged.

At the end of March, officers decided to take an afternoon off and enjoy the first warm, sunny day of the spring. We hadn't had a day off since Christmas. It was quiet in the city since the IED incident at Tripoli

International Airport and by happenstance there were no moves scheduled that afternoon.

The officers agreed to meet poolside at my villa. Nomad declared it was a Fantasy Factory catered event and recruited Arcade to help him spread the word and draft additional security officers as reinforcements to host it.

Nomad and Arcade mixed spritzers of fruit juice and tonic. Flash and Moe dug up some snacks for everyone to share. I brought the music.

That afternoon we gathered by the pool, talked, laughed, and enjoyed the sunshine. It was a brief moment of happiness I relished.

At one point, Belle, lying by the pool, leaned toward me.

"You know what?" she whispered.

"What?"

"I wish I could go back in time and tell my sixteen-year-old self it will all work out and everything will be fine. That one day I'll be lying poolside being served 'cocktails' by former Special Operations and security officers while taking a break from serving my country in a war zone," whispered Belle.

"I thought the same thing," I whispered back, staring at Nomad.

"Would anyone like a refill?" asked Nomad glancing toward me.

"Yes, please, Fantasy Factory director," I called to Nomad over the music, holding up my glass.

"Absolutely," he said smiling and then went to make me another spritzer.

"He likes you," whispered Belle.

"I know," I replied, smiling through my blush. Nomad and I emailed, texted, and squeezed in several additional coffee dates together. We tried to find excuses to talk together in a work-related setting or find brief, private moments to chat alone.

April started off with the first rocket attack in the immediate vicinity of the compound. In early April, unknown anti-Zintan forces staged in the Wadi Rabi'a area a short distance from the compound and fired rockets toward the Sawa'iq Brigade headquarters. The Sawa'iq headquarters sat several kilometers away from the compound, but the rockets fell short of the intended target.

Six GRAD rockets impacted within several kilometers of our compound during the pre-dawn hours that early morning.

I woke with the impact of the first rocket. The explosion reverberated throughout the compound and I felt the concussion in my chest. I'd heard mortars and artillery before in Iraq, but never GRAD rockets—the rockets sounded totally different. The boom sounded much deeper and louder.

Then five more came in before I could fully register the attack. The rockets sounded extremely close. The code red alarm sounded.

I jammed my feet into my boots as quickly as possible and grabbed my radio and body armor.

I ran down the stairs to the bunker. I began to loathe that confined space.

My villa-mates arrived at the bunker around the same time, including Nomad. Security officers then went to the team room in the main villa to discuss the attack. At that time, we didn't know if the rockets were intentionally directed against us or aimed at some other target. We speculated the target may have been the international airport, but I thought that was too far away. Regardless of the intended target, we treated it like an attack on us.

I grabbed my iPad and huddled back down in the bunker. I checked social media to see if any locals heard the explosions. They certainly had, and within the hour there were pictures of the exploded ordinance, fragments of the rockets, and the holes the rockets made. There were no reported injuries.

The other officers began calling their contacts to gather additional information. Many speculated about the cause of the attack and what prompted anyone to fire GRAD rockets inside Tripoli. It was the first major rocket attack since the end of the Revolution.

Eventually Gambler gave us the all clear and I returned to my room and prepared for the day. I went into the office to coordinate with the analysts at CIA Headquarters. They too monitored social media and would see the information on the rocket attack. I wrote a cable back notifying them all US personnel were safe and accounted for. I met with Hunter in the Marine command room and obtained the coordinates for the rocket impacts the Marines compiled.

Using the points of origin and points of impact, I speculated we weren't the intended target. I took the coordinates and a map to the security officers' team room to discuss possible targets with Nomad and Captain. They both agreed the most likely target was actually the Sawa'iq headquarters. The rockets simply fell short.

Arcade and Moe took a vehicle out to obtain a closer look at the rockets in order to determine their make. They were able to confirm the rockets, commonly called GRAD for 'hail,' were 122MM Russian origin rockets.

I explained those were the most common type found in Libya, left-over from the old regime, and frequently fired using weapons systems capable of holding dozens of rockets at once.

Days after the rocket attack, anti-Zintan forces attempted to overrun the Command and Staff College near our Annex. The Zintan kept the opposing fighters at bay and maintained control of the school. However, fighting that day was fierce and within a couple kilometers of us.

The fighting consisted primarily of small arms fire, but I could hear some heavy weapons used as well. Gambler placed the compound under another code red alert. That status meant everyone had to stay indoors, either inside the office or in a villa's bunker. I stayed in the office and researched the attack.

I discussed the recent attacks with Reebok. We shared the concern the fighting had not only increased, but moved alarmingly close. The Zintan provided our first level of outer security, they were our '911', and if the Zintan couldn't protect themselves, how could they protect the compound. There were no Libyan government forces to call on—the US Mission depended on the Zintan militia for outer perimeter security.

We relied on the militia.

The militia remained loyal to the tribe.

I knew about loyalty. I knew money never trumped family. At the end of the day, the militia guards' priority would be their tribe.

Then on April 15th, unknown assailants kidnapped the Jordanian ambassador to Libya. The kidnappers forcibly stopped his diplomatically plated vehicle as he drove home from his embassy to his residence in the diplomatic quarter, removed him from the vehicle, and took him to an unknown location. At first the kidnappers made no demands.

Two days later, on April 17th, unknown assailants kidnapped another Tunisian diplomat as he drove home from his embassy in downtown Tripoli. The kidnappers made no demands for weeks—he simply vanished.

Kidnapping threats began to pour in again. Call-ins, write-ins, walk-ins, and other contacts. It seemed like everyone reported on threats to kidnap diplomatic personnel after the kidnappings of the foreign ambassador and diplomats.

Stress levels on the compound hit an all time high. We all worried about the threats and the increased tensions on the streets of Tripoli. Reebok changed the movement policy and required at least two security officers go on every move off compound.

But I wondered if that would be enough.

I couldn't change the policy, but I could pray. And pray I did.

I also thoroughly researched and monitored and warned.

At the end of April, as I left the office and started walking to my villa, I saw a pile of rubber balls lined up along the side of the path. I looked over in time to see Flash give me a wicked smile then lob a dodgeball at me.

I smiled and ducked easily, picked up a ball and threw it back at him. I hit him right in the face. That began the most epic game of dodgeball Tripoli has probably ever seen.

It was evening, shortly before twilight, and everyone not on duty came to join in the 'fight,' a most appropriate MWR activity. It probably seems silly, but we desperately needed the stress relief.

"Net call, net call, net call," called Blue, "There is a game of dodgeball underway by the main villa."

The off-duty Marines wandered over to join.

A game started between the Marines, with Hunter leading the charge against the other officers on the compound. Each felt honor bound to win and 'fought' with enthusiasm.

We played until we couldn't see anymore and afterward everyone felt just a little bit better. It relived much of the tension and helped us all feel closer as a group.

I cared about every one of the other officers and felt thankful we were in the mess together. That caring is what motivated me just a little bit harder every day. I used my emotion to fuel my drive.

We each high-fived one another at the end of the game.

"I feel like I just scored the winning run in third grade kickball," I said to Flash as I gave him a high-five.

"Well done," said Flash, "You kicked butt."

"So did you," and I moved on to give the next high-five.

That is how I met Tunes.

Tunes stood next in line behind Flash, so I gave him a high five and stopped to chat. He loved the Pacific Northwest and Indie music, so I promptly praised his intelligence and good taste. He was quiet, but so was I. I told him about our breakfast routine, and he joined us from then on.

Nomad didn't join the game, since he was still on duty that night. He finished work as the game wrapped up and wandered over to join me while I chatted with Tunes.

"Well done," said Nomad with a smile, "you dominated the Marines. I'm proud."

"Too bad you couldn't join us," said Tunes.

"It's just as well, wouldn't have wanted to destroy the Marines too much," he joked and then turned to me, "it looked like they thought you'd be an easy mark."

"That's my secret weapon, people always underestimate me. They think I'm sweet and shy, but then bam!"

"Also, tough as nails," added Tunes with a smile. "I think you startled them."

"I have brothers," I said.

"That explains it," said Tunes.

We continued to talk as we walked toward our villas. Once Tunes broke off to his room, Nomad whispered to me, "You are sweet you know."

"But I'm also tougher than I look."

"I know, trust me I know."

In Tripoli, the tension quickly escalated again when at the end of the month ominous rumors began surfacing of a large convoy that left Benghazi and headed toward Tripoli. Its alleged intent was to join with other allied elements to attack opposing forces and take over territory in the greater Tripoli area—territory that included our US Embassy and residence compound.

My immediate concern was the convoy included Ansar al-Sharia members or other terrorists since it came from Benghazi.

The convoy allegedly consisted of Shield forces, primarily Libya Shield Two, which aligned with Ansar al-Sharia and fell under the umbrella of the LROR and MoD. The convoy drove from Benghazi to Tripoli and staged at Camp Twenty-Seven with the LROR under the command of an al-Qa'ida member. They posted messages and photographs on social media announcing their presence.

Postings about the convoy indicated anywhere between dozens or hundreds of vehicles traveled to Tripoli. Local news outlets reported the convoy's arrival at Camp Twenty-Seven, west of the downtown area. I read each article and monitored social media, but our officers noted no visible increase in technicals or militia presence on the streets in our vicinity.

Reebok reminded everyone there was no need to be breathless. We had plenty of other concrete things to worry about.

I agreed. I was concerned about abstract or potential threats, but we also had concrete concerns with which to deal. Meanwhile, the Jordanian ambassador and Tunisian diplomats were still missing, kidnapping threats against us were at an all time high, militia forces were openly attacking the Zintan, and the Libyan government appeared to be collapsing.

I discussed the issue at length with Reebok, Captain, Gambler, and Obi. We were all worried about possible rescue options in the event the situation worsened. In other war zones, the US Military or the host government stood ready to assist in times of emergency.

We could not rely on the host government in Libya. The Libyan government relied on the militias and the militias would not save us. The Benghazi attacks proved that. The US Military was too far away for a rescue during an emergency situation to be practical.

The US Military assets outside Libya were only several hours away, but sometimes several hours was all it took for complete disaster to strike. The GRAD rocket attack earlier that month lasted only seconds and had we taken direct hits it would have been long over before a single US Military asset took off.

We had Marines in Tripoli who would protect us at our facilities, but it was not a large unit.

In Libya, there was no cavalry.

There were no reinforcements coming.

We were on our own.

CHAPTER FIFTEEN

EVACUATION: ROLLING OUT

(JULY 26, 2014)

I thought about the route to the first checkpoint the morning of the evacuation, July 26th, 2014. I couldn't stop myself from thinking over and over and over again how it was the most dangerous part.

We needed to make it through the first check point and then we could breathe a little easier. Ever so slightly easier. Tunisia was still hours and many miles away, but the route would be safer after that first checkpoint.

I felt a great deal of confidence in Nomad and Captain though, and knew if anyone could lead the entire US Mission there safely, it was them. Nomad was an extraordinary warrior and could be very intimidating to those who meant us harm. He was also protective by nature. Captain led the reconnaissance on the route months prior, with several security officers who were currently in the convoy.

I also believed the militias had nothing to gain by targeting or disrupting the convoy.

However, there were those terrorist elements that sought to use the militia fighting as cover to carry out an attack, some had probably already infiltrated Operation Dawn forces. They had the intent and now the capability to conduct an attack against the US convoy or attempt a kidnapping operation. There were so many possible scenarios to consider.

Those same terrorists who joined Operation Dawn maintained contact with Ansar al-Sharia members in eastern Libya, the same group responsible for conducting the Benghazi attacks. Terrorists continued to harbor the same deadly intent to kill Americans.

My mind shifted through the threats like a kaleidoscope of terror.

I also knew, with every fiber of my being, the warriors would do everything within their capabilities to keep me safe. And they were capable of so much.

I knew every last one of them would protect me, would fight for me, and they would die for me if it came down to that. I hoped I was worth that sacrifice while praying it would never come to that. I constantly felt the weight of that responsibility. That was also why I ceaselessly researched and assessed all the possible threats. I felt it was my job to provide timely and accurate warnings to keep us safe on a more strategic level.

I took several deep breaths. In through the nose, hold seven seconds, slowly release. Repeat.

And I continued to pray, the words became a constant stream, a plea in the back of my mind that never stopped.

The sky lightened further; dawn was only a few minutes off, and it was just before 0600. I saw the ambassador walking toward my vehicle and heard a call go out over the radio for Harbor. I couldn't roll down the window of the armored vehicle, so I opened the door to hear what the she wanted. Harbor met her by my door and I realized that although the ambassador saw me first, she wanted to speak with Harbor.

"It's all over social media. Twitter, Facebook, everywhere," she said.

"What exactly is all over?" asked Harbor.

I pulled out my iPad. The wifi still functioned and I quickly pulled up Twitter. Sure enough, the evacuation of the embassy was all over the local pages in Arabic. Tripolitanians saw the embassy vehicles depart earlier and there was widespread speculation the US Mission evacuated. I nodded to Harbor.

"We need to go. Right. Now," said the ambassador.

"We'll depart when our local guards and escorts have cleared the route, all assets are in place, and we have the greatest chance of success. Which should be any moment. Ma'am, you chose this route, and it has extraordinary risk. That is your responsibility. Our responsibility is to mitigate that risk as much as possible for all personnel. We'll do everything in our power to ensure you arrive safely in Tunisia, but we need our local guards and escorts. We need the all clear from AFRICOM."

Harbor and the ambassador spoke a few more minutes, then returned to their vehicles. I closed my vehicle door. Harbor didn't need to see the social media postings. At that point, it made no difference for our safety. Libyans knew about the evacuation, which meant the militias knew, and the terrorists knew.

I took another deep breath and wiped my damp palms on my legs. They began to shake again and I tightened them into fists in my lap before Stitch could notice. I didn't want him to know how I felt. I never felt so scared before in my life.

The radios crackled to life.

"Assets are in place. Evacuation is a go," came Captain's voice, "Chalk one, let's roll out."

As Nomad pulled Chalk one out of the compound, beginning the overland evacuation to Tunisia, my heart started hammering hard in my chest.

All vehicles in Chalk one cleared the gate and after several minutes with no explosions or heavy or small arms fire in our immediate vicinity, I let out the breath I hadn't realized I'd been holding. There was no ambush out of the gate. Chalk one cleared the immediate threat and we could all proceed. Nomad survived, for now.

Chalk two pulled forward to stage at the front gate and Stitch started the engine in our vehicle to move in behind the others in Chalk three. We'd continue staging like that until all the vehicles departed.

Once Flash and Obi pulled Chalk three, vehicle one, into position, the rest of the vehicles followed suit. First, the vehicles full of Marines. Then Stitch and me in the rear.

Chalk two announced their departure a few minutes later. One by one each vehicle cleared the gate, turning left toward the heart of Zintan territory. I again held my breath, waiting—waiting—until Flash pulled Chalk three vehicle one into position.

I couldn't hear any explosions or weapons fire to the south. All the weapons fire remained focused to my north, northeast, and the international airport. The Zintan continued to fire rockets, but I could tell based on the sound that rocket fire was outgoing and not incoming.

Stitch pulled our vehicle into position behind vehicle two of Chalk three.

"How's everyone doing?" asked Stitch.

"Ready to go," said Tunes.

"Okay," mumbled Whirlwind.

"I'm fine," I lied, "You?"

"I'm with Tunes, ready to go," said Stitch.

We all sat silently for a few minutes lost in thought. I thought about my parents, their unconditional love, and our many conversations about how an evacuation was highly unlikely, a worst-case scenario.

The prayer in the back of my mind, became a fully conscious plea for help, repeated over and over again.

I wasn't fine. I'm not afraid to die—I know where I'm going when I do, but I didn't want to die in that war-torn place, where the people no longer wanted us, and for a cause I could no longer clearly define. As fear and anger threatened to overwhelm me, I forced it aside and clung to my faith instead. My new worst-case scenario was that I'd be in Heaven by nightfall and I could handle that. I just wanted to get my friends to safety first. I would not waver.

"Chalk three, let's move," Obi called over the radio.

"Alright everyone, stay alert," said Stitch, "Call out threats."

Gambler, who would depart in the final Chalk, slid open the gate for us. He held up his hand in a slight wave or salute as each vehicle passed.

"Chalk three, vehicle one, clear," Obi called.

"Chalk three, next vehicle, clear."

Stitch pulled up to the gate, drove through and turned left. Tunes, Whirlwind, and I began scanning for threats of any kind.

"Chalk three, last vehicle, all clear," I called and kept the radio in my right hand. Mine was the only female voice over the radio. I never once in my life imagined I'd ever be placed in such a scenario. I felt honored and terrified, but above all maintained my focus. I scanned for threats.

Several two-and three-story buildings lined the road at intervals. The buildings were under construction, they looked dirty and brown, with no windows or doors, and rebar stuck out at odd angles.

Some trees managed to grow in Libya and also lined the road. Few palm trees grew in Tripoli though, which always surprised me. The trees looked scraggly, with pale green sand-covered leaves, making them appear to be suffocating.

Most startling to me were the number of technicals on the road, particularly at that early hour. They were Zintan and operated by two or three militiamen dressed in mismatched fatigues. Almost all of the trucks with mounted weapons headed north toward the fighting and didn't seem interested in our convoy in the slightest. I figured they were reinforcements going to intensify the fighting now that the Americans were leaving.

Tunes, Whirlwind, and I called out each and every technical.

"Friendlies, two technicals at ten o'clock," called Tunes.

"Friendlies, three more on the side street at two o'clock," I said.

We continued as we drove south on that long stretch of road. Rocket impacts left huge potholes in the road in some places and we could see pockmarks on some of the buildings impacted by rockets. In the background, Tripoli International Airport burned.

The further we drove the less we could hear the heavy weapons fire, until the sound disappeared altogether.

We drove through an area at one point that looked like a shoddy strip mall. A small group of local men sat on the side of the road drinking coffee at a cafe and stared intently at the convoy as it drove by them. Several other men milled about or walked along the side of the road, seemingly without purpose in the middle of nowhere.

"Friendlies? Small group of men sitting on our right," I said, "They don't appear armed."

"Similar situation on the left," said Tunes, "several military age men milling about, appear unarmed."

"Roger that," said Stitch calmly and kept driving.

By the time we finished speaking, the men fell away in the distance. The convoy drove fast, with several hundred feet between each vehicle.

Then we passed a tank headed north toward Tripoli.

"Woah," said Tunes.

"Tank on the right," said Whirlwind trying to be helpful, "Probably armed?"

I already knew the militias used tanks in the fighting—knew it, but it was quite another thing to see it. I stared as we zipped past it. It appeared old, possibly from the early Ghadafi era, but clearly it remained fully functional and that was all that mattered to the Zintan and their enemies.

In theory, threats diminished over time and space as more and more vehicles passed without incident, as we drove further from Tripoli, and as the morning passed. We all knew better than to become complacent.

The convoy was large and Chalk three, which included our vehicle, fell near the middle.

"Chalk one, vehicle one at the first checkpoint," Obi called out to our chalk.

He relayed the message from Chalk two, who heard from Chalk one. The distance between vehicles and Chalks was too great for direct communication at that point.

"Chalk two is clear," said Obi, "We're about fifteen minutes out now."

"Chalk three, last vehicle copies," I replied, after the chorus of "copies" from the Marines' vehicles.

That meant Nomad arrived at the first checkpoint. I realized he must be safe, for now, if they were able to radio their position.

Captain probably obtained passage from the guards already. He planned to personally coordinate with the militia commander in charge of the checkpoint, buy our passage if necessary, and receive verbal guarantees of our safety through the checkpoint. Then each Chalk would pass through and he'd stay next to the commander the entire time.

Meanwhile, Nomad and Dolby would provide his protection and stand near the road, by the other guards, to take quick action if a guard became hostile.

Robin and his vehicle would continue through the checkpoint with the rest of Chalk one and take the lead. Robin needed to reach the last checkpoint first, before entering the mountains of Nalut and Amizegh territory.

That was the plan anyway.

As we approached the checkpoint, the vehicles slowed considerably.

I put on my headscarf. No one required scarves or ordered me to wear one, it just seemed prudent since I sat in the front seat and in full view. I adjusted it over my hair and used it to completely cover my body armor. Then I rested my left hand on the butt of my rifle, hidden under my sparkly blue scarf.

Militia members lined the roads on both sides and stared at us hard with varying levels of hostility. I didn't know if they were upset the US Mission was leaving, if they were angry the US didn't do more to help them, or if the militia would rather kill us all than stand by the side of the road and watch us leave.

Intent was very difficult to determine from a hostile stare, especially when they were already on edge from weeks of fighting, and were heavily armed.

I could see two large military transports up ahead, one on either side of the road, along with a huge Libyan flag flying overhead.

All the militia members wore a variety of mixed patterned, camouflaged fatigues. Green pants with desert shirts and berets, or striped pants, brown shirts, and boony cap or desert pants, black shirt, green hats.

I could see the Zintan militia seal on one armed transport and the Warshafana seal on the other transport. At least they used easily identifiable logos, which made it easier for me to identify the militias present. Several technicals and GRAD rocket launchers also sat behind or around the transports.

Upon seeing all the heavy weaponry and hostility, I could feel my heart rate accelerate again. Armored vehicles or not, we were no match for GRAD rockets.

I saw Captain speaking with the militia commander, as planned, off to my right. I could see the militia commander's arm around Captain's shoulders, smiling, and I knew the plan worked.

Dolby must have been off to my left because I didn't see him.

As the vehicle in front of them passed through the checkpoint, I spotted Nomad.

Then I saw only him until our vehicle passed.

Nomad stood at the edge of the road, in front of the transport, next to a guard. He looked very nonchalant in his stance, despite standing out among the Libyans given his height and fair hair, but I knew he could respond to an incident quickly.

As we approached the checkpoint, Nomad's eyes locked on mine. He raised his hand in a small wave as we passed and I raised my hand back.

Stitch drove through the checkpoint.

"Chalk three, last vehicle, cleared the check point," I said into the radio, trying to keep my voice even and calm my pounding heart.

"Roger that," said Obi, "Chalk four, you copy?"

"Roger that," came Triage's reply, "We are fifteen minutes out."

Stitch kept driving and we all breathed a little easier, ever so slightly, now that we passed the first checkpoint. I was amazed at how 'normal' Nomad and Captain appeared but knew they did it for the convoy's protection. I didn't think I could have stood so close to an armed transport manned by hostile militiamen and appeared so outwardly calm.

As the checkpoint fell further into the distance and we continued, Tunes turned to the rest of us.

"So, what next?" asked Tunes as he scanned our surroundings. "'Would you rather'—music edition?"

"Would you rather listen to classical music at the club or dubstep at church?" I asked.

"Dubstep at church, hands down," said Tunes. "Would you rather listen to your favorite song on repeat the rest of your life or only heavy metal?"

"Favorite song," I said.

"Heavy metal," said Stitch at the same time. "Would you rather listen to classic rock in the boudoir or hardcore rap with your parents?"

"Neither," I said, I'd rather go without music in both cases.

"Hm, that's a tough one. Classic rock," said Tunes.

"What's your theme song?" I asked.

"'Born in the U.S.A.,' Bruce Springsteen," said Stitch.

"'Time,' the Mowgli's," I said.

"'Salt and the Sea,' Gregory Alan Isakov," said Tunes.

"You seriously have theme songs?" asked Whirlwind. "Why?"

"Who doesn't?" I asked. I thought it pretty normal—a soundtrack constantly played in my head along to my life. I pulled out my portable speaker instead, "I think I'll play some now. It'll provide some important ambiance. Don't worry, I'll keep the volume down."

"Yes," Stitch, Tunes, and Whirlwind all said at once.

"Alright, this song seems extremely appropriate. Not too obscure, but hopefully you like it. Let me know if you don't and I'll change it. And don't forget to keep calling out any threats."

I hit play on Lorde's *"Glory and Gore."* It was not loud but audible over the sound of the engine and the distant gunfire and explosions.

"I love this song," said Tunes, "I listen to it at my desk with head-phones all the time. This might be my new theme song."

"Me too," I replied.

"Totally rad," said Stitch, humming along.

CHAPTER SIXTEEN

FLASHBACK: COLLAPSE BEGINS

(LATE SPRING 2014)

At the beginning of May 2014, local news and social media continued to report on the large convoy that entered Tripoli and staged at Camp Twenty-Seven near the end of April. The leader of Libya Shield Two, Buka al-Uraybi, even posted a video of himself on social media, showing a large convoy, claiming he entered Tripoli.

There was still no visible increase in militia presence in the vicinity of our compound.

Despite the lack of evidence, I began to gather the reported locations of the various Islamist-aligned forces. What if it was true? I needed to know the potential threat to our personnel.

I printed out a large map of Tripoli and plotted the locations on the map. I next plotted the known locations of the secular-aligned forces and strongholds. Finally, I plotted the location of the US Embassy and residence compound.

It appeared as though the Islamists were attempting to surround the Zintan but remained at a distance from Zintan territory. The Islamists acquired footholds to the south, north, and east of Tripoli. With the Islamist takeover of Camp Twenty-Seven, they had a presence in the west. Although there were multiple Zintan and other allied, sympathetic militia strongholds between our compound and enemy forces, I didn't think it was a good sign.

They were closing in around us.

I briefed the map and reported locations at the next country team meeting. The ambassador and Reebok listened attentively and had many questions about the locations, sources of the reporting, alleged manpower and firepower, and whether the information had been corroborated.

Many unknowns remained and I briefed those as well. The information hadn't been corroborated. We were in the early stages of research, but I briefed the information because of my concerns related to security and stability.

The ambassador asked me to meet separately with the embassy's Regional Security Officer (RSO) to pass along the information.

The next day I met with the RSO, Gambler, and Obi to discuss the information. We held a long conversation about the security situation and our emergency preparedness. Obi asked me to also brief all security officers, which I did the following day.

Whirlwind arrived the day after that. He was a senior officer but looked nervous to be in Libya. He had just gone through a bad divorce and had young children. One of his children had a medical issue and Whirlwind needed the extra money to help pay the bills.

I tried to help him out whenever I could. I gave him the standard intelligence briefing and he often asked for my opinion or thoughts about other issues.

I was scheduled to take leave at the end of May and planned to return to the Pacific Northwest. I cleared the dates one final time with Reebok.

I then talked to Nomad about my home leave plans. He also had home leave that would overlap with mine by a week.

"Well," said Nomad, "How about we meet up stateside?"

"That would be amazing," I replied, "Where?"

"Where are you going?"

"The Pacific Northwest, obviously."

"It would be nice to see the area with a native. Get my own personal tour."

"I think that can be arranged."

"Let's do it then. You tell me where and when, and I'll be there."

"Deal."

Nomad left on his leave shortly after that and I began to plan my vacation.

Days before I departed, another round of GRAD rockets exploded in the vicinity of the compound. That time the rockets landed at night as I walked to Belle's room for an after-work chat. Belle returned earlier that evening after conducting a lengthy meeting and wanted to vent and decompress from the stress. I saw the flash of the impacts and ran the rest of the way to her room.

The code red sounded. A total of four rockets impacted within one to two kilometers of our location. I again felt the concussions deep in my chest and the sound was deafening. Gambler initiated a roll call and ordered everyone to remain in place at the bunkers.

After an hour or so Gambler gave the all-clear for personnel to return to our rooms. I stayed a while longer with Belle and we speculated about what would happen next.

"Being here in a war zone certainly takes a toll," I said, "I'm exhausted. I've worked at least twelve hours a day, often more, for seven days a week, going on ten months now."

"I wonder how the warriors do it and have done it for so long," said Belle.

"I think it becomes addictive. Extreme highs and extreme lows. Constant adrenaline rush and as far as work, everything we do matters. It's high impact," I said. I found it addictive already, and if I did, I figured they must. It was like a legal, lifesaving, world-changing, super-hero high. Batman, Han Solo, and Neo all rolled into one. I chose the red pill and never wanted to go back.

"I agree. You also form relationships in different ways. For example, I know you and I will be friends the rest of our lives."

"I know I could count on every single person here if things went south," I said.

"Right. Everyone here wants to serve his or her country. Is patriotic. Would die for each other."

"I think it heightens emotion too. All emotions. That's also weirdly addictive."

"Right. You just feel things differently."

"And it is an escape from 'normal.' It will be hard to go back to that at the end," I said.

"I don't believe it's possible to ever be 'normal' again," said Belle. And I agreed, there was no going back. I'd never be ordinary again, not that I ever really was.

The next day the ambassador and Reebok discussed options after the rocket incident. They decided to initiate a partial drawdown, cutting personnel. Many embassy officers volunteered to leave, some of their staffers were eager to depart given the heightened threat environment. Reebok also selected officers whose tours of duty were almost over and sent them home early, canceling their replacements.

Although my tour would be over in two months, Reebok designated me emergency essential. He told me to take my personal leave to the Pacific Northwest, but to return at the end of it, ready to work harder than ever. He said they needed my analytic capabilities and Arabic language skills. I was essential to overall security and they relied on me to keep them informed of tactical and strategic threats.

I felt honored he placed so much value on me and had confidence in my capabilities, but I was also worried about what the following weeks would bring. In fleeting moments, the worry felt more like sheer panic.

I hoped I was up to the challenge.

First, I needed a break.

Reebok also ordered officers to increase security precautions at the office and on all moves off the compound. He wanted to ensure the safety of everyone under his watch to the greatest extent possible.

On May 13th, assailants released the Jordanian ambassador to Libya, Fawaz al-Itan, in a prisoner exchange. As part of the exchange, the Jordanians released an al-Qa'ida operative, Muhammad al-Dursi, who Jordanian authorities convicted for his involvement in a 2007 plot to blow up Jordan's main international airport. He was from Darnah.

The group holding the Jordanian ambassador met the plane and conducted the prisoner swap at Mitiga Airfield. I thought LROR, probably in coordination with Ansar al-Sharia, was responsible for his kidnapping.

Shortly after his release, I left for my desperately needed rest and vacation.

On May 16th, Operation Dignity began in eastern Libya. Between his television announcement in February and the commencement of

Operation Dignity, former general Khalifa Haftar apparently remained in the background, slowly pulling together his strategy and allies.

Haftar's major focus, he claimed, was to eliminate extremist terrorist groups. Rather than wait for the politics in Tripoli to catch up with his plan, he started a war against the terrorists in Benghazi by launching attacks against terrorist groups.

Haftar combined forces with LSOF and rumors circulated that the Federalists also joined. They all fought for a common cause and were united in their desire to see Ansar al-Sharia and other terrorists eradicated from their city.

Dignity forces, under the command of Haftar, attacked Ansar al-Sharia strongholds, conducted bombing campaigns, and set up roadblocks throughout the city. Dignity forces referred to themselves as the Libyan National Army, used an official-looking Libyan army logo on their vehicles, and wore army uniforms during fighting.

In reality, it was the start of the civil war in eastern Libya, which various factions of the Libyan government opposed to varying degrees. The prime minister announced that the government did not support Dignity. Islamists came out even more forcefully and strongly condemned the operation.

Ansar al-Sharia fought back hard. They began posting pictures of the fighting on social media as a recruitment tool. They called for their fellow extremists throughout Libya to travel to Benghazi to help them fight.

Some of the Libya Shield elements, led by Buka al-Uraybi, that traveled to Tripoli in the large convoy at the end of April answered that call and returned to Benghazi. Others allegedly remained in Tripoli preparing for their own operation to come later.

I also believed the Islamist-aligned groups had their own strategy and conspired to take control of Tripoli.

I read about Operation Dignity from the Pacific Northwest. I picked Nomad up from the airport and together we drove north. We explored the islands and a national park. We hiked together. Cooked together. Visited the city and local markets together. It was a fantastic and the happiest I'd been in ages. I was completely and utterly head over heels for Nomad.

He was the opposite of me in many ways. He was laid-back, rarely flustered, and never afraid. Or if he was ever afraid, he certainly didn't show it. He believed many people feared intangibles, and he focused on the concrete instead. He took risks, in life and in work, but they were always calculated risks. He taught me the Navy SEAL saying, "two is one and one is none." Or always have a backup. We followed that advice on our many adventures.

We traveled the world together and he became my best friend, and whenever I saw him, I knew we were about to embark on another extraordinary adventure.

I spent the rest of that vacation with my family. My mother wasn't pleased about my designation as emergency essential. She worried for my safety, but also understood why I needed to return. She understood how deeply I cared, and my sense of responsibility to the people and work I cared about. So, instead of growing upset or falling into despair, she prayed even more. My mother is what some people of faith call a prayer warrior.

Her health has deteriorated over the years and she is now fully disabled. She has an autoimmune disorder and chronic pain from it. Her brain is as active and sharp as ever, but her body is not. I think sometimes she feels trapped inside her own body and lack of physical ability. And yet, instead of dwelling on the negatives, she has chosen to use her faith and mental acuity for good. She prays. Constantly.

And I felt her prayers. Even in my lowest, darkest moments I knew beyond a shadow of a doubt my mother prayed for me, probably even at that exact moment when I felt most scared. We share a close connection and she always seems to know when I need her most.

She made many sacrifices for my brothers and me. During our hardest times growing up, she went without to provide for us. She ate less, so we could eat more. She spent every weekend entertaining and playing with us, instead of going out with friends or to parties. She kept us safe.

She protected me. She inspires me. She's my hero and always will be, for as long as I live.

I returned to Libya at the beginning of June 2014. Nomad, who arrived just days before, picked me up from Tripoli International Airport with Moe. For reasons I never learned, the Zintan customs officials didn't want to let me leave the airport. I carried only one suitcase when I returned, met Ali as usual upon arrival, and he escorted me through the process.

Everything seemed fine until we arrived at the last check to enter Tripoli. Then the guards stopped me. They asked where I'd been and where I was going. They spent long minutes studying my passport and visa.

They said they had a new policy and required additional copies of my passport and visa. They took my passport to their office, presumably making copies.

I stood by Ali, who argued with the guards about the temporary detainment, but to no avail. We waited and waited and I tried to remain calm.

I felt nervous, however, and thought I'd be in danger if they kept my passport. I wondered if they'd try to detain me in a prison or other holding facility. I worried about what they might do to a female American prisoner. I prayed they didn't know I was CIA. I briefly entertained the idea of making a break for the exit, but I knew that wouldn't end well for anyone. No international incidents. I'd try to be patient and not panic.

While considering the possibilities, I looked around the arrivals area and tried to take note of any differences in the international airport. There were more militia members than usual. They had new, more official-looking uniforms. The members wore dark blue police style uniforms with the MoI logo. Otherwise, nothing seemed out of place or different.

After nearly an hour, they returned my passport and let me leave. I walked with Ali straight to Nomad, Moe, and the waiting vehicle. Militia members in nearby vehicles began catcalling and honking at me. The security officers blocked me from view and hustled me into our armored vehicle.

I felt much safer once I sat inside the vehicle and locked the doors.

We left quickly, and on the ride back to the compound I told Nomad and Moe what happened. I asked if anyone else had problems returning. Nomad said others were briefly stopped but not held as long.

I told Gambler about the incident at the airport before I did anything else. He added it to the ever-growing list of security concerns. I then went to my room to unpack my bag before going straight back to work.

The atmosphere felt noticeably different after the beginning of Operation Dignity and the partial drawdown. Everyone was more withdrawn and serious. There was a palpable intensity in the air.

The whole country felt hostile to me.

I'd been consumed before, but then became obsessed with analyzing and warning about credible threats. I scoured all sources of information. As a CIA analyst, it was the only way I could protect my friends and colleagues, the ones who served alongside me, took incredible risks for our country.

I stepped up my work. Beginning the next morning, I started providing a daily intelligence briefing. I kept it short and to the point. It was open to all US personnel. Everyone, regardless of position, affiliation, or title. While the group changed from day to day depending on moves, personnel attended when they could.

I focused the intelligence briefing on security and stability issues. I briefed protests, skirmishes in town, and all threats. I provided a brief assessment of credibility. I also provided any other information that could impact the operational moves. I put in incredibly long hours, afraid of missing something that could result in an attack, kidnapping, or other security incident.

"Could you describe how the kidnappings went down?" asked Obi at one briefing.

"We don't have detailed information on how the assailants conducted the kidnappings. The diplomats obviously would have driven with the red diplomatic plates they all have in Libya. That could have made them a more easily identifiable target. In addition, we know from local news and social media that most often the assailants fired on the diplomat's vehicle, forcing it to stop. I expect not all the diplomats used armored vehicles," I said.

"And the non-dip kidnappings?" asked Obi.

"Similar tactics, but we know less. There've been hundreds of kidnappings in the last year. Most are for ransom. Most are against unarmored vehicles or snatch and grabs off the street. The commonality however is that when vehicles were involved, armed men in another vehicle also rammed or fired at the target vehicle to stop it."

"What're the most dangerous neighborhoods?" asked Gambler, "Do you have any data on that?"

"In Tripoli, Abu Salim has high crime, Suq al-Juma is rumored to have an extremist presence."

"Any other areas we should avoid?" asked Nomad.

"Still the well-known ones like Mitiga Airbase and Camp Twenty-Seven, but I'll pass word if I learn of more."

"Dude, why is it so messed up here?" asked Dolby.

"It's the Libyans!" I said, with my best Doc Brown impersonation.

"Huh?" asked Dolby, scowling at me. He looked confused and angry about it.

"Doc Brown. *Back to the Future*," I said, "One of the most important movies of our formative years."

"Seriously, you're such a nerd," said Dolby.

"I prefer intellectual ninja, thank you very much," I said, "But to answer your question, probably because they lived under a brutal dictator for many years."

I also briefed any strategic issues that may impact moves in the near to medium term, such as updates on election planning and the progress of Operation Dignity.

Operation Dignity was underway for several weeks by that point. Haftar's Libyan National Army continued to work with LSOF and together they fought against Ansar al-Sharia. They made some gains but again requested additional assistance. None came.

Ansar al-Sharia used terrorist and guerrilla tactics, which were difficult to combat. They conducted car bombings, suicide attacks, and frequently used IEDs.

The terrorists outnumbered Operation Dignity forces. More terrorists seemed to keep arriving in Benghazi to join Ansar al-Sharia. Terrorists from Darnah moved to Benghazi to join the fight. Al-Qa'ida members from North Africa began to trickle into eastern Libya in greater numbers. Information started circulating of still more fighters returning from Iraq and Syria.

Some of those returning fighters established a nascent Islamic State in eastern Libya. Rumors suggested some of the fighters returned at the request of the former LIFG members. They were the same former LIFG members in Tripoli who publicly presented themselves as focused on peace and prosperity in Libya, while privately plotting a civil war. The fighters returned via Mitiga Airbase, which was under the former LIFG members' control.

Muhammad refused to meet with me any longer. He claimed he was involved in his own preparations to defend his country since the US refused to help.

I continued to eat my meals with Belle, Otter, and Blue. They looked as exhausted as I felt. They frequently stayed up late trying to make contact with local leaders, to gain updates on the status of Operation Dignity, the large convoy that entered Tripoli from Benghazi, returning foreign fighters, and discontent with the government.

Nomad and I didn't have much down time, but every moment of it we spent together. I continued to take breaks from the office for my runs because I needed the stress relief. Nomad started to run with me in the afternoons, just to spend a little time with me.

I provided the weekly intelligence briefing for the ambassador, Reebok, and the country team. I presented much of the same information I gave in the daily briefings but focused on overarching themes. Rather than brief streets x, y, and z saw violence, I discussed the general areas of violence and how that fit into the overall trends we had been following for the past year.

I also researched and provided briefings on any developments that could impact us in Libya related to the upcoming US military operation to capture the prime suspect in the Benghazi attacks, Ahmad Abu Khattalah.

CHAPTER SEVENTEEN

EVACUATION: LONG DRIVE SOUTH

(JULY 26, 2014)

Stitch continued driving south on the main highway through Zintan territory on July 26th, 2014. The farther we traveled from the capital, the less maintained the road became. The southern road suffered more damage from heat and lack of maintenance than from rocket impacts as in the north.

The road stretched in a straight line as far as the eye could see. In the distance, I could see the mountains of Nalut, or the Jabal Nafusa, which literally means the Nafusa Mountains.

To the right and left of the road stretched sand and shrub brush for miles and miles. Some buildings dotted the landscape, but they were few and far between.

"Camel," called Tunes, "We've got camels."

"Oh wow," said Whirlwind, "Those are the first I've seen here."

"Same here," said Stitch.

Camels were a common sight in every other Arab country I visited, but not in Tripoli. Apparently, they were all hanging out in the Sahara Desert.

"I can't get a good picture from here," said Tunes.

He held his phone up against the window on the right side, reaching directly across Whirlwind who just sat there.

"Need help?" I asked.

"Yeah, thanks," he said, passing his phone to me to take the picture.

I obviously couldn't roll the window down to take one, but I tried to get a good angle through my side window. The armored glass distorted the view a bit, but at least I could tell in the frame it was a camel.

I passed the phone back to Tunes and then pulled out my iPad so I could take a few photographs as well.

"You rock," said Tunes.

"Your mom rocks," I teased back, using his favorite expression.

"I know. She'll totally love this too," said Tunes smiling at the picture.

I held my iPad up to the front window and took a few photos of our convoy heading towards the mountains. I could still only see our Chalk, but it was a cool picture.

"Car!" Whirlwind shouted.

We all jumped a bit, startled, and saw the car behind us, moving over to pass on the left. Then I looked at Whirlwind, questioningly.

"Friendly?" he speculated.

"Yeah, looks like he just wants to pass. Totally fine," said Stitch calmly, "Could you let the rest of the Chalk know a vehicle is passing us?"

"Of course," I said.

"Chalk three, a vehicle is passing the convoy on the left. White sedan," I called into the radio.

The Marines in Chalk three took up the call as the sedan passed each vehicle.

"White sedan passed chalk three, vehicle three."

"White sedan passed chalk three, vehicle two."

And so on, until the vehicle drove beyond our Chalk and into the distance.

"Roger that," came Obi's delayed response. I could hear Flash chuckling a bit in the background.

"The Marines certainly like to use the radios, huh?" said Stitch.

I sat back in my seat again after the 'threat' passed. The sun shone down on us, as it rose in the sky, it was going to be a scorcher of a day.

The air conditioner already ran full blast in the Hilux and it barely kept us cool.

"Chalk three, we're coming up on the second checkpoint now," called Obi over the radio.

I looked ahead and as we rounded a small bend in the road, I could see the second checkpoint off to our right. One technical parked on the side of the road with a handful of militiamen. A Libyan flag flew behind the vehicle.

The entire checkpoint looked much smaller than the first, but we still proceeded with caution. Stitch slowed the vehicle again and kept a bit of distance between our vehicle and the vehicle in front.

As we drove through, Stitch raised his hand and nodded his thanks to the guards who nodded or waved back. I kept my gaze on the vehicle in front of us and slightly to the left, scanning for threats and avoiding the guards' stares.

Without a doubt they weren't as hostile or as heavily armed and seemed more interested in the novelty of our convoy and Americans than anything else. Based on their blatant, unnerving stares, I also guessed they hadn't seen a blonde-haired, blue-eyed American woman in a while, if ever. It made me want a thicker scarf to conceal my hair and face.

We continued driving south. We'd already been on the road a few hours, with many more hours to go. I wished we could have taken the coastal road. It was a much shorter distance.

Extremists held territory along the coast road, however. Those terrorists possibly established several training camps in western Libya outside Sabratha. That city was also the location near where the US military was detained the previous December. Sabratha was located on the coastal road about halfway between Tripoli and the Tunisian border.

Instead, we took the long route. Once the immediate threats of militia fighting, civil war, terrorist ambush, and second checkpoint passed, we were able to relax even further.

I pulled out a granola bar and took a small sip of water to wash it down. The men all drank a full water bottle and Tunes pulled out the beef jerky he packed.

"Mom sent it to me in a care package I received right before the fighting started," said Tunes as he shared it with us.

"I will never disparage your mother again," I said, "Mmm—this is tasty."

"Your mom is tasty," said Tunes, without missing a beat.

Stitch laughed at that comeback and it lightened our mood. We put the food and water away after we each had a bit, all while keeping watch as we continued south.

"Chalk three, we're now arriving at checkpoint three," called Obi, as the vehicles began slowing down.

Stitch drove the Hilux through the third checkpoint. The checkpoint consisted of a technical and two guards by the road, although there were several more militiamen in the guard shack I could see situated behind the technical.

Stitch waved and nodded again as we passed, and the guards waved back. I didn't bother with the headscarf again. I unwrapped it from around my neck and tied it around the strap of my go-bag.

"Chalk three, last vehicle, cleared the checkpoint," I called into the radio.

"Roger that," replied Obi.

The road began a long curve right, toward the western border, and Tunisia. The mountains appeared much closer, and the vegetation sparser. The landscape looked barren, sand took over the shrubs, and everything was light sandy brown.

I thought the sand and desert looked different in Libya, and in North Africa, than in the Middle East. We had not passed any sand dunes, although I knew they existed in Libya, instead mountains and plateaus surrounded us. It looked rockier and grittier than other locations I visited.

"Not too much longer now," said Stitch, "Maybe an hour."

"Good, I'm ready to not be in Libya anymore," replied Tunes.

"What are you going to do when you're not in Libya anymore?" I asked, "What's first up when you get home?"

"Shower. Then sleep. Then food," he said. "Or maybe sleep, food, shower. Or food, shower, and sleep. I don't know. But definitely those three things."

"Same here. First, I want a toilet, then sleep for a month, and then gorge myself on food," I said. "What's your favorite post-deployment meal?"

The question was probably the most commonly asked question among Americans in any war zone anywhere in the world. We talked about food a lot. I hadn't met a single person who didn't have a quick answer. The question was generally posed within a day or so before someone's departure.

"Big salad. Huge. With every fresh vegetable that I can possibly squeeze in. Apple pie for dessert. Home made," said Tunes.

"Fresh fish. Wild caught tuna. With grilled vegetables on the side," said Whirlwind.

"Steak," said Stitch, "Then more steak. And potatoes."

"Hamburger. Smothered in peppercorns. With grilled onion, tomato, lettuce, and pickles. Sweet potato fries on the side," I said.

We sat quietly for a while after that, daydreaming of food while gazing out the windows, watching the landscape zip pass. Few vehicles shared the road with us then. Several more passed after the white sedan incident but otherwise all remained quiet.

As the sun continued to rise in the sky, it began scorching the earth. It felt hot, even inside the vehicle. I could see heat vapor rising off the pavement and off the hood of our vehicle. There was distortion in the air from it.

The wind blew hard in the vast expanses of the desert. The wind shook our vehicle and sent waves of sand whipping across the road.

I saw vehicles off to the right up ahead and Stitch slowed down. I recognized Blue and realized Chalk two pulled over and wondered why.

"You think they're okay?" asked Stitch.

"I'll check," I replied as I picked up my phone and called Blue.

It only rang once before Blue picked up.

"What's up?" Blue quickly asked.

"You guys okay, need us to stop?"

"We're good, just making a pit stop."

"Okay. Call if you need help."

"Will do," said Blue and we both hung up.

"They're fine, just needed to make a pit stop," I told the others, "That was Blue from chalk two."

"I could use a pit stop soon myself," said Tunes and the other men agreed.

I stayed silent but hoped somewhere along the way we might find a toilet. Or some trees. I doubted it though.

Tunes and I began chatting about our favorite bands and songs. We needed something to distract us from thoughts of sleep and food, and since we both loved music it was a perfect fit. Whirlwind didn't have much to add, but Stitch loved classic rock and chimed in occasionally with suggestions for us. Tunes and I were avid fans of independent music, from the most obscure to the well known, and could talk music all day long. For two introverts, I thought that was significant.

Another half hour passed and the mountains appeared much more prominent, no longer on the horizon but looming before us.

I knew Moe led the convoy at that point with Robin in his vehicle. By that time, they should've made contact with our allies in the tribe.

Somewhere behind us, Nomad brought up the rear with Dolby and Captain. I had not heard radio confirmation, but I knew if there'd been a problem, we would've heard by then. I believed Nomad was safe, for now, and wondered how he was handling the drive.

"Chalk three, we're pulling over," called Obi.

"Roger that," came the chorus of replies.

"Why are we pulling over?" I asked Stitch, after I rogered up to Obi, "Everything okay?"

"Appears to be, not sure why we're stopping."

Stitch pulled the vehicle off the road and to a stop behind Chalk three. Chalk one was already there, and Chalk two remained a ways back, but was clearly planning to stop. I wondered if Obi learned about some danger up ahead, or if Moe and Robin encountered problems with the tribes. I assessed a hundred scenarios in my mind, none of them good, as Stitch placed the vehicle in park and turned off the engine.

The convoy stopped along the road on a straight stretch of highway that would soon wind its way up into the Jabal Nafusa. We had a clear field of view in all directions. We had cell phone coverage. It was the perfect place to stop.

The men almost as one opened their doors, walked ten to twenty feet off the right side of the road, and took a collective pee. I stepped out of the vehicle before I realized what was happening, blushed bright red, and looked up at the sky. The men clearly couldn't care less that I stood right there.

They certainly didn't care that flying overhead, continuing to follow our convoy through Libya, were aircrafts monitoring our progress. Including the ISR, which I knew a number of the intelligence and policy community officials in Washington were probably watching from at that moment.

"Don't you have to go?" asked Stitch when he finished.

"Yes," I replied, "Not a chance I am going here."

I'd never been so jealous of men before in my entire life.

"What's going on?" I asked.

"Robin is finishing up some last-minute arrangements. Obi said he heard the folks in Tunisia got a late start so they need a little more time to meet us at the border," Stitch replied.

"Couldn't be bothered to wake up early, huh?" someone asked.

We drank a little more water, snacked on the remainder of the beef jerky and I ate another granola bar. I noticed everyone around us taking off their body armor, looked at Tunes who shrugged, so we followed suit. It felt amazing to take off the heavy armor. Almost everyone stood outside the vehicles, milling about, waiting for direction.

"Let's top off the fuel tanks, see who needs more," said Stitch.

Tunes and I helped Stitch untie the rope and the cover from the gas tanks. Stitch found the funnel, handed it to me, and carefully lifted out one of the tanks. He set it on the ground beside me. Whirlwind watched us and helped hold the cover after we removed it.

Stitch filled our vehicle first and then we went around checking and filling any other vehicles in need of a top off. It seemed our vehicle burned through fuel faster, possibly because all the tanks weighed it down.

We helped secure the tanks and ropes and stood around chatting after Stitch finished.

The sun beat down on us as we stood along the side of the road. I could feel sweat dripping down my back from the intense heat and the wind pulled my hair from its ponytail and whipped it around so much I could hardly see.

I walked toward the front of the line of vehicles, stopping to say hello and exchange a few words with the other evacuees along the way.

I saw Obi and Flash at the front, but couldn't see Harbor, and figured he sat inside the air-conditioned vehicle.

The sun and wind made it pretty gnarly to be walking about, but I needed to move. I felt stir crazy from sitting for so long and I hadn't been able to run in weeks, not since the heavy fighting began.

As I approached the front of the convoy, my radio crackled to life. "Attention all personnel, return to your vehicles now," called Obi.

I saw Obi in the distance, waved, and turned around to walk back to our Hilux.

Chalks four and five never arrived at our location. I hoped I'd see Nomad, confirm he was totally fine. The peace of mind would've been wonderful.

"Hey guys," I said as I reached the Hilux, "Anyone know where the other Chalks are? I don't see four or five."

"Yeah, I asked Moe," said Stitch, "One vehicle broke down and instead of ditching it they decided to tow it and that's causing some delay. They're moving our direction, but slower than expected."

"That's unfortunate. We're leaving now? Everything's all set at the border?" I asked.

"Yep, it's time to move out. Robin confirmed they're ready for him at the border, on both sides," said Stitch.

CHAPTER EIGHTEEN

FLASHBACK:
MOVES AND COUNTERMOVES

(JUNE – EARLY JULY 2014)

The US military took months planning the operation to capture Ahmed Abu Khattalah, the lead suspect in the Benghazi attack, and the US president finally approved the concept of operation for the raid that June. The decision was delayed because there was widespread concern for the safety of US Military members entering Benghazi. There was also increased concern about the consequences of conducting the operation on the safety of US Mission personnel in Libya.

I coordinated with the analysts at CIA Headquarters on possible scenarios in response to the capture operation. They analyzed Ansar al-Sharia's potential response, how it might increase the risk to Americans in Libya, and potential international and Libyan government responses, with a focus on whether or not the Libyan government would collapse. They presented their analysis to policy makers, including the ambassador.

In the end, the administration decided the risk was worth the potential gain of capturing Abu Khattalah alive and prosecuting him in a US court for his crimes. Then the US military needed to wait for resources to be in place and all the stars to align on the day that would give them the best possible chance of success.

On the morning of June 15th, Operation Dignity led a massive offensive against Ansar al-Sharia in Benghazi. Dignity Forces conducted a multi-prong assault against their strongholds in the downtown area of the city.

Operation Dignity forces staged out of Benina Airport, on the eastern outskirts of the city, and approached from the north, east, and south.

To the west lay the Mediterranean Sea, where a US military ship and a team of Special Operations Forces waited for the opportune moment to enter Benghazi, Libya.

As night descended, the fighting began to subside. Abu Khattalah, spooked by the fighting, moved to his alternate house along the coast. The moment could not have been more perfect.

US Special Operations Forces entered the city via the Mediterranean Sea, captured Abu Khattalah, and directly handed him over to the FBI.

We anxiously waited in Tripoli while the US military conducted the operation in Benghazi. Most of us remained awake through the night during the operation, hoping for word of its success. We all felt a vested interest in the outcome of the operation since it was to capture the prime suspect in an attack that killed our colleagues.

I felt relieved when it was over and hoped some form of justice might finally come for those we lost that night in September 2012. The second half of June continued much as the first, with security officers and Marines heavily focused on our safety and the increased violence throughout the country.

News of the successful capture of Abu Khattalah broke several days after the operation. The Libyan public expressed surprise and speculated on the possible involvement of Operation Dignity forces. Some even suggested Dignity forces conducted the operation and the US had no involvement.

The Libyan government did not provide an official response. The prime minister remained silent.

Ansar al-Sharia also remained subdued in its anti-US rhetoric, focusing their efforts instead against Dignity forces.

I monitored for threats in response to the capture, but few came across my desk. I actually enjoyed reading some of the positive social media postings regarding the operation. It seemed most people the world over understood, if not condoned, the operation.

After the major Dignity offensive on June 15th, LSOF and the Libyan National Army (LNA) gained some territory in downtown Benghazi. However, Dignity forces appeared to have expended a great deal of resources during their offensive and I believed they probably needed to rest and resupply. Dignity forces and LSOF again requested US assistance in fighting Ansar al-Sharia, a designated terrorist organization. Their requests went unanswered.

Seeing the lull in action, Ansar al-Sharia quickly mustered a response. They fought back with a vengeance and overran compounds used by Operation Dignity forces. In doing so, terrorists gained access to the vehicles and weapons at those facilities, which included heavy artillery.

During that same timeframe, Ansar al-Sharia seized control of a bank in Benghazi. The terrorist group launched its own radio station and multiple social media accounts to spread propaganda. It attempted to project governance through its claimed creation of security forces to "protect" the residents of Benghazi from the LNA. It also attacked and later took control of al-Jalaa hospital in Benghazi.

As fighting raged in Benghazi, a terrorist group calling itself the Youth Islamic Shura Council, with some members affiliated with the Islamic State, increased its activities in Darnah. It staged a massive parade in the streets of the city in April and continued to flaunt its presence in the city. It began using the same savage tactics seen in Iraq and Syria, such as public beheadings and floggings. The Youth Islamic Shura Council would later change its name to Islamic State in Barqa Province, establish sharia police and a sharia court independent from the government.

Crime and violence also increased in Tripoli.

The public was desperate for change.

On June 25th, 2014, the country held its national elections, which the people were waiting, protesting, and calling for since the beginning of the year.

Reebok, concerned about the potential for violence, cancelled all moves that day. I closely monitored the security situation in the city via local news and social media and provided updates to Reebok and analysts at CIA Headquarters throughout the day.

In a decision I did not expect, Dignity forces declared a ceasefire in eastern Libya, and the MoI and MoD deployed forces en masse in Tripoli to provide protection at the polling centers.

Violence stayed minimal and the people turned out to vote.

The election committee set up voting centers in every neighborhood, town, and village in the country. The ambassador, UN officials, and foreign dignitaries visited and monitored election centers. They publicly demonstrated their support for the elections and establishment of a new Libyan government.

Within days, the election committee announced the election results for a new parliament, which they called the House of Representatives. The Islamists didn't fare well in the elections and lost seats. Secularists and independents ruled the day.

The Islamists started plotting in earnest. Forces began amassing in strategic locations throughout the greater Tripoli area, preparing for the onset of open hostilities against the secular-aligned groups.

Kidnappings of foreign workers and foreign businessmen dramatically increased throughout the country, with Italians and Egyptians bearing the brunt of the attacks. Extremists conducted most of the kidnappings for ransom, but they executed some hostages.

I continued providing the daily intelligence briefing to all US personnel in Tripoli. The briefing remained short, and focused only on the most important security developments and stability issues.

"Does the successful election mean they've turned a corner, no more division?" asked Robin one day at the briefing.

"Almost certainly not. The Islamists lost seats and I expect there is some extreme angst about that."

"Any idea what they'll do?" asked Flash.

"They've been threatening for months to overthrow the government, push out the secularists and Zintan from the area. So far, it's been all talk, but I believe they're planning and conspiring to do so."

"How would they do that?" asked Nomad.

"They've said publicly they'll start with the Tripoli International Airport."

"So the fighting, this is the new normal?" asked Belle.

"For now. Although we'll almost certainly see spikes in violence and things could quickly deteriorate with very little additional warning," I said.

I relied on my memory during those briefings. I rarely used notes and when I did it was a simple list of topics on a three-by-five note card. I strongly believe my memorization skills came, in part, from learning Bible verses, quotes, and songs growing up. Rote memorization exercised my brain in a way other activities did not.

Meanwhile, the ambassador shared her views on the success of the elections after the weekly briefing with the country team. While voter turnout was not as high as the embassy hoped, everyone seemed happy the elections occurred at all, and the people did, in fact, vote.

The ambassador remained focused on the political process and the prospects for a stable government and didn't seem as interested in hearing about the spread of extremism in the east or the movement of terrorists west.

I briefed the intelligence anyway, and although the ambassador knew terrorism was a problem and knew the Islamist-Secular divide deepened, I don't think she wanted to acknowledge the spread of extremism. She couldn't let Libya fail, and terrorist expansion did not fit that paradigm. The ambassador stated repeatedly the US would not leave Libya, would stand by the country whose dictator the US had helped overthrow. Libya. Would. Not. Fail.

After the intelligence briefings with the embassy, I normally took a short break and hid in my room for a few minutes. I needed time to decompress.

Nomad, noticing my pattern, began meeting me at my villa if he could. He'd occasionally also brew my favorite coffee and have a steaming cup waiting for me.

After one such briefing, I hurried back to my villa. As I walked up the stairs to my room, I ran into Triage who was heading into the team room.

"I saw that boy making you coffee," said Triage.

"Yes, he does that sometimes," I said with a smile.

"And I've seen you do the same," said Triage.

"He always pays me back later though."

"You know, of any people I've ever met, you two couldn't be more perfect for each other," said Triage and then continued down the stairs.

At the end of the month, on June 30th, extremists released the two Tunisian diplomats whom they held hostage since early spring. The extremists demanded a prisoner exchange. It took several months to negotiate, but in the end the Tunisian government allegedly released two terrorists in exchange for their diplomats.

Analysts never confirmed the identities of the kidnappers.

Early July was the calm before the storm.

Tripoli seemed to be moving forward on a positive trajectory after the elections. The public expressed excitement about the new government. A Libyan woman started a new campaign on social media that became an instant sensation. Locals throughout the country began posting photos of their lives and beautiful places in Libya.

Reebok needed to take vacation to attend an important family event and departed Tripoli. Harbor arrived in his place and served as my acting boss during his absence.

Harbor called officers into the office for an all-hands his first night in Tripoli. He told us he'd do his best to run things in Reebok's stead. He emphasized the importance of communication given the tenuous security situation. He also gave us July 4th, Independence Day, off work and encouraged all personnel to take some time for rest and relaxation on the holiday.

Later that night, I stopped by to introduce myself to Harbor. He reminded me of my stepfather because he was also a veteran and served during the Vietnam War.

"Good evening, sir. I'm your CIA analyst."

"Yes, I've heard good things about you. How long have you been here?"

"I've been here since last July, so my time's almost over."

"Is this your first war zone?"

"No. You?"

"No, I've been around."

"Well, I usually give all new arrivals an intelligence briefing, if you'd like one. Plus, I'm available literally anytime, of course. All day, every day."

"Thanks. I received a briefing from other CIA analysts before I departed Washington D.C."

"Perfect," I said and went on my way. I knew I'd end up briefing him before too long. The analysts at CIA Headquarters tended to focus on bigger strategic issues, plus it was their day job, whereas I lived and breathed Libya on a daily basis for a year—no other officer knew Libya better than I did at that time. But my time in Tripoli was winding down and he would work with my replacement, a vivacious and extroverted analyst I looked forward to trading places with soon.

The morning of July 4th, we held a five-kilometer race. Gambler put out the call for runners to participate. Nomad and I walked the route, using a navigation system for accuracy, and I drew a map of the compound with the route for the race.

Mid-morning we held the race, running lap after lap after lap around the compound. A handful of people participated and the rest cheered us on. Stitch took first place. I came in second. I enjoyed teasing Stitch beforehand about beating him in the race, knowing I didn't have a chance, but I still tried my best to keep up.

Afterward we all jumped in the pool to cool off. It was already a sweltering day.

Everything changed after that.

It was my last brief moment of "fun."

When I was eight years old, in second grade, I received my first A- on a report card. Up to that point, I'd only ever received straight A's and I was devastated. I returned home sobbing.

"I failed," I sobbed to my mother and crumpled into her arms.

"What happened?"

"It's terrible,"

"What's wrong?"

"I got my report card today," I admitted and handed it over. My mother skimmed down the list of A's.

"You have all A's again."

"No, I don't. I got an A-. I don't understand. What did I do wrong?"

"You didn't do anything wrong," she said, and I'm sure she held back a smile then.

"But I tried so hard," I sobbed, unable to let it go. I felt crushed. Gutted.

"It's still an A," she said.

But I knew it wasn't the same.

My mother gave my brothers and me one dollar for every A and I thought I wouldn't receive that dollar. I needed it because I'd picked out a gift for my mother I'd been saving all my report card money for a year to purchase. I found a small Precious Moments figurine depicting a little girl sewing needlepoint with the word mother on it. My mother loved those figurines, but they were too expensive, and she'd never buy one for herself.

I was determined to buy it for her and she had no idea. Thankfully, I received that last dollar and the kind, elderly woman in the shop wrapped it up in beautiful paper for me. I proudly gave it to my mother on her birthday, and then it was her turn to cry.

That event perfectly captures my perfectionism, sense of personal responsibility, drive, and depth of emotion. And I was eight.

That was my level of determination back then, when I was eight.

My determination was far greater by the time the civil war broke out in Libya.

Some claimed it was the hottest July they could remember. Electricity again became a major problem due to the lack of fuel. The oil fields reopened after the change in prime minister and national elections, but production was slow to begin.

Fuel shortages spread through the country and gas lines appeared again at most gas stations in Tripoli. The lack of fuel combined with the extreme temperatures led to shortages in electricity and rolling blackouts.

Militia violence simmered as all sides postured for power. Low-level fighting occurred throughout the city and remained intermittent, with minimal casualties. Intentions were unclear and the identities of those involved even more so.

Harbor and I ended up discussing the situation at length. I reviewed the increase in violence and political instability during the past several months. Harbor noted that it seemed volatile, leaderless, and directionless.

I agreed and explained how local fighting groups often pushed hostilities to the brink of war, but then pulled back at the last minute. As time passed, and hostile incidents became more frequent and volatile, the line marking the brink in Libya moved ever closer. Each incident reset the baseline further along the spectrum toward all-out conflict.

I liked to refer to the current situation as a simmering morass of muted angst. I believed the next hostile incident could push them right over the edge and provided that assessment to all who would listen, including in cables back to CIA Headquarters.

Haftar, the leader of Operation Dignity in Benghazi, made a public statement announcing his intention to "liberate Tripoli from terrorists and illegal militias" with the assistance of military forces and tribes in Western Libya. He called for the GNC to step down, its members to be prosecuted, and the democratically elected House of Representatives (HOR) to retain power. He specifically called out the Libyan Muslim Brotherhood as his enemy.

After Haftar's televised coup announcement in the spring, Libyans had a difficult time believing his public claims. However, he since started a major operation in Benghazi and therefore his announcement seemed to give people pause. It remained unclear if Haftar had enough allies, manpower, firepower, and time to wage a war in both major cities.

The Islamists, however, took it quite seriously.

In early July, a previously unknown group calling itself Operation Dawn circulated threats on social media, which were then picked up by local media, threatening to liberate Tripoli International Airport from Zintan control. It remained unclear who led the effort or hid behind the threat. Operation Dawn was a new name, a new entity in the ever-evolving power struggle in Libya. The group, however, clearly sided with the Islamist-aligned elements operating in Tripoli.

The Zintan countered the threats and claimed the tribe and its allied militias would take offensive, not defensive, action in the looming showdown.

On the evening of July 12th, a Misratan contact called Blue. The contact served on the Misratan local council. He called to inform Blue, and requested Blue relay to the ambassador that the Misratans planned to launch Operation Dawn in the morning in cooperation with the

Misratan's allies. The assault would begin at 0500 and be directed against Tripoli International Airport.

The Misratan contact wanted the ambassador and US Mission to know Operation Dawn sought only to attack the Zintan and not the United States. The contact felt it wise to warn the ambassador since the US Mission personnel were located so near the Airport. However, the contact's warnings did not provide any guarantee the Misratans would refrain from bombing US facilities in pursuit of their Zintan targets.

Blue relayed the information to Harbor and me. Harbor then passed the information to the ambassador and called for another all-hands in the office. While threat reporting came in fairly frequently, we had never received such specific and seemingly credible information on timing and targets.

Harbor shared the information during the all-hands. He requested that everyone ensure their go-bag was packed and ready in the event an attack did occur.

Gambler said any outbreak in fighting would likely result in a code red. In that event, everyone should report to the closest bunker and await further direction.

I also briefed our concern that extremist elements could be involved. I shared that Operation Dawn was led by the Islamist-aligned bloc and given their association with terrorists, they could use any fighting as cover for an attack directed against us. Either way, if the target was the Zintan, we sat squarely inside the target area.

The all-hands ended. Most officers left the office for the night and returned to their rooms. There was a strong sense of foreboding in the air. I could feel the tension escalate and my own heart rate increased in response. I wondered if this was it, if we would see the beginning of the next phase in the Revolution, an all-out civil war. I only hoped there would be no casualties among our officers or the women and children who could also become trapped in the violence.

I stayed behind and spoke with Gambler for a few minutes.

"What do you think the chances are of an all-out fight?" I asked.

"Normally, I'd say slim, but given the specificity, I'm inclined to believe it."

"Chances seem higher this time."

"You still sound skeptical."

"No, you're right, this is different. I'm just worried. If this is the start of a civil war, I don't think it'll end anytime soon."

I returned to my villa and placed my go-bag and Glock on the nightstand in my room, body armor by the door, and running shoes on the floor next to my bed.

Nomad did the same. He also placed his rifle next to his gear.

If we were very lucky, we could get almost six hours sleep before the war would allegedly start. Nomad and I talked for a little while before going to bed. I hated the idea of being stuck in the middle of heavy fighting and not being able to defend ourselves or mount a response. I felt trapped already. And I didn't want to die there, caught in someone else's war. At that point, I wondered why the administration even wanted us in Tripoli when it clearly had no intention of doing anything outside monitoring the situation.

I believed the US should be countering the terrorists, not watching them expand their territory to our doorstep, we should be stopping the extremists before they rested control of the government, not waiting to see the casualties mount.

"I wonder if we'll try to evacuate. If they actually fight," I said.

"Evacuate?" asked Nomad.

"Well, we conducted a drawdown already. Seems like a logical next step. But the ambassador said her guidance from the administration is that we won't leave. No matter what."

"Do you think we should leave?"

"Well, it depends. There are many other options short of evacuation and our mission here is important. We could fall back to a safer place or draw down further. We've paid such a high price to be here already. At the same time, we shouldn't stay if a war starts and our hands are tied, if we're just waiting here to die without being able to take action. We've had dozens of opportunities to intervene, to diplomatically or militarily pick a side, but have done nothing. Now it may be too late," I said.

"If there is fighting, it'll probably involve GRAD rockets again and other heavy weapons."

"Yes, if it's anything like in the past."

"There's no way to defend against such things in our current circumstances. We'd need to change our posture, otherwise it's just a matter of time until they're at the front gate," Nomad said.

"True, and we've not been allowed to do anything proactive to protect ourselves here."

I prayed myself to sleep that night. I hoped the next day would be peaceful, but I knew Libya better than that.

CHAPTER NINETEEN

EVACUATION: BORDER CROSSING

(JULY 26, 2014)

"You know anything about this next stretch of road?" asked Tunes the afternoon of July 26th, 2014.

"Looks like it'll be different than the rest," noted Stitch.

"Yes. It's up through the Jabal Nafusa. I haven't seen it myself but based on photographs and Internet research it'll be a climb up. There's a steep, narrow road and it's pretty rocky. They're not pointy mountains, more plateau than traditional mountains."

"Pointy?" asked Tunes with a smile.

"Jagged? It's descriptive, isn't it?"

"Your mom's descriptive."

I grinned and got back in the Hilux with the others. I was thankful Tunes rode in my vehicle.

"Any threats out this far we know about?" asked Stitch.

"No, but we lack information in this area, so it's more a matter of an intelligence gap than a lack of threat," I replied, "No dots in this area to connect."

"Well, alright," said Stitch, "Let's keep a sharp eye out. Narrow, winding roads are the perfect place for an ambush."

Tunes, Whirlwind, and I buckled up and began scanning our surroundings once more.

"Chalk three, rolling out," called Obi, and we were off again.

We spaced the Chalks once more so there were at least ten minutes between each. Chalk three's vehicles followed Chalk two once again, and we moved back into the original order.

Except Chalk one, vehicle one. Nomad was still somewhere in Libya far behind me. I thought of him as I scanned the desert.

There wasn't much to see, no buildings, very few vehicles besides the convoy, and almost no vegetation.

Stitch drove the Hilux up into the Jabal Nafusa and the road was just as narrow and winding as I expected. We drove incredibly slowly which made me a bit nervous. I couldn't see around the hairpin turns in the road, which turned into unpaved dirt by that point.

Everything around us looked dry and dead. The sun beat down on our vehicles. Nothing stirred except the sand and dirt kicked up by our vehicles and blown by the wind in the air around us.

I stared out the windows and remained quiet. I scanned for threats as Stitch cleared the mountain pass.

I put some music on again. I hoped it would help cut the tension. I played Mumford & Sons' "*After the Storm*" and we listened to it in the background as we climbed into the mountains.

After thirty minutes or so Stitch drove around one last bend in the road and we could see far into the distance. The road then wound steeply down the other side. Before we started down, Stitch paused and pointed.

There, in the distance, I could see the border crossing.

Stitch drove the downhill side of the steep, winding road in the Jabal Nafusa toward the border crossing. Tunes, Whirlwind, and I continued to scan for potential threats, but we had a wide field of view and nothing looked suspect.

The crossing looked deceptively close from the top of the mountains, but it took another half hour before we heard Chalk one call out their arrival. Chalk one arrived with a lead-time of an additional half hour. Robin needed time to coordinate with his contacts and set up arrangements for the crossing of the vehicles.

"It looked so close. I could see Tunisia," said Whirlwind longingly, "I think I could even smell it. It smelled marvelous, just for a moment."

"We're almost there though. Another half hour," I replied.

"You think Robin is handling things okay?" asked Tunes.

"Yes, he's a meticulous planner and could talk his way into or out of just about any situation. He's the perfect person for this," I said.

I liked Robin, but as an introvert, his constant chatter became overwhelming to me at times. It took us some time to work out an understanding, but I finally asked very bluntly one evening when we were alone outside drinking coffee if he would mind very much being silent. Just for a little while.

From then on whenever we sat together, with no one else around, he was silent. We simply enjoyed the brief quiet together. I greatly appreciated his understanding, since unlike him I was confined to the compound most of the time. I could never escape the constant social interaction. It overwhelmed me sometimes and I craved the silence.

"Chalk two, arriving at the border crossing," called out Blue on the radio.

"Roger that," replied Obi, "We're ten miles out."

"Only ten minutes?" I asked, "It looks farther than that."

"And then another ten or so until our turn," replied Stitch.

We entered the Libyan village by the border crossing. It consisted of a single mosque, with a tall minaret, and several small buildings set back from the road. The buildings all looked rundown and like they were under construction. A heavy layer of dirt and sand covered everything in sight.

I took a few photographs as we drove slowly though the village.

"Chalk three, arriving at the border crossing," called Obi.

Stitch slowed considerably and pulled in behind the last vehicle. Chalk two vehicles still waited in front of us, so I assumed the crossing must be taking more time than they anticipated.

The border crossing looked derelict.

A shack on the right side of the road boasted a large map of Libya painted on the side, with the map colored in to look like the Libyan flag. I imagined the writing in Arabic at some point probably said something about departing Libya but the paint was so faded and dirty I had a hard time reading it. All I could make out for sure was 'Free Libya' in Arabic.

A metal, canopy-like structure stood on the left side of the road. The road passed along the shack on the left, curved through the canopy structure, and then turned up and over a hill out of sight.

Chalk two vehicles took that route. Approximately every five minutes one vehicle pulled forward, stopped at the shack, drove left, up under the canopy, and disappeared over the hill.

"What do you think is taking so long?" asked Stitch.

"No idea," I replied, "I honestly thought they'd simply wave us through."

Before long, ours was the next vehicle in line. Stitch pulled up to the shack where Robin waited with a linguist and the border guards. I unlocked and cracked my door to speak with Robin.

"Hi, what do you need?" I asked.

"I need all your passports. They want to put an exit stamp in each one," said Robin.

I quickly collected passports and handed them to Robin, concealing my surprise in view of the border guards.

"Here you go," I said.

"I'll be back in a few minutes," said Robin, "Also, I need some additional cash. Five thousand. Could you get some from Whirlwind and wrap it in something so they can't tell exactly what it is I'm carrying?"

"Yes, of course," I said.

While Robin took our passports over to the guards, then stepped into the shack on the right side of the road, Whirlwind dug out the five thousand dollars.

"Anyone have an envelope or something similar?" I asked.

"Nope. Didn't think to put an envelope in my go-bag," said Tunes.

"Me neither," I replied as I took my knife out of my boot. I used it to cut off part of my sparkly blue scarf. I wasn't going to keep the scarf anyway, so it didn't matter if I destroyed it. I wrapped the cash several times in the scrap of my scarf. Add 'passing five thousand dollars to a shady border guard to obtain safe passage' to my list of things I never expected to do in my life.

A few minutes later, Robin returned holding our passports. I cracked the door again. As I opened it, a gust of blistering heat and sand blew into my face.

"Wow, it's hot out there," I said, wiping my hand across the beading sweat and bits of sand on my forehead. "Here's the cash."

Robin took the cash in one hand and handed me the passports with the other.

"Fancy," he said, glancing at the scarf, "Double check these, make sure the exit stamp is in there. Keep them with you, they'll ask for them at the Tunisian border as soon as you cross to the other side of the hill."

"Okay," I said opening the first passport.

"Whirlwind..." then I flipped through pages until I found the exit stamp with the correct date.

"...Yes," and set it on my lap.

"Stitch...yes."

"Mine...yes."

"Tunes...yes. We're all set Robin."

"Good. Now pull forward, over the hill, you'll see the Tunisian crossing right away," said Robin, "And I'll see you soon."

Stitch put the Hilux back into drive and pulled slowly forward. He drove to the left, under the canopy structure, and over the hill. In front of us loomed the much more formidable Tunisian border crossing.

The Tunisian crossing looked huge, particularly in comparison. A wide metal canopy structure crossed over the road, which split into multiple lanes. The left side had several permanent, solidly built structures. Multiple guard posts lined the lanes. It looked clean and whitewashed.

The Tunisian border guards looked much more prepared and trained than the Libyans. A row of guards stood on the left side of the one open lane. Clean-cut, shaven, with matching uniforms.

Stitch pulled the vehicle up to the first guard.

"Passports," the guard said in accented English.

I handed the passports to Stitch who handed them to the border guard. I stared at the border guard, but he kept his eyes trained on Stitch.

"Pull forward," the guard said.

"Thank you, sir," said Stitch and slowly pulled forward.

We passed under the canopy, lined with security guards who successively waved us through, until we reached the other side. I saw the other vehicles pulling into a staging area on the left. I sunk back into the seat, finally allowing myself to relax a bit. I wiped my sweaty palms on my pants and wiped the remaining sweat and sand from my face. I closed my eyes for a moment and breathed a deep sigh of relief.

We made it.

We successfully entered Tunisia.

I felt so relieved I was in Tunisia, but equally worried about Nomad, who would be last to arrive. As I wondered where he was along the route, I scanned my surroundings from inside the vehicle.

Several Tunisian National Guard vehicles lined the right side of the road. The vehicles were white with the military logo painted on the side. The men looked particularly well-trained and capable. They all wore matching desert camouflage fatigues and carried large rifles. Next to them sat several US Embassy vehicles from Tunis.

To the left, Chalks one and two lined up along the side of the road, backing in their vehicles, sometimes three or four deep. They tried to arrange the parked vehicles in a way that would allow them to pull out quickly and in the same Chalk order. Stitch slowly drove over to the last empty slot in line, backed in, and put the vehicle in park.

Stitch let out a huge sigh.

"Wow it's hot," he said.

"I still need to get out, stretch my legs," I said.

"Great, can you help me with the fuel again? We need to top everyone off."

"Sure. Tunes, Whirlwind you in?"

"Yep," said Tunes.

"I'll wait here," said Whirlwind. I glanced back at Whirlwind with concern. He appeared pale, sweaty, and jittery, and I worried about his health.

Stitch, Tunes, and I exited the vehicle and began the process of untying the rope from the truck bed, pulling off the cover, and taking out the fuel tanks. By the time we finished we were covered in sand, dust, and sweat once again.

"Green is diesel. Red is gas," he said, handing me the funnel.

Stitch filled our Hilux's tank first, then started walking around to the other chalk leaders asking who needed fuel. A long line started to form to pick up the extra fuel.

"We'll also be stopping for gas en route, so you just make sure you have enough for another hundred miles or so," said Stitch.

Stitch continued to handle the fuel situation with Tunes as Obi marched over from the other side of the road, near the Tunisians, to talk to me.

"The Tunisia National Guard offered to escort the ladies to their facilities," said Obi.

"I don't mind staying here and helping," I said. I thought he meant to give the women a place to rest out of the heat, but I'd rather stay with the group and help.

"They have a bathroom," said Obi, being a little more explicit.

"Oh, thank God," I said, relieved beyond belief. "Yes!"

As we stood there discussing the escort to the facilities, Obi received a text message from the ambassador.

"She said they're lost."

"What?"

"The ambassador says they're lost."

"Isn't she still in the convoy, following a long line of vehicles in front of her, with the US government watching overhead?"

Obi just nodded his head, flabbergasted, as the Tunisian National Guard vehicle pulled up to take me to their facility.

I took the front seat and chatted in Arabic with the Tunisian National Guard member driving. He waited a few minutes and other female officers joined us in the back seat and he drove us to their facilities next to the border crossing.

We hurried into the facility and found our way to the bathroom, which was neither clean nor sanitary. But it was a private toilet and that was all I cared about. I would've celebrated a hole in the ground with a door I could close. They even had toilet paper. And they didn't charge for the toilet paper, as many public toilets did in the Middle East and North Africa. We finished and hustled back to the vehicle.

"Shukran jazilan," I said, or thank you very much.

"Afwan," he replied, or you're welcome.

He drove us back to the staging area and as I exited the vehicle, I thanked the driver again, and said "Allah Ma'ik" or God be with you. He seemed unsure how to handle a car full of American women, but he was extremely polite though a bit red in the face. He seemed shy and a bit embarrassed to me.

I felt so much better after using the bathroom, but I still figured I'd be lucky if I didn't have permanent bladder damage.

CHAPTER TWENTY

FLASHBACK: OPENING SALVO

(MID-JULY 2014)

Operation Dawn started thirty minutes late, but once it began it did not stop. At approximately 0530 on July 13th, 2014, forces under Operation Dawn's command launched a barrage of heavy weapons fire directed at Tripoli International Airport.

Throughout the day, the Marines monitored the fighting in their command room. They noted more than fifty GRAD rocket launches that morning, each launch contained multiple rockets, and the Marines worked to determine the barrages' points of origin and points of impact. In addition to the 120mm GRAD and 60mm rockets, they witnessed an enormous amount of anti-aircraft artillery fire, including 14.5mm.

I didn't see the initial barrage, but I certainly heard it. I woke around 0400, checked the time, and began sifting through social media to search for references to an impending attack. I found none. I lay quietly in bed, trying to rest as much as possible, and saying another prayer for safety.

I listened to the world outside and felt tense. 0500 came and went. I started preparing for the day. I hoped the rumors of attack were false once again, but I still prepared for the worst.

Around 0530, when the initial barrages hit the airport, the whole compound shook as if the earth opened up to swallow us. The windows rattled in their frames. Anything not tied down or secured shook or fell over. Explosion after explosion echoed in the morning air. The compressions even vibrated the curtains and bedding. They reverberated through my body.

My adrenaline spiked. My hands began shaking and sweat trickled down my back.

The code red alarm sounded. I grabbed my go-bag and put my Glock in my holster. I had just finished adding my holster and magazine pouch to my belt when the initial barrage hit. The ambassador had a no-visible-weapons policy for most US personnel, but at that point I didn't care. If there was to be a war, I would be armed. If we were overrun, I wouldn't go down without a fight.

Nomad also quickly grabbed his gear and together we moved down to the bunker. Our villa-mates Dolby and Triage met us there. We waited until the initial barrages ceased, and the security officers in my bunker decided to move us as a group to the main villa.

"We need to walk to the main villa. Can you do this?" Triage asked me.

"Yes. I'll come with you," but I could hear the quaver in my own voice and my hands shook. I clenched them into fists, but my breath came in gasps.

"I'll go first, then Dolby and you. Nomad take the rear," said Triage.

Nomad stared at me, "Ready?"

"Okay, I got this," I said, my voice shaking with fear.

I felt terrified and tried desperately not to appear that way. I'd never walked outside during a major bombing campaign before. That was completely outside my realm of experience.

"Alright, let's move with a purpose," said Nomad.

I knew I needed to get to the office to write cables and relay information back to CIA Headquarters. Security officers needed to be there to coordinate among the team. Plus, we didn't know if or when the fighting would stop. I took several deep breaths. My hands shook more. My heart pounded so hard it hurt.

We left the villa together. Triage led us out the back door, followed by Dolby, me, and then Nomad. We hustled as quickly as possible to the main villa.

Anti-aircraft and other heavy weapons fire continued. Halfway to the main villa the next barrage of rockets hit the international airport. We walked south and in the direction of the airport. I heard the rocket's impact and saw the huge billows of black smoke rising into the sky. The sound was deafening. I resisted the urge to cover my ears, I kept my head down, and marched onward.

I thought the impacts shared some similarities with fireworks. Not little fireworks, but the massive ones that rocked the end of celebrations and games. I knew I'd never like fireworks again. Never.

We reached the main villa within minutes and I split off and walked to the office. Nomad and the security officers walked to their team room. I logged onto my computer and began the long process of researching and compiling information related to the onslaught. I coordinated with Harbor and decided to cable the information to CIA Headquarters with my research into the fighting.

The ambassador called for an Emergency Action Committee (EAC) meeting at the embassy facility. Normally, she held EACs in the office in order to discuss pertinent classified information, but the embassy personnel deemed it unsafe to travel. The ambassador ordered Harbor to do so instead.

That afternoon, Harbor asked Stitch and me to accompany him to the EAC. Nomad and Moe drove us to the compound and provided our protection en route. After the ambassador began the EAC, she asked me to provide an intelligence briefing on the status of fighting and prospects for more.

I provided my assessment that the fighting would probably continue for the foreseeable future. Our contacts claimed both sides were committed to the fight and the Zintan were preparing a response. The next day could possibly be worse.

I detailed how the morning's fighting shutdown Tripoli International Airport. All airlines cancelled flights indefinitely. We couldn't confirm that rockets impacted and destroyed the runway, but they did hit multiple planes, which was the source of the fires and billowing smoke. Either way, Operation Dawn caused significant damage to Tripoli International Airport.

The Intelligence Community was still working to confirm the full extent of the damage.

The other EAC participants reviewed what each knew about the status of fighting from their contacts and sources. The ambassador and Harbor discussed the status of their respective facilities and the need to stock up on provisions in case the fighting lasted a while. Harbor explained that he was already well prepared with enough food, water, and fuel to last weeks. The embassy would seek to obtain more, they hadn't planned ahead.

All participants agreed to continue to monitor the situation and pass all threats or other relevant information. No one proposed leaving Libya, the ambassador didn't mention whether the administration would send us help or conduct a rescue operation.

After returning to my normal work location, I drafted a cable back to CIA Headquarters about the EAC. I worked late into the night, trying to determine what the next few days might bring. I heard nearby rocket fire and explosions off and on throughout the day, but it simmered down some by that evening.

As the day wore on and fighting continued, Gambler put us into a modified code red status. We needed a safe way to move outside, walk between buildings, and continue our work on the compound. He therefore required every person to wear body armor outside at all times and instituted a buddy system so no one could go outside alone. He recommended we keep our go-bags with us at all times wherever we went.

No one slept much that night or the rest of the week.

Fighting did, in fact, intensify the next several days. The Zintan initiated their response around 0300 the morning after Operation Dawn began. The Zintan set up their rocket and artillery batteries in the fields and affiliated bases around us.

I tried to differentiate between outgoing and incoming rockets.

The outgoing rockets sounded even louder, probably given their close proximity to the compound. The outgoing made a harsh, loud, scraping sound with each explosion. Metal on metal. One after the other, after the other, after the other.

The incoming had a distinct loud high pitch whine immediately before impact.

The Zintan placed some rocket batteries in the open field east of our location, the direction my bedroom windows faced. Each launch rattled my windows. The smell in the air grew acrid. Smoke continued to billow from the airport. The scent of gunpowder permeated the air, filled my lungs, and made the sky hazy.

In addition to the heavy weapons fire, clashes erupted throughout the city. Militia forces on both sides engaged in small arms fire, used rocket propelled grenades, and any other portable weapons they had at their disposal.

No neighborhoods escaped the violence. Artillery shells and misfired grenades and rockets fell on homes, roads, and businesses throughout Tripoli.

Operation Dawn sought to oust the Zintan-allied forces from all affiliated bases, compounds, and territory. The Zintan held the line at the Iron Bridge, the edge of their territory, which lay south of downtown Tripoli.

Fighting was usually worst in the early morning hours, around dawn before and after the first call to prayer, and then quieted somewhat in the afternoons during the heat of the day. I began to connect the morning call to prayer with the inevitable onslaught. I remembered being in Cairo years prior and finding the sound hauntingly beautiful as the call echoed up and down the Nile River. Even throughout my year in Tripoli, I enjoyed hearing the call spread from minarets throughout the city, it was such a unique sound. However, it would now forever be tied in my mind as a trigger for impending bloodshed and fear.

By evening the fighting began again, off and on, until engaging in all out battle once again around dawn the next day.

The ambassador called us to the embassy every day for an EAC. She usually held the meeting in the morning during the heaviest fighting, but sometimes in the afternoon. Security officers drove Harbor, Stitch, and me each time ensuring we made it safely there and back.

They attempted to alter our routes, but the main road between the facilities became a Zintan staging area, and the security officers avoided it.

On July 19th, the ambassador responded to a threatening social media posting of a man pointing a weapon toward the camera with a threatening picture of her own—it depicted her at a range firing a large revolver in the general direction of the camera. While some Libyans found it amusing, others did not, and it served to heighten tensions further. I thought as the US Ambassador to Libya, she would help mitigate the threat against our lives. Instead it seemed like she taunted the extremists, antagonizing them. It was disheartening, and I showed the postings to Harbor, Gambler, and Obi for their security planning.

Meanwhile, I stayed so completely focused and consumed with work during the day I soon didn't have time to feel scared or worried about the fighting. I didn't feel anything until I returned to my villa at night. There, with the fighting raging around us, Nomad held me close and helped me remain calm.

"Have you ever been in fighting like this before?" asked I late one night.

"Yes, but it was different," said Nomad, "I've never witnessed such a high quantity of heavy artillery used, directly over my location, during such an extended period of time."

"It's been non-stop for almost a week already."

"And my prior experiences were with other Special Operations Forces and combat troops. I have never been in the middle of intense fighting before with civilians I'm charged to protect."

"And me."

"Especially you. I've never been in the middle of an intense firefight before with a woman I adore."

I nodded, looked into his eyes, "Why aren't people more worried about us?"

He didn't have an answer, but I knew the act of worrying assumed people knew or cared what was happening to us. I felt isolated. I felt alone. I also felt I had no real perspective on such things. I wasn't a warrior. Month's earlier six rockets spooked Washington enough to conduct a drawdown.

That week, at least six rockets were launched in each barrage, and there was no mention of evacuation.

My greatest concern was eventually Operation Dawn forces would start counter-battery fire—at the Zintan positions—in the field I could see from my bedroom window.

The second week of fighting grew worse. Operation Dawn forces intensified their attacks and the fighting lasted throughout the day. The brutal heat of the afternoons didn't sway the dedication of the militia fighters or the severity of the war.

The Marines could no longer keep track of the exact numbers of heavy weapons fired each day given the sheer volume. The militias fired hundreds of rockets, mortars, and anti-aircraft weaponry every single day that week.

Operation Dawn forces also incorporated new tactics that revealed the extremists within their midst. A suicide car-bomb exploded outside the Zintan controlled Seven April Camp, to the west of the embassy. Clashes at the Hamza Barracks, just to the east of the embassy, resulted in the gruesome deaths of Zintan-affiliated forces.

In addition to the heavy bombing campaign around the international airport, artillery and rockets fired between the opposing forces also struck civilian targets in Tripoli proper. They destroyed homes. Businesses and hotels in the downtown area sustained heavy damage. The death toll rose. Most locals had nowhere to run and no government, law enforcement, or security element to turn to for help. The women and children of the country were caught in another brutal war between authoritarian men and had no way out.

To the east, Dawn forces in the Wadi Rabi'a area continued to hammer Zintan forces at and around the airport. Dawn forces eventually pushed back the Zintan and claimed control of al-Afiya hospital.

The al-Afiya hospital was the primary medevac point in Tripoli for all US Mission personnel. Triage made the arrangements on behalf of the entire US Mission with the al-Afiya chief medical officer, who died in the fighting. After the loss of the hospital, we no longer had a viable medevac option.

Despite the ambassador's prior vehemence to stay the course in Libya, we began to discuss options. At a minimum, we needed a new route to move personnel in and out of the country. Reebok needed to return, and for others, it was time to leave. We decided to evaluate those same routes for potential full-scale evacuation. We needed a way out in an emergency.

I also wondered what would constitute an emergency, if not our current situation, but I kept my personal opinion to myself.

Harbor, Stitch, and I continued to provide briefings and updates at the daily EAC. We conducted each trip during heavy fighting and I felt extremely thankful to have the security officers' protection.

My whole life I'd never once considered the possibility I could find myself in my current predicament. I was trapped in a war zone, with no apparent way out, during a civil war. I knew others relied on me and so I remained focused on our immediate requirements. I felt responsible for each life there. They were counting on me to warn them of additional or imminent threats.

The embassy facility manager announced the sewage tanks were full and they had no way to empty them. She relied on local staff to do so. The local staff had not reported for duty since fighting broke out. She sought alternate options to dispose of their human waste. The ambassador made jokes about the predicament, but I didn't think it was funny. I thought they shouldn't rely on local staff as much as they did, especially when it negatively impacted their health and safety.

The facility manager also revealed that, due to the fighting, local businesses would not make deliveries so the embassy had a difficult time obtaining food. They'd thus far been able to make alternate arrangements, but they had no reserves. Access to water also became an issue. The embassy hadn't stored enough extra supplies and had no well.

The RSO (State Department Regional Security Officer) at one point recommended embassy personnel begin considering the possibility at some point they might want to think about, possibly, putting together a go-bag, or at least think about what they might include in a potential go-bag should one be required.

I couldn't believe what I heard. I had my go-bag packed and ready from day one. I wondered how some people could be so ill-equipped and unprepared in such a place. I considered my go-bag an essential item and carried it with me whenever I attended a meeting, but I also realized some people relied entirely on the Marines and security officers for their safety.

Once word got out about their circumstances, embassy staff began to panic.

CHAPTER TWENTY-ONE

EVACUATION: TUNISIAN AIRFIELD

(JULY 26, 2014)

While we continued to wait on the Tunisian side of the border on July 26th, 2014, I walked back over to our vehicle to check on Whirlwind. He kept saying he felt fine, nothing was wrong, but wanted to stay in the vehicle. I didn't push it. I didn't know what exactly what was wrong, but he looked unwell.

I saw US Embassy Tunis staff passing out bottles of cold water. The water looked amazing. Our remaining water was warm and almost gone and I was extraordinarily dehydrated by then, so I walked over to request bottles for Whirlwind and me.

"Could I get a water please?" I asked.

"Aren't you CIA?" asked the embassy employee, looking me up and down.

"Yes."

"These aren't for you."

"Seriously? You won't give me water?" I asked.

"Fine, just this once" he said, handed me a bottle, and on he moved.

I found Belle as I chugged it down. I needed to walk away before I tackled the guy and took all his cold water. *What a jerk*, I thought. I didn't understand why an embassy employee would refuse to give another American water, especially in our current circumstances, and then act like it was a special favor when he did. It made no sense, but it was totally in keeping with the State Department's notorious pretentiousness.

"Want to go for a walk about?" I asked.

"Yes. I'm getting stir-crazy," said Belle.

"Me too."

"You worried about Nomad?"

"Yes, I am. I'll be worried until he arrives."

"He'll be across that border before you know it."

Belle and I continued to stroll around the staging area. We walked behind the vehicles on the left side of the road, all the way to the end. We stopped and gazed off into the distance. More sand and desert filled the landscape, as far as I could see. The desert had that same rocky, gritty quality. We could also see more mountains in the distance, but I didn't know the name of the mountain range.

After a few minutes we started our return to the vehicles. It was late afternoon and extremely hot.

"You know what the temperature is?" I asked.

"The thermometer on the dash of our vehicle indicated it's 140 Degrees Fahrenheit," said Belle.

"Certainly feels close."

"And super windy, if you didn't notice."

"The wind really blows the sand around. It'll probably take me a month to get it all out of my hair."

"Yeah. I can't wait to take a shower and sleep. I'm exhausted," said Belle.

As we approached the vehicles, Tunes, Blue, and Otter walked over to join us. We chatted for a bit about the drive, the border crossing, and the conversations in our vehicles.

"I can't believe they made us get exit stamps," said Otter, "What was that about?"

"Maybe word hasn't made it down here that their country is in complete chaos," speculated Tunes.

"Come on guys, it's just a minor civil war, they have protocols to follow," joked Blue.

I broke off from the others and walked to my vehicle again. I wanted to double check on Whirlwind. However, the ambassador intercepted me as I reached our row in the Chalk lines. I wished I'd seen her coming and had time to prepare.

"I didn't hear the call on the radio you'd arrived," I said, surprised. "How are you?"

"Not well. We got lost on the way here."

"I thought everyone took the same route? And ISR focused and remained on your vehicle specifically?"

"The escort took a wrong turn," she emphatically stated, "I'm not making it up."

"Well, I am glad you're here now. Soon we'll be in Tunis."

"Yes, I wanted to talk to you about that. I couldn't find Harbor."

"What about Tunis?"

"I spoke to the US Ambassador in Tunis and he said you may not stay there."

"What?"

"We'll stop at an airfield along the route and the Marines and embassy staff will fly out on AFRICOM planes, including me."

"We must continue to Tunis, we need to turn in our weapons and vehicles there."

"Then you'll have to leave immediately. It's very arrogant to think you can do whatever you want. I've told Harbor this time and time again. I tried to find him, but he's missing. Where is he?"

"I'll find him for you right now."

"You know this decision isn't up to me, don't you?"

"It's not my decision either. Or Harbor's. I'm sure it's under discussion as we speak in Washington. The administration, Secretary of State, CIA Director, Secretary of Defense, and other leaders are probably working out the details now. We don't have many options," I replied.

"He said you'll have to leave immediately."

"We can't even have one moment's rest?" I asked. I felt angry and knew my face flushed from it. "I'll find Harbor now."

I walked around until I spotted Harbor and then relayed the entire conversation. He looked very annoyed, didn't appreciate their attitude, and assured me leaders were in direct communication in Washington.

"I understand Tunis is also an unstable environment, but it's certainly safer than where we just came from. What about some basic human decency?" I asked.

"Well, that's all that was needed."

"To save their lives, one more time, and kick us to the curb?"

"Yes, and it probably won't be the last time either," Harbor said as he walked away to find the ambassador.

I didn't know what to say or think. I was so tired my thoughts felt jumbled and incoherent. The idea of immediately leaving Tunis and getting on a plane later that night made me feel sick. I hadn't really slept in weeks and felt tired to my core, incredibly hungry, and so very thirsty.

As I stood there wondering where to go next, what to do, and on the verge of collapse, my radio squawked.

"Last vehicle is approaching the border. Chalk one, vehicle one," came Dolby's voice.

"Nomad—" I whispered.

Nomad arrived at the border crossing, which meant he'd be in Tunisia in just a few minutes. I strode as quickly as I could without drawing attention to the side of the road, in front of the vehicles, where I could see the border crossing.

Within minutes, I saw Nomad's vehicle crossing over into Tunisia. They slowly drove up to the guard, handed over their passports, and continued down the road. I smiled to myself as he approached and held up my hand in a small wave.

I breathed a sigh of relief and my steady prayer stream switched from a plea for safety to a rush of thanks and then back. We'd made it to Tunisia, but we still had a long way to go.

Nomad's eyes found mine and he nodded in return, looking at me for just a moment, before turning his eyes back to the road. He drove to the end of the line of vehicles and backed in.

I stayed where I was, by the side of the road, but I could see Nomad, Dolby, and Captain exit their vehicle and walk over where Obi and Harbor stood. I returned to my vehicle to check on Whirlwind.

"You still okay?" I asked Whirlwind after opening his door.

He slowly nodded.

"Do you need anything?"

He slowly shook his head.

I was worried about him and assumed he was also dehydrated. I grabbed the last bottle of our warm water for him out of the back. Even though it was warm, it should do the trick. I stood there and demanded he drink the whole thing.

"Better?" I asked after he finished.

He nodded, with slightly more vigor. I nodded back then walked around to find Stitch to let him know Whirlwind seemed to have some dehydration or heat related illness.

Triage stopped me on the way and asked how I was holding up.

"I'm surviving. I'm trying to drink as little water as possible, so I'm dehydrated, but not bad. I'm hungry, but not starving, and incredibly tired."

"Here, take these, and drink up. You need to maintain your alertness and health," said Triage handing me some Vitamin C and an energy drink. "We need you to remain in top performance as right seat. You're doing great so far, but don't forget we still have a long way to go."

"Awesome! Thanks, Triage. How are you doing?"

"Doing just fine. Hang in there."

"I will," I said as he walked away.

He always looked out for me. It felt nice that he cared enough to seek me out and give me Vitamin C. It was a simple thing, but it mattered to me and could keep me from becoming sick. His encouragement also helped. I continued to find Stitch.

"Any idea when we're leaving?" I asked Stitch when I spotted him.

"As soon as we get our passports back. Then we're off to Tunis. They're discussing the route now, but it sounds like we'll definitely stop by the airfield in southern Tunisia first."

"Hopefully we'll make it to the airfield before dark."

Obi walked over then to fill us in on the plan.

We'd depart as soon as possible. We'd drive to southern Tunisia via back roads. Someone heard there was a protest scheduled for the main road that would interfere with our route, so they had to change it at the last minute. The Tunisian National Guard would lead us on the back roads to the airfield, and then escort our remaining officers all the way to Tunis. It would take many additional hours.

"Attention all personnel. Passports are ready for pick-up," came a call over the radio. I couldn't identify the voice. "Chalk leaders will have all passports for each Chalk. Report to your Chalk leader."

Several minutes later a Tunis Embassy official walked over with a stack of passports and handed them to Obi. He split the stack with Stitch and together they started calling out names and passing out the passports.

"Whirlwind?" called Obi.

"I can take his to him," I said, right as Whirlwind called, "Here."

Stitch handed Whirlwind his passport and asked how he was doing. Whirlwind said he was fine and then walked back to our vehicle. Stitch looked at me and I shrugged. I didn't know anything more about Whirlwind's health.

"Carlson."

"Here," I called and accepted my passport.

I opened it to double check the stamp and verified it was in there. I then returned to the vehicle.

After a few moments, Tunes entered the back seat, and we saw Stitch walking our way with several cold water bottles in his arms.

"How did you score those?" asked Tunes after Stitch sat inside.

"I can be very persuasive," said Stitch, "Drink up."

"All personnel return to your vehicles," called Obi over the radio, "Chalk one, ready when you are."

Everyone climbed back into their vehicles and anxiously waited for several more minutes.

"Chalk one, rolling out," called Dolby. He, Nomad, and Captain were back in the lead.

Stitch pulled out at the rear of Chalk three and I picked up the radio.

"Chalk three, last vehicle, in position," I called.

"Roger that," replied Obi.

We were finally on our way. The stop at the border lasted hours and I felt desperate for some rest that night.

"Do you think they might have beds at the airfield?" I asked.

"I doubt it," said Stitch.

"I think Harbor wants to arrive in Tunis as soon as possible anyway," said Tunes, "I heard him talking to Nomad and he seemed pretty intent on it."

As the Chalks began moving, Stitch followed suit, and we drove in the full convoy on our way to the southern Tunisia airfield. All the vehicles drove with no separation in between the Chalks, just one long convoy that stretched for what seemed like miles. We stayed on the main highway for quite a while.

When the convoy started passing more populated areas, we pulled off the main highway and started traversing back roads. The convoy followed the winding road through small villages. As we continued, I noticed more and more locals lining the road or sitting outside to watch our passage.

"We must look like a parade," said Stitch.

"This is probably the single biggest event to happen in their villages in years," I said, "Other than *Star Wars*."

The nerd in me felt super excited to be in the same area where a *Star Wars* movie was filmed. Tunes and I geeked out about it for a while and it was a nice distraction from the stress.

As we continued to drive, I noticed by the locals' dress and an occasional flag that some of the villagers were Berber rather than Arab.

Many children waved, cheered, and smiled as we drove past. I began smiling and waving back to all the children. All the villagers looked friendly, but the children were particularly enthusiastic.

Parts of the convoy occasionally needed to slow or stop for various animals crossing the road in the villages, mostly goats and chickens. The houses in the villages resembled mud huts, we drove on dirt roads, and villagers gathered around porches to smoke and cook their evening meals. I felt like we were transported to another time.

I looked up at the sky and out at the landscape. The sun started setting over the horizon, which made the desert and the convoy driving through it look eerie. The wind died down and the air became noticeably cooler.

We arrived at the airfield as the last rays of light disappeared from the evening sky. The desert turned pitch black and only the floodlights at the airbase provided light of any kind. No light shone from any other streetlights, buildings or houses. As far as I could determine, electricity was the exception and not the rule in that part of the country.

The Tunisian National Guard directed the convoy into the airfield. The vehicles driven by security officers lined up along the right side of the staging area, while the other vehicles carrying the Marines and embassy staff continued to the edge of the runway where the two AFRICOM cargo planes waited.

Since the embassy staff drove several of our vehicles we needed to take to Tunis, we had to wait at the airbase until they finished unloading those vehicles and turned them back over for the drive north.

None of the embassy staff or the ambassador sought me out to say goodbye. Stitch said they ignored him and the security officers too. So much for saving their lives, I thought.

The unloading took several hours. While we waited, I used the bathroom again and searched for food and water.

US Embassy Tunis staff met the convoy at the airfield and again brought water. The staff also brought pre-packaged meals. Someone again told me I couldn't have the food or water because I was a CIA officer.

By that point, I didn't care. Tunes, Whirlwind, and I marched into the room with the food and each took a meal. We sat down and ate and dared anyone to say a word. I was starving and hadn't eaten a proper meal in more than twenty-four hours.

"Unreal," said Tunes, "Don't they realize we saved them yet again. And this is how they treat us?"

"Sadly, I'm not surprised anymore," I said.

"I wish I could at least update my status on Facebook with this," said Tunes, "Stopped for dinner in southern Tunisia, service was terrible."

When we finished eating, I took another meal container for Stitch along with several apples and waters for our vehicle. I walked out with my head held high, my arms loaded with provisions, and seething with anger.

I finished setting the food down in the Hilux when an emergency call came over the radio.

CHAPTER TWENTY-TWO

FLASHBACK: EMERGENCY ACTION

(MID JULY 2014)

Later in mid-July 2014, the ambassador decided those staffers who panicked over our devolving circumstances needed to leave as soon as possible, but options for their departure were extremely limited.

Ultimately, the ambassador decided the best option was to send those eleven US citizens out on a Libyan Air commercial flight from Mitiga Airbase. It was the same Airbase extremists and former LIFG officials controlled and I believed they used to send fighters to and from Iraq and Syria to join the Islamic State.

Harbor and I immediately objected. We reviewed the body of intelligence reporting on Mitiga Airbase, which was located east of the city along the coast. We requested the ambassador reconsider. She claimed she had the assurances of a former LIFG member, one of the leaders of Operation Dawn the Americans could use his airbase and depart Libya safely.

She trusted him—she said he was handsome and charming. I thought that was a terrible reason to trust someone and I knew how often appearances could be used to deceive. I assessed intentions below the surface and outside of the public realm. I didn't trust the LIFG leader's claims.

The LIFG leader told the Libyan public and the ambassador he opposed the Islamic State and denied his close ties to al-Qa'ida. I didn't think that made him our friend. I firmly believed the enemy of our enemy was not our friend. Just because the Islamic State was enemies with a certain terrorist or al-Qa'ida, that didn't make them a friend of the US. I didn't think we should overtly work with or support that LIFG leader in any way. Period. End of story. Full stop, in my mind. But apparently not the ambassador's mind.

Harbor and I pointed out that, in addition to the clear threat to US citizens, using Mitiga Airbase would also infuriate the Zintan, in whose territory we resided and on whom we continued to rely for some outer security. The ambassador was resolute and said the arrangements were already made. The eleven personnel would leave later that day in mid-July, a week after the fighting started.

After Harbor, Stitch, and I returned, we discussed the airbase option. I described in detail the intelligence reporting on extremist connections to the Mitiga Airbase. I felt extremely concerned and called back to CIA Headquarters for further guidance on how to handle our dissent.

Harbor ultimately asked me to return to the embassy one more time, despite the persistent heavy fighting all around us, to attempt to change the ambassador's mind. I did as he asked. I thought, without a doubt, if something happened to those US citizens the ambassador would blame me. I thought she would cry intelligence failure and claim she hadn't been told the risks.

Nomad and Flash drove me back to the embassy once again, under the constant barrages of rocket fire and explosions, and I met one on one with the ambassador. I again went through our intelligence and CIA's assessment of the airbase. I knew I had a huge responsibility to successfully present the information. I felt the weight of every one of their lives on my shoulders during that briefing.

But she cut me off.

"I understand the risks. I hear you. I understand, but it's my call."

"Yes, ma'am, but this is not an intelligence gap. There are dots everywhere. All the information points to threat."

"Sometimes we have to make difficult decisions for the greater good. Despite the risks, I think it's worth it to get them out of Libya."

"Do they know the risks?"

"It doesn't matter, they're already on their way to the Mitiga Airbase. The airline called and told them to get there as soon as possible. Apparently, planes take off at Mitiga when they are full and they were waiting on the Americans to depart."

I felt I had the breath knocked out of me. I failed to protect them. I warned, but was ignored. What then was the point? Of any of it?

I believed extremist groups already operating at the Mitiga Airbase would set out to kidnap the Americans once they learned about a planned departure. I thought their early departure from the airbase was probably the only thing that saved their lives. Once the embassy personnel left, social media postings noted the departure of Americans almost instantly and Libyans speculated the Americans had begun an evacuation.

The ambassador also engaged in a policy discussion with me that afternoon about the possibility of a full-scale evacuation.

"It's time for us to evacuate. What do you think?"

"There will be consequences if we depart. As you know, terrorism is a key issue in the region and of utmost importance. Multiple terrorist groups are entrenching. It will soon be a major safe haven. If we leave, we lose insight into that and it will take a long time to get it back."

"State isn't the military. We're not prepared for combat. Staying in our current circumstances, doing nothing, is a death sentence."

"What about falling back to another location? Then we could continue our mission."

"It's too complicated and too expensive to start over in another location."

Then I became upset. I couldn't believe the decision might come down to money and lack of political will.

"I agree we shouldn't sit here waiting to die, but I think we could've done something sooner or we could take action now. There were so many times we could have provided support or intervened. I don't understand what's happened here. The administration chose Libya, claimed it was important, but there's no policy or strategy. We just stood back and watched the country crumble around us. Now all our lives are in jeopardy, and for what?"

"The US did plenty, but Libyans didn't appreciate it. Now we must leave before more damage is done. Libya isn't worth losing another life for."

"But what I struggle with is the thought that if we leave, everything we've sacrificed so far is in vain. If it's not important, why were we ever here? We're not mindless drones here to do the administration's bidding. It's not a game. We're real people. I'm a real person with real thoughts and feelings. I'm not expendable, but my life seems to mean nothing to the administration. I thought our mission here, that Libya, was important for our national security. That it was worth risking my life for. We all did. Why does the administration continue to place people in harm's way when it has no long-term strategy? Why are they so ready to sacrifice American lives for no concrete purpose?"

That night, I couldn't sleep. I woke throughout the short night with terrible nightmares of the Mitiga Airbase, kidnapping, and the sound of explosions. I'd tried so hard to change the ambassador's mind, risking my own life to do so. I felt responsible for everyone's safety. Nomad came to help me as I covered my ears, curled into a tight ball on the bed, but I refused to cry. I desperately tried not to think about the 'what-ifs.' They were safe. No one was hurt yet. No casualties this round.

Nomad also tried to comfort me. He told me it wasn't my fault. I did everything I could and he admired my courage in risking my life to try. I reminded him the attempt risked his life too, since he took me there, but it was a wasted effort and yet another unnecessary risk since the eleven had already departed.

After the Mitiga incident, discussions of full-scale evacuation routes began in earnest during the daily EAC.

The embassy's primary evacuation plan was to request AFRICOM send cargo planes to the international airport to evacuate us. Obviously, that wouldn't work in our current situation. The airport was literally up in flames and the vast quantity of anti-aircraft weapons being fired would preclude any aircraft, AFRICOM or other, from flying into Tripoli airspace.

But we'd been planning for an evacuation since our arrival in the country. We discussed multiple other options, by land, by sea, and by air. We discussed options that didn't include evacuation, such as relocating operations to an alternate site.

During one such discussion, rocket fire impacted the embassy facility. Their alarm sounded and all personnel took cover. Harbor, Stitch, Captain, Robin, and I were all at the embassy for the EAC and evacuation discussions.

The Ambassador demanded someone call the Zintan and order them to stop firing at the embassy. I guessed it was probably Operation Dawn forces firing our direction but at the Zintan.

However, the embassy did not have any Arabic linguists left, they were all sent out via Mitiga that week.

Robin dialed up his Zintan contact and handed me the phone. I was the only Arabic speaker on the embassy facility except for the ambassador. As the phone rang, Robin told me what he wanted me to say. I again felt the extraordinary responsibility I'd just been handed. I didn't know if my Arabic was good enough and tried to recall the correct vocabulary as explosions sounded outside. A direct impact overhead would kill us and it was falling all around.

I tried to focus on the call, my Arabic, and not fear.

The Zintan militia commander answered the phone.

"Hello. I am with the US Embassy. We have been hit. Someone fired on the embassy. Please help us," I said as plainly as I could. I spoke slowly, clearly, and loudly to be heard over the sound of the firefight on both ends.

"I understand," the commander replied.

"Can you send help?" I asked.

"We are in the middle of a battle. We will try," he answered.

"Can you stop the shooting around the US Embassy?"

"We will try. We will try."

"Go with God," we said to each other and then I hung up and we waited. I alternated between pacing the room and huddling in the corner depending on the proximity of the fight outside.

I knew I wasn't the linguist that Robin had wanted, but I'd like to think he was provided what was needed—an analyst who knew just enough Arabic to convey the message and happened to be at the embassy during the firefight.

Blue's location was also hit with rocket fire and he made similar calls to Misratan contacts.

Within the hour, all rocket fire ceased. The Zintan militia commander understood and sent forces to help secure our location.

Harbor, Stitch, Captain, Robin, and I quickly returned. Gambler tasked a damage assessment and Nomad led the others in conducting a thorough search of the compound looking for unexploded ordinance and impacts.

They found impact points at every villa. Blue found 14.5mm rounds in the walls of his bathroom. The rocket that struck the compound destroyed our small kitchen facility. Thankfully, no one was in the kitchen at the time due to Gambler's quick reaction.

I wrote a summary of the damage and cabled the information back to CIA Headquarters.

I refused to cry and bottled up my fear. I tried to focus instead on my responsibilities. I would need that focus for the days ahead, because the afternoon lull in fighting didn't last long.

The rocket impacts and indirect fire spraying the compounds seemed to spook the ambassador. She went from her 'we will not fail' mantra to the opposite extreme and wanted viable options to leave as soon as possible.

In conjunction, the Zintan lost more territory. The fighting moved closer to our location. I expressed my concern that soon the major roads would be cut off by enemy forces. Tanks reportedly appeared on the southern roads near the airport and Qasr Bin Gashr and north of our location near the Iron Bridge.

A stray rocket hit on or near a large oil storage tank at a facility by the embassy. Black smoke filled the sky for miles around us. The air began to smell heavily of burning fuel mingled with the spent artillery.

Harbor and Stitch discussed other options with Captain, Obi, and Gambler and presented those options to the ambassador. I listened and provided CIA's assessments related to each option as it was presented.

The embassy could draw down further and relocate their staff to an alternate facility. Security officers could conduct reconnaissance on the southern airfield in Zintan territory to determine whether it could be used as a temporary base or evacuation platform. We could establish a new location away from the heavy fighting.

We ruled out the coastal road.

We ruled out sea options, because the fighting lay between our facilities and the Med.

We ruled out using Mitiga again or other airports around Tripoli. Harbor refused to allow any more officers to transit Mitiga and the other landing zones in the greater Tripoli area were too close to the anti-aircraft fire.

Many other options were reviewed and ruled out.

The ambassador approved a trip to the Zintan's southern airfield in Libya, Harbor's preferred option. She gave them the green light to leave the next morning.

That evening, the ambassador called us for what would be our final EAC. It was late at night and the fighting continued to rage around us. Nomad and Triage escorted Harbor and me to the meeting and provided our protection. I could hear frequent small arms fire that sounded alarmingly close.

When Harbor and I walked into the ambassador's office, the other senior country team members were already present. She expressed her concerns with the deteriorating security situation. She explained we had to maintain a position of neutrality in the conflict, which had grown untenable.

She turned to the Marine captain and asked his view. He recommended leaving. His men were cannon fodder in our current circumstances. They were forced to guard a facility during a heavy bombing campaign in a civil war but were under orders to maintain a strictly defensive posture. He didn't believe ducking behind a sandbag was an effective defense against heavy enemy weapons fire.

One by one, the ambassador turned to each senior member and asked for his or her opinion.

"Harbor?" she asked last.

"I defer to you. I think we have several viable options to remain as we've previously discussed. However, we cannot and will not remain without you or without the Marines, of course."

"Alright. It's time for the next meeting with Washington," said the ambassador, "Harbor, will you join me?"

I waited outside the ambassador's office with Triage and Nomad. I guessed the ambassador would recommend evacuation. I sat close to Nomad, but didn't touch, wanting the comfort of his nearness. We all sat in silence, waiting. After the meeting Harbor joined us and we left.

By that time it was pitch black outside and Triage and Nomad drove blacked out. They wore their night vision goggles to see the way.

Harbor and I couldn't see anything. There were no streetlights, no other vehicles about, and electricity in the area didn't appear to be operating. The only light that evening came from explosions I could see briefly in the near distance as rockets hit their targets and tracer rounds streaked through the sky.

Later that night, I asked Harbor what he thought would happen. I wanted to know if the administration would decide in favor of an evacuation.

Harbor said security officers would conduct the reconnaissance trip the next morning and he thought we'd be using it before too long. There would be a SVTC with Washington the next afternoon and he thought a decision would be made then.

"Do you really think it's safe to leave?" I asked. I had my doubts. I thought it was a huge risk.

"At this point, no. There is no safe option," said Harbor.

"Right, we risk our lives with every option."

"I don't like the idea of evacuating, but we can't stay here in this current environment. If someone is hurt, there's no longer a way to treat him or her. We can't defend ourselves or guard against rockets and heavy artillery. Others need to leave, such as yourself, because your tour of duty is finished. The longer we stay now, the more the risk increases. The danger grows exponentially each day."

"I understand, but I still hope there is a fallback option. Otherwise it just feels like losing."

But it already felt like we'd lost. The US intervention was an utter failure and rather than correct the course, the administration chose to continue making the same mistakes it made in every other conflict the US engaged in throughout the region. The administration continued to do the bare minimum to keep up the appearance that they still had a strategy and all it cost them was other people's lives, bloodshed, and money.

I didn't sleep much that night either. Explosions, rockets, small arms and artillery fire sounded throughout the short night. I thought about the day ahead. Nomad would go on the trip to the Zintan airfield and then there'd be the SVTC.

The next morning, Nomad and half the other security officers departed just after dawn. They left during heavy fighting. It left the compound vulnerable, but they believed if the reconnaissance trip resulted in a viable fallback or evacuation option, it was worth the risk.

I worked in the office all morning. I provided updates on the fighting to Harbor and coordinated with analysts at CIA Headquarters.

The analysts mentioned several times they heard the evacuation was a go. AFRICOM had a list of assets they would provide for the evacuation on Saturday via the southern border. AFRICOM obtained its information from the embassy in Tripoli.

I told the analysts we hadn't yet selected a route, the officers hadn't returned from the trip to the Zintan airfield, and we hadn't even been told to evacuate.

Shortly after, security officers returned to the compound from the trip to the southern Zintan airfield while the rocket and artillery fire continued all around our location.

Their trip concluded immediately prior to the SVTC with Washington. The officers briefed Harbor on the results. Captain believed it was the best option available. The runway would support large cargo planes, it sat far from the fighting, and was located in friendly territory. He thought we could even use it as a fall back option to maintain a presence in the country to continue our mission in Libya.

As the SVTC began, I jogged to my room to take a much-needed break. Nomad said he'd meet me there.

As I went, I thought once again it would have been nice for the administration to determine what was or was not in US national security interests and have a strategy for what it would or would not do to ensure those interests, before putting us in harm's way.

CHAPTER TWENTY-THREE

EVACUATION: FAREWELL IN TUNIS

(JULY 27, 2014)

"A-lyst, A-lyst, Stitch."

"Go for A-lyst."

"We have a medical situation. I need you to get my medical kit from the back of the Hilux and bring it to me at the front of the convoy as quickly as possible."

"Right away," I replied.

I untied the ropes and yanked the cover aside as quickly as I could. Triage and Flash soon joined me and together we found the medical kit and Triage ran it to the front.

"Do you know what happened?" I asked Flash after Triage left.

"A US Embassy official has severe heat stroke," Flash replied, "They have a medical doctor here, but no medical kit."

"No medical kit?"

"Nope."

I thought I should be surprised, but only felt disappointment and concern for the injured man, of course. Stitch and Triage prepared for any eventuality on any moves and constantly practiced emergency medical care. They even ran drills and we were all required to carry a small medical kit.

"I hope that man is okay," I said.

I chatted with Flash a while longer, since we were parked right next to each other. Shortly after the medical emergency we received word it was time to leave again, for the last, long push to Tunis.

"All personnel report to your vehicles," Obi called.

I said farewell to Flash who joined Obi at their vehicle. I saw Stitch, Tunes, and Whirlwind walking toward my vehicle. They looked exhausted, but particularly Stitch. His eyes drooped and he seemed ready to drop.

"Everything okay?" I asked Stitch.

"Yeah, he'll be okay. He needed an IV," he replied, "Do you mind switching seats with me and driving this next stretch of road?"

"Sure," I said, "Do you know if we're taking the highway or back roads?"

"A mix of both, but mainly highway," Stitch replied.

Stitch and I then rearranged our seats. We needed to switch our rifle positions so Stitch had his next to him and I had mine wedged between the driver's seat and the center console. I was careful to keep the muzzle clear of the pedals.

Once we finished rearranging weapons, I pulled out my portable speaker and iPad.

"It's time again," I said, "I need music and it will help keep me awake."

"Perfect," said Tunes, "What're you going to play?"

"My 'Mellow with an Edge' playlist. I think you'll like it. But it starts with Sylvan Esso's 'Hey Mami.' That okay?"

"Sweet."

"That cool with everyone else?" I asked.

After they agreed I hooked up my iPad and speaker and set it up to play. Then we waited, and waited, and waited. It seemed like it took forever for the vehicles to finally begin moving. More hours wasted. I was losing patience when the Chalks began to pull out.

"Chalk three, last vehicle, rolling," called Stitch over the radio.

I drove us out of the airbase. Tunes had the first song queued up for me and as soon as the wheels started to roll he hit play.

The song filled the vehicle. Extremely loud this time. Stitch held the radio up to the speaker for a minute so that the song filled the airwaves in all the vehicles in the convoy. No one said a word. We all listened and kept driving.

I drove through most of the night. We passed through more villages and towns.

One town was pretty hopping and pedestrians crowded everywhere, randomly crossing the street between our vehicles. I had to slam the brakes on more than one occasion to avoid an accident and for a while drove bumper to bumper with the vehicle in front of me, which was now Obi and Flash since the Marines departed.

We stopped for gas, bathrooms, and coffee around 0300. The Tunisian dinar came in handy and I bought us each a coffee.

I looked around for Nomad but didn't see him anywhere. I assumed he must have stayed with his vehicle but was too exhausted to look further.

When I returned, Tunes offered to take a turn driving, and I climbed into the back seat next to Whirlwind. The portable speaker had run out of power, so Stitch and Tunes began chatting. I couldn't hear them very well over the engine and stared out the window, willing myself to remain awake until the end.

Shortly, we were back on the road and Tunes drove us the rest of the way to the US Embassy in Tunis.

As we neared the US Embassy we could see the lights illuminating the huge American flag on top. I smiled. I thought it looked like a beacon of hope for our exhausted and traumatized convoy.

Tunes pulled into the embassy compound following the guards' directions followed by Obi's vehicle at 0700 Sunday morning, July 27th, 2014. We entered via the front gate but wound our way around the compound to the back entrance and the main building. I breathed a prayer of relief. I couldn't manage more than that. I couldn't form coherent thoughts.

Reebok waited there along the side of the road as we pulled vehicles in, one behind the other, in three rows. Each person slowly exited their vehicle and stretched out a bit. Some people jumped up and down, others performed yoga-like moves, and I walked over to Reebok.

He gave me a hug in welcome and greeted each person as they walked by him. I knew he wanted to be there in Tripoli with us, was probably extremely disappointed he wasn't part of the evacuation, and was worried for our safety.

Our counterparts in Tunis had carts set up along the sidewalk.

"Everyone listen up," the deputy shouted, "We need to clear the weapons right now and turn in all accountable property. The first cart is for radios and phones. The second cart is for ammunition. The third cart is for pistols. Place your rifles on the ground next to the last cart. Make sure to unload and clear all your weapons before placing them on the carts. Once you are finished, gather all your personal belongings. You won't be coming back to these vehicles. Take your personal belongings with you into the back door of the embassy where your colleagues will direct you to our office. Leave everything else in the vehicles. Let's move," he said.

I picked up my rifle first, removed the magazine, cleared the weapon, and put the ammunition on the second cart and the rifle on the ground. I then did the same to both Glocks Gambler had issued me. Next, I carried all the extra magazines, my phone, and my radio over to the carts and put them on the corresponding piles.

Stitch was called away to assist with some security related matter, so Tunes and I helped clear his weapons and placed them on the carts.

"You think clearing weapons is the best idea when we've been pushed past the point of exhaustion?" Tunes muttered out loud, barely able to keep his eyes open.

"It's a terrible idea," I whispered back, "I've never been so tired in my entire life."

But we continued. Next, we went from vehicle to vehicle seeing who else needed help and assisted them with clearing weapons and carrying extra magazines to the carts.

Once we loaded everything onto the carts, I could see what an arsenal we carried with us. And I knew that didn't even include the grenades, which I wasn't going to touch. I figured someone else could handle those, and assumed every vehicle probably carried six or more.

Tunes and I returned to our vehicle, pulled out our go-bags, and removed our backpacks from the truck bed. Luckily, the garbage bags worked to keep the gas stench out of our gear. Just Libya. I wasn't sure Libya would ever wash off.

"Where to?" asked Tunes.

"Over here guys," called Belle.

Belle waited by the door with Blue and Otter. Tunes and I walked over to join them, while I looked around again for Nomad. I didn't see him. Together the five of us entered the embassy and walked upstairs to the office.

Within minutes, the room filled. We all looked worn out, dirty, and hyped up on adrenaline.

I'd been up almost thirty hours straight. After surviving thirteen days of intense fighting. After spending over a year in a continuously devolving security environment. After spending more than a decade of my life dedicated to counterterrorism. I felt tired to the very core of my being.

The chief in Tunis stepped forward to make an announcement.

"Welcome to Tunis everyone. I'm glad you made it here safe and sound. I know you're exhausted and it's been a long few days, but unfortunately I have some bad news. It's not over yet.

"The ambassador has ordered you to leave—you may not stay here any longer than absolutely necessary. Everyone must leave later today or tomorrow. The security officers must go first. Our support office has already reserved flights for some security officers. You can pick up your itineraries from him and pay at the airport once you arrive."

My mind literally couldn't process what he said. I reeled in shock.

"In thirty minutes the embassy shuttles will meet you outside, immediately inside the front gate. Some will take the security officers for a short stop to shower and clean up and then on to the airport. Other shuttles will take the rest of you to wait at the hotel for your flights. I'm really sorry. We ordered some pizza and there's plenty of cold water in the fridge. Please at least eat something before you leave," said the Tunis chief.

There was stunned silence. No one moved or said a word. My hands started trembling. I felt cold, shaky, and sick to my stomach. I scanned the room for Nomad, he was already looking at me, and I stared back. I felt tears prick my eyes and blinked them away. I couldn't believe this was happening.

Then Harbor stepped forward.

"You should be incredibly proud of what we have accomplished. You're responsible for safely evacuating the entire US Mission out of Libya. There were no casualties. You did it without complaint and showed uncommon courage. What you have done is extraordinary and no one else will probably ever know. But we know. I know. It has been an honor to serve with each and every one of you," said Harbor.

He then walked around to each person in the room, shook their hand, looked them in the eye, and thanked that person for serving our country.

After that, officers filed out of the room. We picked up our bags on the way out and stumbled toward the front exit of the embassy. We walked through the lobby, across the State Department seal set in the marble, and out the front door. We made our way over to the front gate.

I walked next to Nomad and we stood together to wait.

Otter realized he forgot his jacket and walked back to the entrance. He tried to re-enter but was barred from doing so.

"But I'm an American," said Otter to the embassy guard, "Isn't this illegal?"

The guard apologized but wouldn't let him enter, so Otter returned to the front gate and waited with us. He claimed losing one more article of clothing after leaving behind his entire wardrobe didn't matter to him anyway. But I could tell it did. It was probably the only jacket he owned after the evacuation.

Blue pulled out a bottle of Scotch. An eighteen-year-old Glenlivet. He took a sip and then passed the bottle around. No one asked how he obtained the bottle. We each drank some, silently sharing our relief we made it that far.

Nomad then pulled me aside to say goodbye.

"I don't know what to say. I have to leave. I have no choice. I hoped for more time," he said, cupping my face.

"I know," I said.

I took short, shallow breaths—my whole body shook. My palms were clammy but I felt cold all over.

The shuttles pulled up. Nomad stared into my eyes and he leaned down and kissed me.

"I have to go now," Nomad said again.

"I know," I replied and whispered, "You saved my life."

"And you saved mine. I relied on you so much. We all did. More than I think you realize."

"When—where—will I see you?"

"I'll find you."

Then he turned and walked away.

In that moment, I felt completely shattered. I wrapped my arms around my waist, as if I could physically hold myself together when I felt as though I were breaking into fragments.

I felt so scared for so long, but I held myself together when our world was falling apart. I handled it and contained the fear. I knew more than anyone how fortunate we were no one died or was injured. We were fortunate there were no casualties. It was a miracle.

I truly thought we wouldn't all make it out alive.

Although the evacuation was considered a success, it felt like anything but that. It felt like we'd given up. Lost. It felt like all the sleepless nights, tears, hard work, and worry no longer had meaning. I thought our mission was important, so important people fought for it, spent millions on it, and some even died for it. I dedicated my entire life to it.

But instead we stood by as the country fell apart around us. We watched as Libya became a terrorist safe haven, about to be taken over by Islamic extremists.

While I risked my life to brief the impending conflict and spread of terrorism, my government watched and waited, did nothing, and then gave up.

And I knew, beyond a doubt, I'd never be the same again.

> "Think, too, of the great part that is played by the unpredictable in war. Think of it now, before you are actually committed to war. The longer a war lasts, the more things tend to depend on accidents. Neither you nor we can see into them—we have to abide their outcome in the dark."

—THUCYDIDES— The Peloponnesian War, *1.78*

LESSONS LEARNED

AFTER THE EVACUATION from Libya, I returned to CIA Head-quarters and continued to serve as a North Africa counterterrorism analyst for the following year. Part of me wanted to resign immediately, but my mother's advice prompted me to remain a while longer. She recommended I wait a year, saying anyone who has suffered a traumatic event should wait a full year if possible before making any major life changing decisions.

I'm glad now I waited.

It gave me the opportunity to plan my finances for a career change, pray for guidance, and write this memoir.

It also gave me time to begin to recover from my post-traumatic stress. I'd already figured out how much fireworks bothered me, but I had no idea how traumatized I actually was until I flew into Seattle the first time after the evacuation. I almost lost it in customs when the officer returned my passport and said, "Welcome home." I held it together until I walked into the arrival's hall and saw my mother. In that moment, I started sobbing and couldn't stop and not gentle streaming tears, but full on ugly sobs. In front of everyone. My mother wrapped me in her arms, then the rest of the family around us, and they held me until I could leave. I'm still claustrophobic. I still cry when I hear fireworks. It's still a struggle and some days are harder than others.

Most importantly, during that year, I learned about the extraordinary efforts of the military and intelligence communities during the evacuation. I learned about the dedication and hard work other officers expended in an effort to help us during Libya's descent into civil war. Although I felt alone in Tripoli, I learned many others participated behind the scenes. Some I knew about, most I did not.

I learned that although we were on our own in Libya, we were never really alone.

The CIA's operation center closely monitored the situation and reacted to all security incidents affecting us in Tripoli. The Middle East North Africa Task Force provided twice-daily updates on the region frequently including our status. CIA sent it to every cleared individual in the entire national security community and senior policy makers. The CIA also responded to every request for information, immediate cable, and imminent threat we sent. Collectors throughout the world met with sources and contacts to obtain information about Libya and threats to Americans there, which CIA then sent to us in Tripoli.

The Director of National Intelligence, responsible for the President's Daily Briefing (PDB), kept the administration informed of important developments, especially with regard to our safety and security. Analysts stayed late countless nights to write PDB updates. Briefers woke early to research and provide the information. I spoke to a few who needed the latest information from the field, but I know there were many others toiling to support the briefers.

The open source center went into the office weekends, overnight, holidays, and any time they learned about a threat or security situation, which meant they were in the office a lot. They called me directly to provide warning on multiple occasions. During the evacuation, officers provided twenty-four-hour coverage from the moment they learned of the evacuation until we reached safety in Tunisia. They poured over militant and terrorist associated social media searching for even a hint of threat against us.

The NSA also provided twenty-four-hour coverage during the evacuation. Officers listened to and translated anything and everything available to them from Libya in an attempt to identify threats to Americans, our convoy, or our facilities in Tripoli.

The NGA (National Geospatial-Intelligence Agency) monitored from high above. They sought out enemy locations, militant compounds, or gatherings of hostile forces. NGA paid particular attention to those forces within the vicinity of the US Embassy and residence compound in Tripoli and provided warning of any they found.

The FBI continued to investigate the Benghazi attacks and to build cases against those terrorists responsible for the deaths of the four Americans killed that day and the deaths of many other US citizens at the hands of Libyans. They will continue to do so. I'm confident the FBI will not give up in its pursuit of justice.

AFRICOM planned unceasingly to respond to another disaster in Libya. AFRICOM developed numerous concepts of operations—trained, and drilled. AFRICOM attempted to train Libyan forces and sent military members into Tripoli to do so. The AFRICOM Commander placed Libya as one of his top priorities and his staff regularly briefed him on security issues. I also personally briefed the commander and deputy commander because they wanted to know details about all the issues we faced on the ground in order to plan accordingly. They were prepared to respond if we came under direct attack.

The Marine Corps was also prepared to respond if we came under direct attack. I have no doubt those Marines who flew nearby during the evacuation would have intervened if even a single bullet was fired in our direction. They would have done so in grave danger of their own lives. In addition, the Marines who served on our compound in Tripoli risked their lives every day to protect us and defend against a possible attack. I slept at night because the Marines did not.

The Libya analysts also put in countless hours pouring over every report or scrap of news about the country. They were the ones who provided assessments to policy makers, congressional leaders, and the administration. I relied on them every day. They made me smarter. They kept me informed. They enabled me to keep my head above water on those days I felt like I was drowning.

We also had the prayers of hundreds, if not thousands of people like my mother who pray for our warriors overseas. God heard those prayers. I know he did, and that faith sustained me, even when I couldn't utter a simple prayer myself, and even when I began to doubt.

At the end of that year, I faced a choice. Another choice in the long series of choices that have formed my life, and it was a difficult one. How could I leave my career? It becomes a lifestyle, an identity, and I made so many personal sacrifices during my years of service. However, I was also angry. I felt expendable. I disagreed with the administration's policies. The hurt and frustrations consumed me.

Because my mother still hasn't had her dinner. The one like her grandmother, where all her children return home after the war ends, and victory is declared, and she's able to breathe that long, deep final sigh of relief that we all survived. We all came home.

She hasn't had it, because the wars aren't over. Because I still have family in the Armed Forces. Because one brother remains in active duty and will likely deploy again. Because soon it will be the next generation going to serve in the same wars.

I didn't want to become bitter.

That final decision to leave was much more difficult than I anticipated. Ultimately, it came down to one of the guiding principles of my life—there is always a choice. Always. Even in the most heinous circumstances, it's there. That God-given choice, and I strove to base all my choices on my values and faith.

I could choose anger. I could choose hate. I could choose to wallow in my misery and blame others for what happened.

Or I could choose the hope of something better. I could choose to move on. I could choose to return to my family. I could choose to use my experience to somehow help others.

I could choose to remain in the darkness, or I could move forward into the light. For me, it was that simple and that hard.

I chose the light.

Even throughout this accounting, the details I've provided about my past and upbringing focused on the positive. That's intentional. That's the lens through which I choose to view my life. I could dwell on the heartache or complain about everything bad that's ever happened to me. I could wade through the dregs of the adversity I've overcome. That's not me.

Instead, I choose to remember the good. I have been greatly blessed. I've lived an extraordinary life.

But I have to make that choice every single day. Every. Single Day.

As with other traumas, it's not possible to "get over it" or "move on" or "put it behind me." It's always there and I won't forget it. It's a part of me now. To this day, it's difficult for me to write or talk about my experience in Libya. I'm not perfect, far from it, and it's so easy to fall back into the anger and blame. And I have to make that choice again. Life isn't about forgetting, it's about choosing.

Faith is also a choice.

My faith is my choice.

I often think about the X-Files when I try to explain my faith to people. It's a strange comparison, I know. In that show, Agent Mulder is consumed with his belief in aliens and proving their existence. He has a poster that reads, "I want to believe." He means in aliens of course, but I think it's the same with any kind of belief or faith system. He wants to believe, so he chooses to believe.

It's the same for me, and for anyone else who believes in anything. I want to believe, so I choose to believe. For me, it's not in aliens—although I haven't given up hope—but in something more, a higher calling and purpose.

I believe there is a path for me. My faith and the values I've learned have led me to make the choices I have in my life. I haven't always liked the path and I haven't always understood. I most definitely didn't understand some of what occurred in Libya. I've struggled to make sense of what happened there and why I was chosen. Tactical commander? Really? Me?

However, we don't always receive what we want, sometimes we're provided with what we need.

I was provided Nomad, when I needed to feel safe.

I was provided Belle, when I needed a friend.

I was provided a team with unique skills, when we needed to evacuate.

I was provided specialized officers, when we needed a route to escape.

I was provided the Marines, when we needed to secure the compound.

I was provided many, many other things and people when we needed them, most of which I cannot share.

And maybe, just maybe, my path led me to Libya, because I was provided to them. Maybe it wasn't about what I needed, but about what they needed. Maybe they needed a former preacher's kid with a deep understanding of Christianity, a career in counterterrorism, security-focused Arabic vocabulary, who could relate to military men, knew how to use weapons, could communicate effectively, had a freakishly good memory, and a dedicated perfectionist, with a sense of responsibility, skilled in survival, who would do anything necessary to keep her people safe.

I'd like to think so.

Together we saved the lives of more than 150 US personnel. We accomplished it without incident. We avoided injuries. We didn't lose a single American life in our daring escape.

I believe we were brought together in Libya for that purpose.

Religion is a divisive thing. That's why I speak of faith and not religion. Religion is polarizing.

However, religious freedom is one of the founding principles of our country. It is a constitutional right. That right doesn't extend to one religion, it extends to all religions, and one of the things we swear to defend and uphold when we join government service.

That freedom doesn't apply to one religion, it applies to all.

Terrorism is an entirely different matter. Terrorism is a tactic employed by many different people with many different agendas and religions. Terrorism is in no way tied to a single belief system. It is not Islamic any more than it is Christian. It is neither. It is a tactic, not a belief system. It is abhorrent. It is done by individuals embracing the dark. The subsequent backlash against an entire race or religion by other people is also those individuals embracing the dark.

I believe there's good and bad in us all. We all possess the light and the dark in equal measure. It's how we choose to act that shows who we really are and what we really believe. Yet again, it's our choices.

I now pour my energy and focus into the next generation.

The next generation has known nothing but war. Our country has been at war their entire lives. Some have known devastating loss as a result. I hope to help and guide them as they process that loss.

I volunteer with an organization that assists survivors and provides support directly to military families, the Tragedy Assistance Program for Survivors (T.A.P.S.). They help anyone grieving the loss of a military loved one. They provide a 24/7 helpline and host activities and camps for survivors. It's a phenomenal program that focuses on survivors helping other survivors heal.

I also help my family in the Pacific Northwest. I want to teach my nieces and nephews some of the lessons I've learned. They have no idea where I worked or what I've done, but it's the values that matter. Some of them will almost certainly be our future warriors and spies.

When I decided to stay in the Pacific Northwest with my family, I parted ways with Nomad. We needed each other during and immediately after those extraordinary circumstances, and we spent several years together, helping each other. In the end, he chose to delve deeper into his career and I needed to leave that world behind.

I recently had a moment of clarity. One of those rare moments when I could see so clearly how all of my choices, my faith, and path led me to exactly where I needed to be. It was a silly, fun moment, but profound all the same.

When the Wonder Woman movie came out, my mother and stepfather bought it and invited my middle brother, his daughters, and me to family movie night at their house. It was a tradition she started when we were children and one they're continuing for the next generation.

My nine-year-old niece sat beside me and was absolutely, utterly enthralled. When the young Diana learned to fight, my niece punched and kicked the air along with her. She bounced along to the music in the fight scenes with many gasps of wonder and "oh wow."

There's a scene where they must cross no-mans-land, and the other characters tell Wonder Woman she can't cross because no man can survive.

"Did you hear what they said?" I whispered to her. "No man can cross it."

"But she's not a man, she's a woman!" gasped my niece.

"Exactly," I said.

"She's going to get the bad guys," squealed my niece as the character did exactly that.

"Why'd she choose to do that?" I asked.

"She wanted to save people. I'm going to save people one day too," said my niece, and we were off again, following the adventure.

My family and I will now continue our adventure together, through this extraordinary life that has been given us. Through the horrors and the blessings, through the light and the dark, our choices will continue to define us and our faith will continue to sustain us.

> *"It is useless to attack a man who could not be controlled even if conquered, while failure would leave us in an even worse position."*
>
> —*THUCYDIDES*— The Peloponnesian War, *6.18*

THE END

LIST OF US PERSONNEL

The administration - Former US President Barack Obama, his advisors, and cabinet members

Embassy:
The ambassador - The former US Ambassador to Libya, Deborah
    Jones
Facility Manager
Foreign Service Officer
Regional Security Officer

Other:
Me - CIA Analyst
Arcade - Security Officer
Belle - Other Officer
Blue - Other Officer
Captain - Other Officer
Dolby - Security Officer
Flash - Security Officer
Gambler - Information Security Officer
Harbor - Deputy, acting chief in Reebok's absence
Hunter - Marine Staff Sergeant, also known as 1 Actual
Moe - Security Officer
Nomad - Security Officer
Obi - Security Officer Team Lead
Otter - Other Officer
Reebok - Chief of the compound, my boss
Robin - Other Officer

Stitch - Special Operations Forces (SOF) Representative
Triage - Security Officer
Tunes - National Security Agency (NSA) Officer
Whirlwind - A senior Officer

Washington D.C.
Analysts – CIA Headquarters-based officers covering a range of topics on Libya including terrorism, politics, economics, military, and open source information.

GLOSSARY OF TERMS, ACRONYMS

AFRICOM - US Africa Command
Cyranaica / Barqa - Northeastern region of Libya
EAC - Emergency Action Committee
Fezzan - Southern region of Libya
GNC - Libyan General National Congress
GPF - General Purpose Force
IED - Improvised Explosive Device
ISR - Intelligence Surveillance Reconnaissance aircraft,
        also known as drones
JCP - Libyan Justice and Construction Party
LIFG - Libyan Islamic Fighting Group
LROR - Libyan Revolutionary Operations Room
LSOF - Libyan Special Operations Forces
MARSECFOR - Marine Security Force
MEDEVAC - Medical Evacuation
Misrata/Misratan - City east of Tripoli, large Islamist-aligned militia
MoI - Libyan Ministry of Interior
MoD - Libyan Ministry of Defense
MRE - Meals Ready to Eat
MSG - Marine Security Guards
NFA - Libyan National Forces Alliance
NGA - National Geospatial-Intelligence Agency
NSA – National Security Agency
QRF - Quick Reaction Force
RSO - State Department Regional Security Officer
SVTC - Secure Video TeleConference
Tripolitania - Northwestern region of Libya
Zintan - Large secular-aligned tribe and militia based south of Tripoli

SELECT BIBLIOGRAPHY

CHAPTER TWO:

Cruickshank, Paul; Lister, Tim; Robertson, Nic. (2013, March 20). New al Qaeda document sheds light on Europe, U.S. attack plans. http://www.cnn.com/2013/03/20/world/new-qaeda-document/

Pargeter, Alison. (2006, November 30). Libyan Fighters Join the Iraqi Jihad. Terrorism Monitor Volume, 4(23). http://www.jamestown.org/single/?tx_ttnews%5Btt_news%5D=988&no_cache=1#.VSR3HVz0iS0

Reed, Matthew M. (2014, February 3). Federalism and Libya's Oil. http://foreignpolicy.com/2014/02/03/federalism-and-libyas-oil/

Joscelyn, Thomas. (2015, March 3). Osama Bin Laden's Files: The Arab Revolutions. http://www.longwarjournal.org/archives/2015/03/osama-bin-ladens-files-the-arab-revolutions.php

Vanderwalle, Dirk. (2012). A History of Modern Libya. Cambridge University Press. 2nd edition.

CHAPTER FOUR:

Housley, Adam. (2013, September 11). Sources: US weapons stolen in Libya raids, fueling Special Forces pull-out. http://www.foxnews.com/politics/2013/09/11/us-military-weapons-equipment-stolen-in-libya-raids/

Tombokti, Reem. (2013, July 25). UAE embassy attacked with RPG. https://www.libyaherald.com/2013/07/25/rpg-attack-on-uae-embassy/

CHAPTER SIX:

Goldman, Adam. (2014, February 10). Video shows U.S. abduction of accused al-Qaeda terrorist on trial for embassy bombings. http://www.washingtonpost.com/world/national-security/video-shows-us-abduction-of-accused-al-qaeda-terrorist-on-trial-for-embassy-bombings/2014/02/10/7f84927a-8f6b-11e3-b46a-5a3d0d2130da_story.html

RT (formerly Russia Today). (2013, October 3). Tripoli embassy attack sparked after Libyan officer killed by Russian woman – FM. Retrieved from http://rt.com/news/russian-embassy-libya-attack-693/

RT (formerly Russia Today). (2013, October 3). Gunmen attack Russian embassy in Libya's Tripoli. http://rt.com/news/libya-russian-embassy-attack-651/

Stephen, Chris. (2013, October 2). Gunmen attack Russian embassy in Libya's capital Tripoli. http://www.theguardian.com/world/2013/oct/02/gunmen-attack-russian-embassy-tripoli

CHAPTER EIGHT:

Bright, Arthur. (2013, October 10). Did US operation in Libya lead to PM's kidnapping? http://www.csmonitor.com/World/Security-Watch/terrorism-security/2013/1010/Did-US-operation-in-Libya-lead-to-PM-s-kidnapping-video

Chivers, C. J., Mazzetti, Mark, Schmitt, Eric. (2013, June 21). In Turnabout, Syrian Rebels Get Libyan Weapons. http://www.nytimes.com/2013/06/22/world/africa/in-a-turnabout-syria-rebels-get-libyan-weapons.html?_r=0

Karadsheh, Jomana. (2012, July 28). Libya rebels move onto Syrian battlefield. http://www.cnn.com/2012/07/28/world/meast/syria-libya-fighters/

Libya Herald. (2013, October 10). Breaking News: Zeidan kidnapped. http://www.libyaherald.com/2013/10/10/breaking-news-zeidan-kidnapped/

Libya Herald. (2013, November 17). Gharghour massacre death toll now at 47. http://www.libyaherald.com/2013/11/17/gharghour-massacre-death-toll-now-at-47/

Mahmoud, Khalid. (2013, November 22). Tripoli Supreme Security Committee Chief on militias, protests. http://english.aawsat.com/2013/11/article55323141/tripoli-supreme-security-committee-chief-on-militias-protests

Mzioudet, Houda. (2013, October 10). Libyans react to Zeidan's kidnapping. http://www.libyaherald.com/2013/10/10/libyans-react-to-zeidans-brief-kidnapping/#axzz3WrBvkVmQ

Sullivan, Kevin. (2014, October 28). A Tunisian teenager's path from top student to aspiring suicide bomber. http://www.washingtonpost.com/world/national-security/a-tunisian-teenagers-path-from-top-student-to-aspiring-suicide-bomber/2014/10/28/8b8a9fd2-5974-11e4-8264-deed989ae9a2_story.html

Tunisia Live. (2013, October 30). Attack on hotel in Sousse. http://www.tunisia-live.net/2013/10/30/attack-on-hotel-in-sousse/

CHAPTER TEN:

African Globe. (2014, January 23). Libyan Regime Stokes Anti-Black Tensions In South. http://www.africanglobe.net/africa/libyan-regime-stokes-anti-black-tensions-south/

Al-Sahli, Ayman; Wroughton, Lesley. (2013, December 28). U.S. military personnel freed after brief detention in Libya. http://www.reuters.com/article/us-usa-libya-military-idUSBRE9BR05W20131228

Carter, Chelsea J.; Starr, Barbara. (2013, December 28). Official: 4 U.S. military personnel detained by Libya released. https://www.cnn.com/2013/12/27/world/africa/libya-americans-detained/index.html

Chappell, Bill. (2013, December 5). American Teacher is Killed While Jogging in Benghazi, Libya. http://www.npr.org/blogs/thetwo-way/2013/12/05/248998059/american-teacher-is-killed-while-jogging-in-benghazi

New Zealand Herald. (2014, September 23). Kiwi shot in Libya: In 'wrong place at the wrong time.' http://www.nzherald.co.nz/nz/news/article.cfm?c_id=1&objectid=11329828

Wahab, Ashraf Abdul. (2014, January 25). Janzour schools and colleges closed over security fears. https://www.libyaherald.com/2014/01/25/janzour-schools-and-colleges-closed-over-security-fears/

CHAPTER TWELVE:

Al Arabiya News. (2014, January 27). Libyan militiaman released in Egypt after diplomats freed. http://english.alarabiya.net/en/News/middle-east/2014/01/27/Libyan-militiaman-released-in-Egypt-.html

BBC News. (2014, January 20). South Korean trade official kidnapped in Libya. http://www.bbc.com/news/world-africa-25812248

BBC News. (2014, January 27). Egyptian diplomats released after Tripoli kidnapping. http://www.bbc.com/news/world-africa-25907945

CBS News. (2014, February 14). Libya Major General Khalifa Haftar claims gov't suspended in apparent coup bid; PM insists Tripoli "under control." http://www.cbsnews.com/news/libya-major-general-khalifa-haftar-declares-govt-suspended-in-apparent-coup-bid/

CNN. (2014, January 26). Some Egyptian diplomats abducted in Libya reportedly released. http://www.cnn.com/2014/01/26/world/meast/libya-egypt-kidnap/

CNN. (2014, January 26). Some Egyptian diplomats abducted in Libya reportedly released. http://www.cnn.com/2014/01/26/world/meast/libya-egypt-kidnap/

Eljarh, Mohamed. (2014, February 6). February Is a Make-or-Break Month for Libya. http://foreignpolicy.com/2014/02/06/february-is-a-make-or-break-month-for-libya/

Laessing, Ulf; Shennib, Ghaith. (2014, February 18) Libyan militias threaten parliament, deploy forces in Tripoli. https://www.reuters.com/article/us-libya-politics/libyan-militias-call-on-parliament-to-hand-over-power-in-five-hours-idUSBREA1H1KD20140218

Lake, Eli. (2014, April 23). Jihadists Now Control Secretive U.S. Base in Libya. http://www.thedailybeast.com/articles/2014/04/23/jihadists-now-control-secretive-u-s-base-in-libya.html

Libya Herald staff. (2014, January 27). Egyptian diplomats set free after LROR head released. https://www.libyaherald.com/2014/01/27/egyptian-diplomats-set-free-after-lror-head-released/

Sang-Hun, Choe. (2014, January 20). South Korean Trade Official Abducted in Libyan Capital. http://www.nytimes.com/2014/01/21/world/asia/south-korean-trade-official-abducted-in-libyan-capital.html?_r=0

Shennib, Ghaith. (2014, January 25). Egypt diplomats kidnapped in Libya over militia chief's arrest. http://www.reuters.com/article/us-libya-egypt-kidnapping-idUSBREA0O06220140125

CHAPTER FOURTEEN:

Al Hayat News. (2014, April 30). Libya: «Buka» from changing car oil. http://www.alhayat.com/Articles/2076246/

Amera, Hani; Laessing, Ulf. (2014, March 21). Bomb explodes on runway of Libya's main airport in Tripoli. http://uk.reuters.com/article/2014/03/21/uk-libya-security-idUKBREA2K1TE20140321

Barbash, Fred. (2014, March 17). Navy SEALs board mystery tanker Morning Glory near Cyprus. No one hurt, Pentagon says. http://www.washingtonpost.com/news/morning-mix/wp/2014/03/17/navy-seals-board-tanker-morning-glory-near-cyprus-no-one-hurt-pentagon-says/

Good Morning Libya. (2014, May 1). Buka [al-Uraybi] enters Tripoli. https://www.youtube.com/watch?v=BMpoVQ9oQ5U

Libya Herald. (2013, January 22). Terrorist source claims Libyan connection with In Amenas attack. http://www.libyaherald.com/2013/01/22/terrorist-source-claims-libyan-connection-with-in-amenas-attack/

Mahmoud, Khalid. (2014, April 6). Al-Qaeda flags raised in Eastern Libya. http://english.aawsat.com/2014/04/article55330898/al-qaeda-flags-raised-in-eastern-libya

Middle East Eye. (2014, April 18). Libyan kidnappers of Tunisian diplomat demand prisoner exchange. http://www.middleeasteye.net/news/libyan-kidnappers-tunisian-diplomat-demand-prisoner-exchange-1150195590

UN Security Council. (2014, November 19). Security Council Al-Qaida Sanctions Committee Adds Two Entities to Its Sanctions List. http://www.un.org/press/en/2014/sc11659.doc.htm

CHAPTER SIXTEEN:

Al-Khalidi, Suleiman. (2014, May 13). Jordanian envoy to Libya freed, Jordan sends back jailed militant. http://www.reuters.com/article/us-libya-jordan-ambassador-idUSBREA4C0F920140513

Al Jazeera. (2014, May 13). Fighter swapped for abducted envoy to Libya. http://www.aljazeera.com/news/middleeast/2014/05/jordan-kidnapped-envoy-libya-freed-201451345959878942.html

BBC News. (2014, June 15). Libya crisis: More deadly clashes in Benghazi. http://www.bbc.com/news/world-africa-27862365

El Gomati, Anas. (2014, June 10). Khalifa Haftar: Fighting terrorism or pursuing political power? http://www.aljazeera.com/indepth/opinion/2014/06/khalifa-hifter-operation-dignity-20146108259233889.html

Keilberth, Mirco; Mittelstaedt, Julian von; Reuter, Christoph. (2014, November 18). Islamic State's Gradual Expansion into North Africa. http://www.spiegel.de/international/world/islamic-state-expanding-into-north-africa-a-1003525.html

Middle East Monitor. (2014, June 18). Haftar plans to move towards Tripoli. https://www.middleeastmonitor.com/20140618-haftar-plans-to-move-towards-tripoli/

Morajea, Hassan. (2014, May 19). Libyan armed groups fight over capital. http://www.aljazeera.com/news/middleeast/2014/05/libyan-armed-groups-fight-over-capital-2014519101950444140.html

Lundquist, Lisa. (2014, June 13). Libya. http://www.longwarjournal.org/archives/2014/06/the_interior_ministry_said_its.php

CHAPTER EIGHTEEN:

Adaki, Oren; Barr, Nathaniel; Gartenstien-Ross, Daveed. (2014, July 15). Libya: Hifter's Stalled Anti-Islamist Campaign. http://waronth-erocks.com/2014/07/libya-hifters-stalled-anti-islamist-campaign/

Adaki, Oren. (2014, July 30). Ansar al Sharia, allies seize Libyan special forces base in Benghazi. http://www.longwarjournal.org/archives/2014/07/ansar_al_sharia_alli.php

BBC News. (2014, June 11). #BBCtrending: Amid chaos, Libyans look on the bright side. http://www.bbc.com/news/blogs-trending-27796839

DeYoung, Karen; Goldman, Adam; Tate, Julie. (2014, June 17). U.S. captured Benghazi suspect in secret raid. http://www.washingtonpost.com/world/national-security/us-captured-benghazi-suspect-in-secret-raid/2014/06/17/7ef8746e-f5cf-11e3-a3a5-42be35962a52_story.html

Human Rights Watch. (2014, November 27). Libya: Extremists Terror-izing Derna Residents. https://www.hrw.org/news/2014/11/27/libya-extremists-terrorizing-derna-residents

Karadsheh, Jomana. (2014, June 2). Islamist militants strike back against Benghazi renegades; 15 killed. http://www.cnn.com/2014/06/02/world/africa/libya-violence/

Kirkpatrick, David D. (2014, June 17). Brazen Figure May Hold Key to Mysteries. http://www.nytimes.com/2014/06/18/world/middleeast/apprehension-of-ahmed-abu-khattala-may-begin-to-answer-questions-on-assault.html

Middle East Eye. (2014, July 1). Conflicting reports over Benghazi hospital attack in Libya. http://www.middleeasteye.net/news/conflicting-reports-over-benghazi-hospital-attack-libya-10862226

UN Security Council, (2014, July 23). Security Council Press Statement on Libya's Elections. http://www.un.org/press/en/2014/sc11489.doc.htm

Yahia, Mona. (2014, July 1). Tunisia: Kidnapped Tunisian Diplomats Released in Libya. http://allafrica.com/stories/201407020105.html

CHAPTER TWENTY:

Al Arabiya Institute for Studies. (2014, August 25). Libya Dawn: Map of allies and enemies. http://english.alarabiya.net/en/perspective/alarabiya-studies/2014/08/25/Libyan-Dawn-Map-of-allies-and-enemies.html

Bosalum, Feras; Laessing, Ulf. (2014, July 12). Heavy fighting breaks out near Libya's Tripoli airport, seven dead. https://www.reuters.com/article/us-libya-security/heavy-fighting-breaks-out-near-libyas-tripoli-airport-seven-dead-idUSKBN0FI07420140713

Security Council Report. (2014, June 30). July 2014 Monthly Forecast Libya. http://www.securitycouncilreport.org/monthly-forecast/2014-07/libya_11.php

CHAPTER TWENTY-TWO:

Lamothe, Dan. (2014, September 25). Before Libya evacuation, Marines were concerned about ambassador's plan. http://www.washingtonpost.com/news/checkpoint/wp/2014/09/25/before-libya-evacuation-marines-were-concerned-about-ambassadors-plan/

Hosenball, Mark; Spetalnick, Matt. (2014, August 31). Libyan armed faction takes over U.S. Embassy annex in Tripoli. http://www.reuters.com/article/us-libya-security-usa-idUSKBN0GV0MH20140901

Vandiver, John. (2014, July 26). US military assist in Libya embassy evacuation. http://www.stripes.com/news/africa/us-military-assists-in-libya-embassy-evacuation-1.295357

Yaakoubi, Aziz El; Markey, Patrick. (2014, July 25). Libya seeks ceasefire as south Tripoli a militia 'war zone'. http://www.reuters.com/article/us-libya-security-airport-idUSKBN0FU2CC20140725

OTHER:

Central Intelligence Agency. The World Factbook: Libya. https://www.cia.gov/library/publications/the-world-factbook/geos/ly.html

Director of National Intelligence. Counter Terrorism Guide: Ansar al-Sharia. https://www.dni.gov/nctc/groups/ansar_al_sharia.html

Ferran, Lee. (2015, August 20). State Department Screwed Up Tripoli Escape, Won't Say How. http://abcnews.go.com/International/state-department-screwed-tripoli-escape-wont/story?id=33158837

Final Report of the Select Committee on the events surrounding the 2012 terrorist attack in Benghazi: https://www.congress.gov/congressional-report/114th-congress/house-report/848/1

Military Times. (2014, July 28). New details emerge on Libya embassy evacuation. https://www.militarytimes.com/2014/07/28/new-details-emerge-on-libya-embassy-evacuation/

U.S. Embassy, Libya. https://ly.usembassy.gov, https://www.facebook.com/usembassytripoli, https://twitter.com/usaembassylibya

U.S. Ambassador to Libya. (2013-2015). https://twitter.com/safiradeborah

Seck, Hope Hodge. (2014, September 25). Marines reveal details of tense embassy evacuation from Libya. http://www.marinecorpstimes.com/story/military/pentagon/2014/09/25/marines-reveal-details-of-tense-embassy-evacuation-from-libya/16219927/

Virtual Reading Room Documents. Clinton Email Collection: https://foia.state.gov/Search/Results.aspx?collection=Clinton_Email

ACKNOWLEDGMENTS

FIRST AND FOREMOST I want to thank my family who has encouraged and prayed for me every single day of my life. A special thank you to my mother, you are my hero and my tether to this world. You gave me a thirst for life, adventure, and sense of purpose; you helped me become the person I am today. Thank you for understanding during those final days when I couldn't talk at all, only email "I'm okay." I'm sorry the worst-case scenario turned out to be true. To my bonus dad, for teaching me how to drive a manual and shoot archery. I'm sorry John Kerry announced the evacuation so many hours before I could tell you I was safe. To my brothers and their families, but especially Adam and his girls for giving me purpose in the aftermath. And to my more recent additions, Dale Craft and his boys, thank you for giving me hope. You all are my joy.

I also want to thank my literary agent Greg Johnson of Wordserve Literary for believing in this book, encouraging me to continue when I was ready to give up, and for sticking with me through the unexpected lawsuit. I will always be grateful. Thank you also to Mark Zaid and Bradley Moss for representing me in that lawsuit against CIA. Without you, this book might never have become a book.

Thank you to CIA's PRB staff, in spite of the lawsuit. I truly appreciate the many, many hours you spent reviewing my manuscript and working with me to find substitute language rather than use redactions.

Thank you to my editor at Fidelis Books, Gary Terashita, of Post Hill Press and the entire team who helped bring this book to fruition. It was a pleasure working with you on this project.

While I can't name names, thank you to the officers I served with in Libya, especially those who were there with me at the end. You know who you are. A special thank you to "Nomad" and his family; I'm forever thankful for our time together and our many adventures. Thank you also to Denise Coyle, for helping me later process what happened in Libya.

My heartfelt gratitude to the analysts at CIA Headquarters I relied on while I was in Libya. Again, I can't name names, but you know who you are. You made me smarter. You kept me informed. You helped me keep my head above water on those days I felt like I was drowning.

A special thank you to my friends and support network who stuck with me over the years: my phone a friend Rosa Smothers, my oldest friend Emily Verdonk, my childhood friend Elizabeth Hemmert, my best pool time pals, and so many more I cannot name. To my social media support network for your advice and encouragement, especially Fred Burton, JC Finley, David Priess, Nada Bakos, Cindy Otis, and Tracy Walder. And to my friends and colleagues in emergency management, especially Kyle Bustad and Ed Reed, for giving me roots and purpose.

Thank you to those who have made the ultimate sacrifice for our country, those wounded in service, and those who lost the battle to the demons that haunted them after. And "Arcade," may you rest in peace.

And a final thank you to the Customs and Border Patrol Agent at SeaTac International Airport who said, "Welcome home." I will never forget that moment when I finally, safely made it home.